# Mini Music

# Guitar Scale Dictionary

All the essential scales and modes in an easy-to-follow format!

Alfred Music Co., Inc.
P.O. Box 10003
Van Nuys, CA 91410-0003
**alfred.com**

Copyright © MMXV by Alfred Music Co., Inc.
All rights reserved. Printed in USA.

*No part of this book shall be reproduced, arranged, adapted, recorded, publicly performed, stored in a retrieval system, or transmitted by any means without written permission from the publisher. In order to comply with copyright laws, please apply for such written permission and/or license by contacting the publisher at alfred.com/permissions.*

ISBN-10: 1-4706-2287-4
ISBN-13: 978-1-4706-2287-9

Cover guitar photos courtesy of Gibson USA and Fender Musical Instruments.

Library of Congress Control Number: 2014955653

 **Alfred Cares.** Contents printed on environmentally responsible paper.

# Contents

Fundamentals of Scale Theory ........................... 5
    The Major Scale ........................................... 5
    The Sharp Keys ........................................... 6
    The Flat Keys .............................................. 8
    The Natural Minor Scale ............................ 10
The Modes of the Major Scale ......................... 11
    Ionian ......................................................... 11
    Dorian ....................................................... 11
    Phrygian .................................................... 12
    Lydian ....................................................... 12
    Mixolydian ................................................. 13
    Aeolian ...................................................... 13
    Locrian ...................................................... 14
Pentatonic and Blues Scales ............................ 15
    Parallel ....................................................... 15
    Relative ..................................................... 15
    Using Pentatonic Scales ............................. 16
The Blues Scale ............................................... 16
    Using the Blues Scale ................................ 17
The Harmonic and Melodic Minor Scales .... 17
    The Harmonic Minor Scale ........................ 17
    The Melodic Minor Scale .......................... 18
Modes of the Harmonic
and Melodic Minor Scales ............................... 19
    The Modes of the
    Harmonic Minor Scale ............................... 19
    The Modes of the
    Melodic Minor Scale ................................. 20
Symmetrical Scales .......................................... 21
    The Chromatic Scale ................................. 21
    The Whole Tone Scale .............................. 21
    The Half/Whole Diminished Scale ............ 22
    The Whole/Half Diminished Scale ............ 23

|  | A♭ | A | B♭ | B | C | D♭ | D | E♭ | E | F | F♯ | G |
|---|---|---|---|---|---|---|---|---|---|---|---|---|
| Aeolian | 28 | 48 | 68 | 88 | 108 | 128 | 148 | 168 | 188 | 208 | 228 | 248 |
| Aeolian ♯11 | 37 | 57 | 77 | 97 | 117 | 137 | 157 | 177 | 197 | 217 | 237 | 257 |
| Aeolian Major | 27 | 47 | 67 | 87 | 107 | 127 | 147 | 167 | 187 | 207 | 227 | 247 |
| Augmented | 34 | 54 | 74 | 94 | 114 | 134 | 154 | 174 | 194 | 214 | 234 | 254 |
| Augmented 9 | 35 | 55 | 75 | 95 | 115 | 135 | 155 | 175 | 195 | 215 | 235 | 255 |
| Augmented ♯9 | 39 | 59 | 79 | 99 | 119 | 139 | 159 | 179 | 199 | 219 | 239 | 259 |
| Augmented ♭9 | 35 | 55 | 75 | 95 | 115 | 135 | 155 | 175 | 195 | 215 | 235 | 255 |
| Augmented Dominant | 38 | 58 | 78 | 98 | 118 | 138 | 158 | 178 | 198 | 218 | 238 | 258 |
| Augmented Dominant ♯9 | 39 | 59 | 79 | 99 | 119 | 139 | 159 | 179 | 199 | 219 | 239 | 259 |
| Augmented Dominant ♭9 | 38 | 58 | 78 | 98 | 118 | 138 | 158 | 178 | 198 | 218 | 238 | 258 |
| Augmented Minor/Major 7 | 39 | 59 | 79 | 99 | 119 | 139 | 159 | 179 | 199 | 219 | 239 | 259 |
| Blues, Diminished | 35 | 55 | 75 | 95 | 115 | 135 | 155 | 175 | 195 | 215 | 235 | 255 |
| Blues, Major | 25 | 45 | 65 | 85 | 105 | 125 | 145 | 165 | 185 | 205 | 225 | 245 |
| Blues, Minor | 31 | 51 | 71 | 91 | 111 | 131 | 151 | 171 | 191 | 211 | 231 | 251 |

# Contents

|  | A♭ | A | B♭ | B | C | D♭ | D | E♭ | E | F | F♯ | G |
|---|---|---|---|---|---|---|---|---|---|---|---|---|
| Chromatic | 33 | 53 | 73 | 93 | 113 | 133 | 153 | 173 | 193 | 213 | 233 | 253 |
| Chromatic Augmented | 34 | 54 | 74 | 94 | 114 | 134 | 154 | 174 | 194 | 214 | 234 | 254 |
| Diminished, Half/Whole, Symmetrical | 34 | 54 | 74 | 94 | 114 | 134 | 154 | 174 | 194 | 214 | 234 | 254 |
| Diminished Tritonic | 41 | 61 | 81 | 101 | 121 | 141 | 161 | 181 | 201 | 221 | 241 | 261 |
| Diminished, Whole/Half, Auxiliary | 33 | 53 | 73 | 93 | 113 | 133 | 153 | 173 | 193 | 213 | 233 | 253 |
| Dominant ♯9 | 42 | 62 | 82 | 102 | 122 | 142 | 162 | 182 | 202 | 222 | 242 | 262 |
| Dominant 13 | 43 | 63 | 83 | 103 | 123 | 143 | 163 | 183 | 203 | 223 | 243 | 263 |
| Dominant ♭5 | 41 | 61 | 81 | 101 | 121 | 141 | 161 | 181 | 201 | 221 | 241 | 261 |
| Dominant ♭5♭9♯9 | 41 | 61 | 81 | 101 | 121 | 141 | 161 | 181 | 201 | 221 | 241 | 261 |
| Dominant ♭9♯11 | 43 | 63 | 83 | 103 | 123 | 143 | 163 | 183 | 203 | 223 | 243 | 263 |
| Dominant ♭9♯11♭13 | 43 | 63 | 83 | 103 | 123 | 143 | 163 | 183 | 203 | 223 | 243 | 263 |
| Dominant ♭9♯9 | 42 | 62 | 82 | 102 | 122 | 142 | 162 | 182 | 202 | 222 | 242 | 262 |
| Dominant ♭9♯9♭13 | 42 | 62 | 82 | 102 | 122 | 142 | 162 | 182 | 202 | 222 | 242 | 262 |
| Dominant, Bebop | 39 | 59 | 79 | 99 | 119 | 139 | 159 | 179 | 199 | 219 | 239 | 259 |
| Dorian | 29 | 49 | 69 | 89 | 109 | 129 | 149 | 169 | 189 | 209 | 229 | 249 |
| Dorian Pentatonic | 31 | 51 | 71 | 91 | 111 | 131 | 151 | 171 | 191 | 211 | 231 | 251 |
| Dorian, Bebop | 40 | 60 | 80 | 100 | 120 | 140 | 160 | 180 | 200 | 220 | 240 | 260 |
| Four Semitone Tritone | 36 | 56 | 76 | 96 | 116 | 136 | 156 | 176 | 196 | 216 | 236 | 256 |
| Harmonic Minor | 28 | 48 | 68 | 88 | 108 | 128 | 148 | 168 | 188 | 208 | 228 | 248 |
| Hybrid Scales | 37 | 57 | 77 | 97 | 117 | 137 | 157 | 177 | 197 | 217 | 237 | 257 |
| Ionian Augmented | 27 | 47 | 67 | 87 | 107 | 127 | 147 | 167 | 187 | 207 | 227 | 247 |
| Jazz Minor | 29 | 49 | 69 | 89 | 109 | 129 | 149 | 169 | 189 | 209 | 229 | 249 |
| Locrian | 30 | 50 | 70 | 90 | 110 | 130 | 150 | 170 | 190 | 210 | 230 | 250 |
| Locrian ♮2 | 32 | 52 | 72 | 92 | 112 | 132 | 152 | 172 | 192 | 212 | 232 | 252 |
| Locrian ♮6 | 32 | 52 | 72 | 92 | 112 | 132 | 152 | 172 | 192 | 212 | 232 | 252 |

# Contents

| | A♭ | A | B♭ | B | C | D♭ | D | E♭ | E | F | F♯ | G |
|---|---|---|---|---|---|---|---|---|---|---|---|---|
| Lydian | 24 | 44 | 64 | 84 | 104 | 124 | 144 | 164 | 184 | 204 | 224 | 244 |
| Lydian Pentatonic | 26 | 46 | 66 | 86 | 106 | 126 | 146 | 166 | 186 | 206 | 226 | 246 |
| Lydian ♯9 | 26 | 46 | 66 | 86 | 106 | 126 | 146 | 166 | 186 | 206 | 226 | 246 |
| Lydian Augmented | 28 | 48 | 68 | 88 | 108 | 128 | 148 | 168 | 188 | 208 | 228 | 248 |
| Lydian ♭7 | 26 | 46 | 66 | 86 | 106 | 126 | 146 | 166 | 186 | 206 | 226 | 246 |
| Major | 24 | 44 | 64 | 84 | 104 | 124 | 144 | 164 | 184 | 204 | 224 | 244 |
| Major and Dominant Scales | 24 | 44 | 64 | 84 | 104 | 124 | 144 | 164 | 184 | 204 | 224 | 244 |
| Major, Bebop | 40 | 60 | 80 | 100 | 120 | 140 | 160 | 180 | 200 | 220 | 240 | 260 |
| Melodic Minor | 29 | 49 | 69 | 89 | 109 | 129 | 149 | 169 | 189 | 209 | 229 | 249 |
| Melodic Minor, Bebop | 40 | 60 | 80 | 100 | 120 | 140 | 160 | 180 | 200 | 220 | 240 | 260 |
| Minor Scales | 28 | 48 | 68 | 88 | 108 | 128 | 148 | 168 | 188 | 208 | 228 | 248 |
| Mixolydian | 24 | 44 | 64 | 84 | 104 | 124 | 144 | 164 | 184 | 204 | 224 | 244 |
| Natural Minor | 28 | 48 | 68 | 88 | 108 | 128 | 148 | 168 | 188 | 208 | 228 | 248 |
| Pentatonic, Major | 25 | 45 | 65 | 85 | 105 | 125 | 145 | 165 | 185 | 205 | 225 | 245 |
| Pentatonic, Major 13 | 25 | 45 | 65 | 85 | 105 | 125 | 145 | 165 | 185 | 205 | 225 | 245 |
| Pentatonic, Minor | 30 | 50 | 70 | 90 | 110 | 130 | 150 | 170 | 190 | 210 | 230 | 250 |
| Pentatonic, Minor 13 | 30 | 50 | 70 | 90 | 110 | 130 | 150 | 170 | 190 | 210 | 230 | 250 |
| Phrygian | 29 | 49 | 69 | 89 | 109 | 129 | 149 | 169 | 189 | 209 | 229 | 249 |
| Phrygian Major | 27 | 47 | 67 | 87 | 107 | 127 | 147 | 167 | 187 | 207 | 227 | 247 |
| Phrygian ♮6 | 32 | 52 | 72 | 92 | 112 | 132 | 152 | 172 | 192 | 212 | 232 | 252 |
| Phrygian Pentatonic | 31 | 51 | 71 | 91 | 111 | 131 | 151 | 171 | 191 | 211 | 231 | 251 |
| Symmetrical Scales | 33 | 53 | 73 | 93 | 113 | 133 | 153 | 173 | 193 | 213 | 233 | 253 |
| Tetratonic | 36 | 56 | 76 | 96 | 116 | 136 | 156 | 176 | 196 | 216 | 236 | 256 |
| Three Semitone Tritone | 36 | 56 | 76 | 96 | 116 | 136 | 156 | 176 | 196 | 216 | 236 | 256 |
| Tritone | 37 | 57 | 77 | 97 | 117 | 137 | 157 | 177 | 197 | 217 | 237 | 257 |
| Two Semitone Tritone | 37 | 57 | 77 | 97 | 117 | 137 | 157 | 177 | 197 | 217 | 237 | 257 |
| Whole Tone | 33 | 53 | 73 | 93 | 113 | 133 | 153 | 173 | 193 | 213 | 233 | 253 |

# Fundamentals of Scale Theory

Most of the music we hear and play conforms to a system of scales and keys. Each key is made up of just seven of the twelve possible pitches. Let's look closely at scales and keys, first in major, then in minor. These scales are the basis of all that is to come in this book, so take your time and let it all sink in!

## The Major Scale

Remember "do, re, mi, fa, sol, la, ti, do" from childhood songs? This syllable series is always sung to the major scale. The major scale is the source of many scales in our culture.

Let's look at a C Major scale. There are seven notes; the last note repeats the first an octave higher. An octave is the distance of twelve half steps. The note an octave above middle C is also named C, but sounds higher. Below are the distances between each of the C Major scale notes. This series of whole and half steps is used for every major scale, no matter what the starting note is.

W and /\ = Whole step

H and ⌒ = Half step

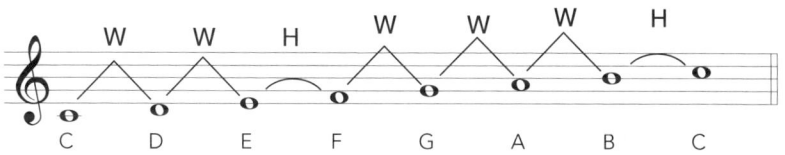

There's an octave between the first and last notes of the C Major scale above. This is called a one octave scale. By repeating the pattern of whole and half steps, you can create a two octave scale, as shown below.

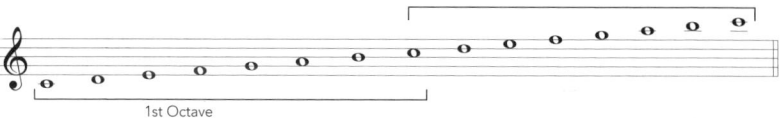

Because this whole/half pattern is used to construct the other eleven major scales (you guessed it, one for each note), it's crucial to memorize it. We'll also need names for the scale steps. The first note of any scale is the root or tonic. The second note is called the second degree, the third note is called the third degree, and so forth. We're now ready to create other major scales, as long as we keep a few things in mind:

1. To spell a major scale correctly, all seven letters of the musical alphabet must be used.

2. The tonic note is repeated at the end of the scale.

3. Scale degrees 3–4 and 7–8 are separated by half steps. All other scale degrees are separated by whole steps.

# The Sharp Keys

The C Major scale contains no sharps or flats. Since the C Major scale contains no sharps or flats, the key of C also contains no sharps or flats. You have learned that the same series of intervals—W W H W W W H—is used to construct all major scales. Let's construct another major scale, this time starting on a G root.

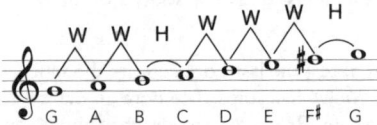

Notice that an F♯ occurs as scale degree 7. If we follow the pattern of whole and half steps for major scales, the F must be raised to F♯ so that there's a whole step between scale degrees 6 and 7 and a half step between scale degrees 7 and 8.

We could not have accomplished the same thing using G♭ instead of F♯ because one letter of the musical alphabet would be missing (F), and all major scales must contain each letter of the musical alphabet.

Let's try creating another major scale, this time with D as the root.

Two sharps are needed to complete the formula of whole and half steps for a D Major scale. As before, sharps are used rather than flats so that each of the seven musical alphabet letters is included. Now let's list all the major keys containing sharps. There's a total of seven sharp keys. Notice that each new key has one more sharp than the one before it.

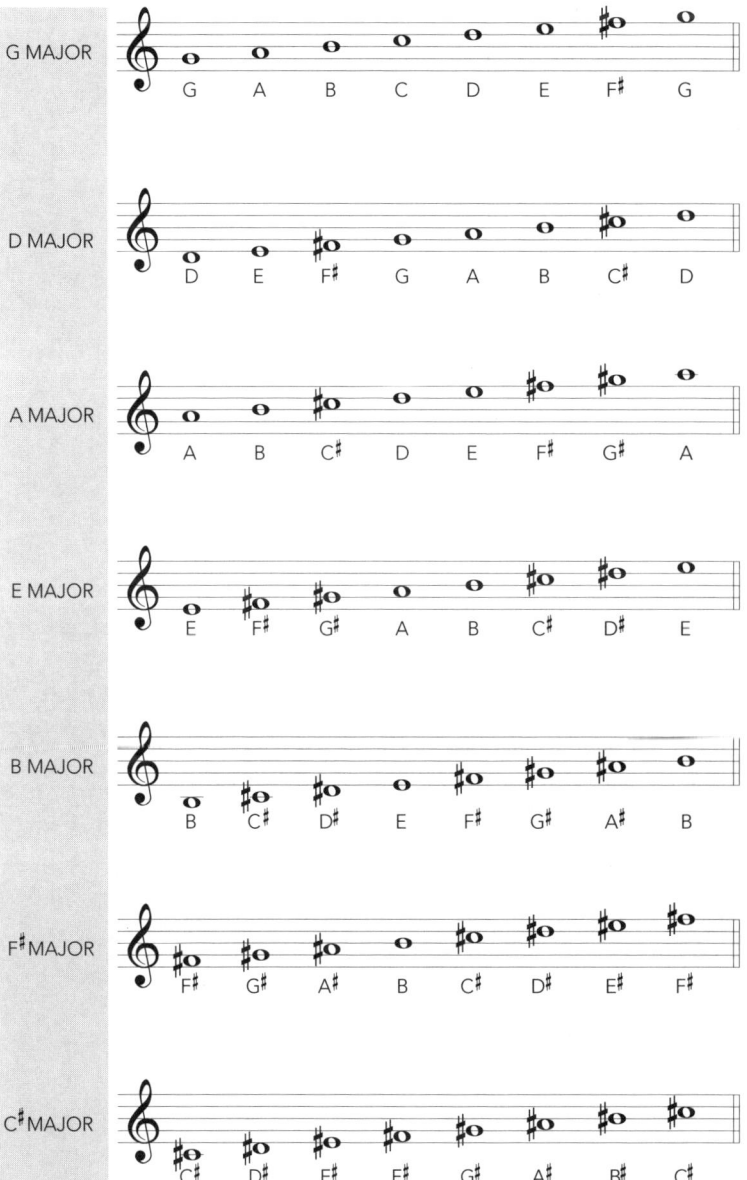

# The Flat Keys

Let's take a look at the major scales that have flats. There are seven such instances, known as the flat keys. Here is an F Major scale:

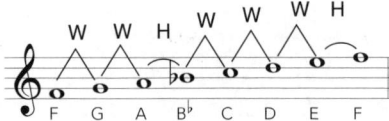

A flat is needed to correctly generate the scale. B♭ lies a half step above A and a whole step below C. Play these notes on your guitar and your ear will help you confirm this.

Here is a B♭ Major scale: This time, two flats are needed to correctly generate the scale.

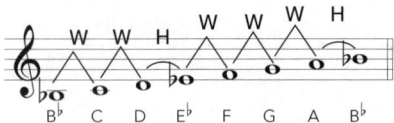

The flat keys appear less commonly in rock and classical guitar music because they contain less open strings than the sharp keys. However, they are very common in jazz because saxophones and trumpets are most comfortable in those keys.

Below are all seven flat-key major scales. Each new key has one more flat than the last.

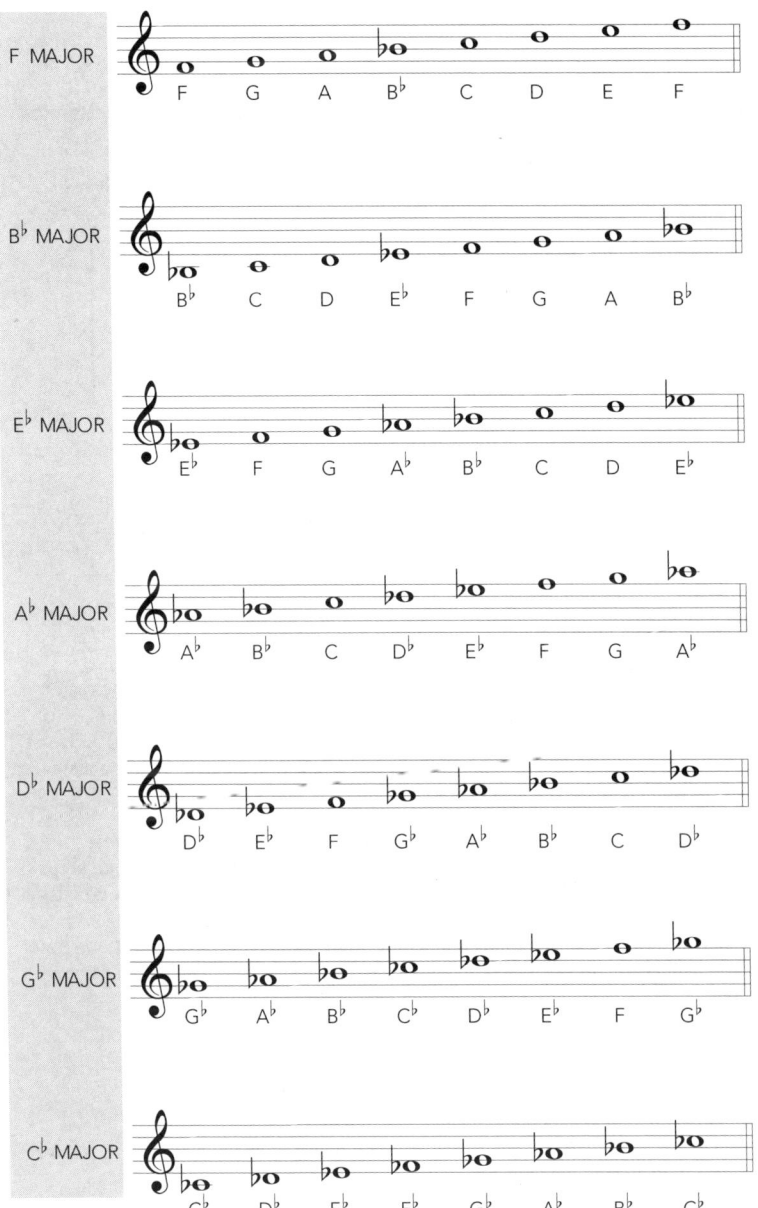

# The Natural Minor Scale

We know that C Major and A Minor are relative keys — keys that share the same key signature but which have different roots. The scale built on the root of the relative minor key is called the *natural minor scale*. Using all seven letters of the musical alphabet, we construct the natural minor as follows:

Here is how the A Natural Minor scale is derived from the C Major scale.

> 1. Begin on the root of the relative minor key (one and one half steps — or three frets — below the root of the major key).
> 
> 2. Proceed upwards from the root until you've gone through all seven letters, using the same notes as the relative major scale.

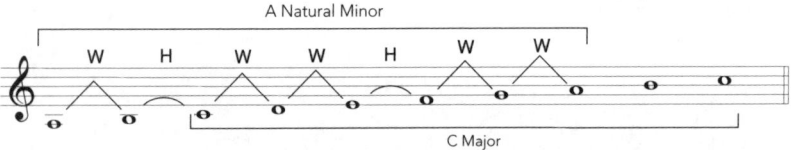

Notice that the pattern of whole and half steps is different from that of the major Scale. The half steps now occur between scale degrees 2 and 3, and 5 and 6. Also, notice that if you count up six notes from the root of the major scale, you arrive at the root of the natural minor scale. So, you can count up to the 6th degree instead of down one and a half steps if you prefer.

It is also possible to turn this thinking around and determine the relative major key, and thus the key signature for the natural minor scale, by counting up three steps from the root of the minor key. For instance, let's determine the notes of E Natural Minor. Count up from E through the musical alphabet three notes, starting with E: $E_1$–$F_2$–$G_3$. So, G is the relative major key. Since G Major has one sharp (F#) we now know that E Natural Minor will read as follows:

E–F#–G–A–B–C–D–E.

# The Modes of the Major Scale

A *mode* is a reordering of a scale. In other words, if you play a scale, such as the major scale, but start and stop on a note other than the root, you are playing a mode of that scale. For instance, if you play the notes of a C Major scale, but begin and end on D, you are playing a mode.

The modes of the major scale are important resources for contemporary improvisation.

Because there are seven notes in the major scale, there are seven modes—one for each note. They fall into two families: *major family* (those with a major 3rd—♮3), and *minor family* (those with a minor 3rd—♭3).

There are two popular ways of learning the modes. In the *derivative* approach, a mode is a reordering of a *parent* major scale, as described in the first paragraph of this chapter. In the *parallel* approach, a mode is an alteration of a major scale.

## Ionian

The *Ionian* mode is the major scale from root to root. The C Ionian mode is a plain old C Major scale (see p. 5). All that's new is the name. *Ionian* and *major* are synonymous.

## Dorian

In the derivative approach, you create the *Dorian* mode by starting on the 2nd degree of the major scale. In this case, D to D within the C Major scale creates the D Dorian mode. In the parallel approach, the Dorian mode is a major scale with a ♭3 and ♭7. Dorian is a minor family mode because of the ♭3.

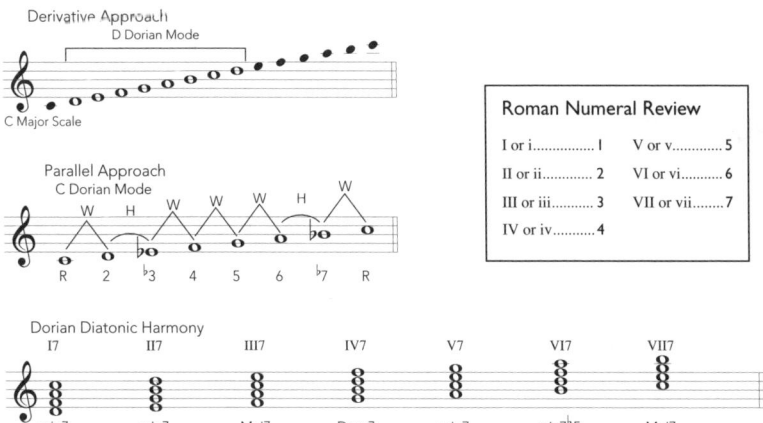

Roman Numeral Review

| | |
|---|---|
| I or i............1 | V or v............5 |
| II or ii............2 | VI or vi............6 |
| III or iii............3 | VII or vii............7 |
| IV or iv............4 | |

# Phrygian

In the derivative approach, you create the Phrygian mode by starting on the 3rd degree of the major scale. In this case, E to E within the C Major scale creates the E Phrygian mode. In the parallel approach, the Phrygian mode is a major scale with a ♭2, ♭3, ♭6, and ♭7. Phrygian is a minor family mode because of the ♭3.

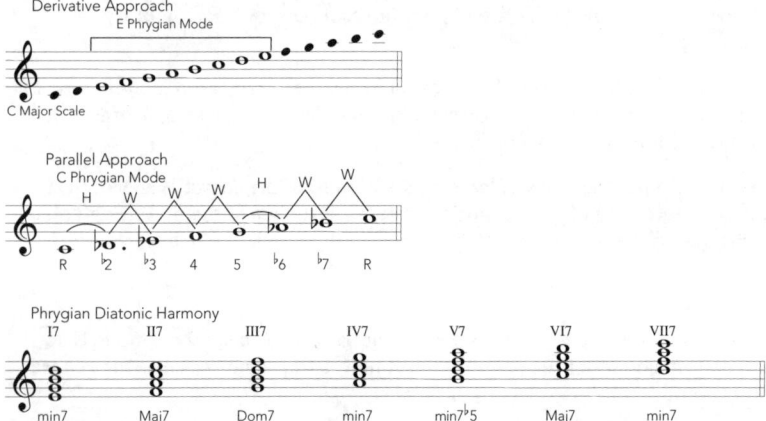

# Lydian

In the derivative approach, you create the Lydian mode by starting on the 4th degree of the major scale. In this case, F to F within the C Major scale creates the F Lydian mode. In the parallel approach, the Lydian mode is a major scale with a ♯4. Lydian is a major family mode because of the ♮3.

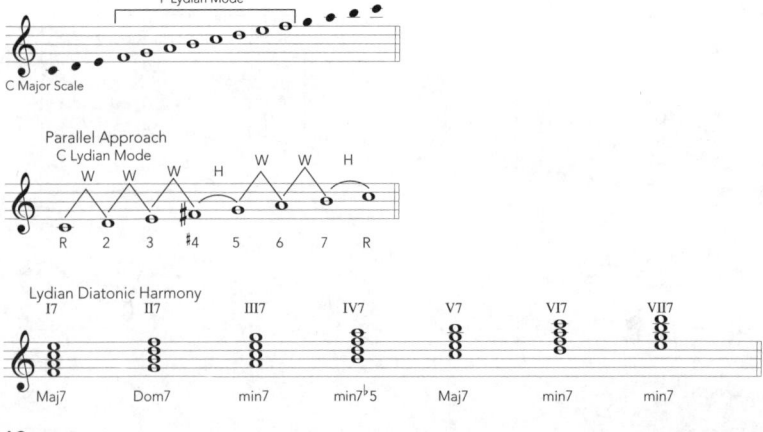

# Mixolydian

In the derivative approach, you create the Mixolydian mode by starting on the 5th degree of the major scale. In this case, G to G within the C Major scale creates the G Mixolydian mode. In the parallel approach, the Mixolydian mode is a major scale with a ♭7. Mixolydian is a major family mode because of the ♮3.

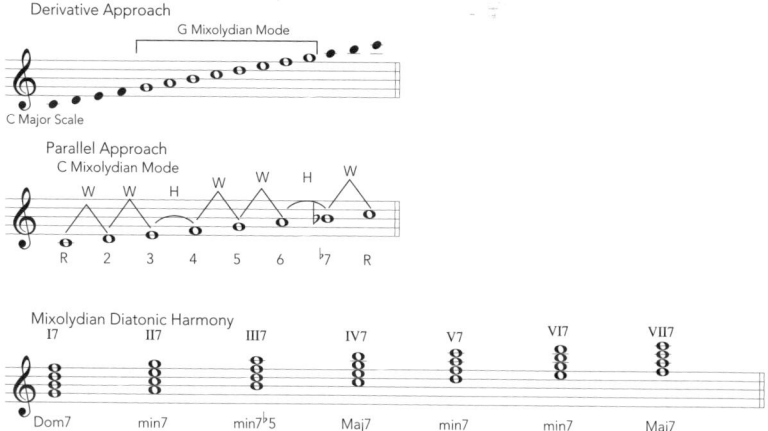

# Aeolian

In the derivative approach, you create the Aeolian mode by starting on the 6th degree of the major scale. In this case, A to A within the C Major scale creates the A Aeolian mode. In the parallel approach, the Aeolian mode is a major scale with a ♭3, ♭6, and ♭7. The Aeolian mode is the same as the natural minor scale, and is therefore a minor family mode.

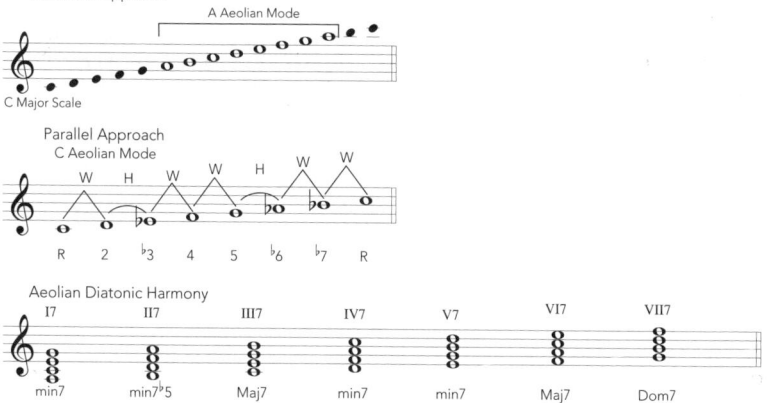

# Locrian

In the derivative approach, you create the Locrian mode by starting on the 7th degree of the major scale. Here, B to B within the C Major scale creates the B Locrian mode. In the parallel approach, the Locrian mode is a major scale with a ♭2, ♭3, ♭5, ♭6, and ♭7. Locrian is a minor family mode because of the ♭3.

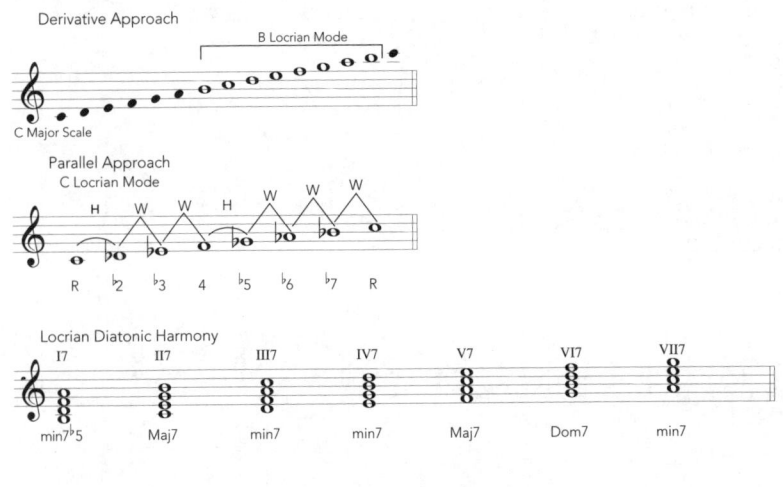

As with all music theory, once you learn a concept in a simple key like C Major, you can generalize the idea to fit any key. The following is an example of the kind of question that comes up all the time:

**Question:** *"What are the notes of a G Phrygian scale?"*

**Answer:** In parallel thinking, the Phrygian mode is a major scale with a ♭2, ♭3, ♭6, and ♭7. So, the G Phrygian scale would read G–A♭–B♭–C–D–E♭–F–G. In derivative thinking, the Phrygian mode is built on the 3rd degree of a major scale. G is the 3rd degree of the E♭ Major scale. So, G to G within the E♭ Major scale creates the G Phrygian mode.

# Pentatonic and Blues Scales

## Parallel

A pentatonic scale contains five different notes (the Greek word "pente" means "five"). Pentatonic scales are used in many musical styles. The *major pentatonic* and *minor pentatonic scales* are the most commonly used. The two scales shown below, C Major Pentatonic and C Minor Pentatonic, are parallel scales. In other words, C Minor Pentatonic is the parallel minor of C Major Pentatonic, and vice-versa.

> The major pentatonic scale formula is R–2–3–5–6.
> The minor pentatonic scale formula is R–♭3–4–5–♭7.

## Relative

Major and minor pentatonic scales can be derived from the major scale. A two-octave C Major scale is shown below. The upstemmed notes show the C Major Pentatonic notes, and the downstemmed notes show the A Minor Pentatonic notes. Recall that C Major and A Minor are relative scales and keys — they share the same notes and key signature.

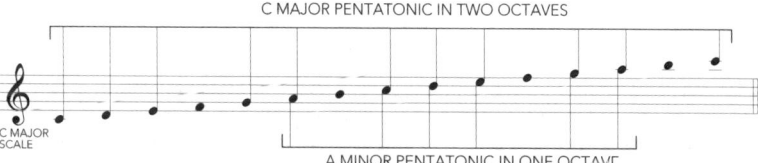

A common major scale fingering is shown in Figure A below. The black circles indicate the pentatonic scale notes contained within it. Figure B extracts these pentatonic notes, with major pentatonic roots in squares and minor pentatonic roots circled. Since both scales, major and minor, share the same notes, it is the context that makes one sound either major or minor. Also, it has a lot to do with phrasing. In other words, if you gravitate towards the major root in your improvising, the scale will sound major, or, if you emphasize the minor root, it will sound minor.

### Fingerings

Figure A: The major scale

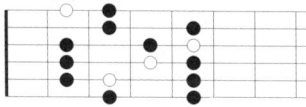

● = Pentatonic scale notes
○ = Other major scale notes

Figure B: The pentatonic scales

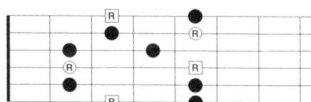

Ⓡ = Root of the minor pentatonic scale
☐R = Root of the major pentatonic scale

## Using Pentatonic Scales

Pentatonic scales are used to improvise over chord progressions. The trick is to know when to use which scale. Here are five tips:

1. A major pentatonic scale works with a major chord, a major 7th chord, or dominant 7th chord of the same root.

2. A minor pentatonic scale works with a minor chord, a minor 7th chord, or a dominant 7th chord of the same root. However, the ♭3 of the minor pentatonic scale clashes with the 3 of the dominant 7th chord, so it should be used carefully.

3. For any major or minor chord, you can use the relative major or minor pentatonic scale.

4. You can improvise over a diatonic major-key chord progression with the major scale or major pentatonic scale whose root is the same as the key.

5. You can improvise over a diatonic minor-key chord progression with the minor scale or minor pentatonic scale whose root is the same as the key.

## The Blues Scale

The *blues scale* is a minor pentatonic scale with an added ♭5, for a total of six notes.

The ♭5, called a *blue note*, forms a juicy, pungent *tritone* interval against the scale's root. Tritone is just another name for an augmented 4th (or diminished 5th) interval. Sometimes we call it a tritone because it is a distance of exactly three whole steps (six half steps). The *dissonance* (tension) of the blue note creates lots of excitement and can really add spice to your improvisations.

Be careful to *resolve* the ♭5 to the perfect 5th one half step above it. The term resolve implies reaching a resting point. In this case, reaching the *consonant* (harmonious) perfect 5th after playing the dissonant (clashing, tense) ♭5 is reaching a point of rest (resolution). The root, ♭3 and 5 of a blues scale are consonant tones. They can be used freely and don't have to resolve to another scale tone. The 4, ♭5 and ♭7 are dissonant tones. Unless you resolve each of them, they will sound like "wrong notes." For variety, let's look at the blues scale in the key of A.

The A Blues scale dissonances and their resolutions to consonances

## Using the Blues Scale

The blues scale works well over dominant 7th chords of the same root. For instance, try playing an A Blues scale over an A7 chord. You can also use the blues scale anytime you can use the minor pentatonic scale, although sticking to dominant 7th chords of the same root is your best bet. This is because the blues scale contains the R, 5, and ♭7 of a dominant 7th chord. Plus, the ♭3 of the blues scale is often bent up one half step to the 3 of the dominant 7th chord. This is shown below.

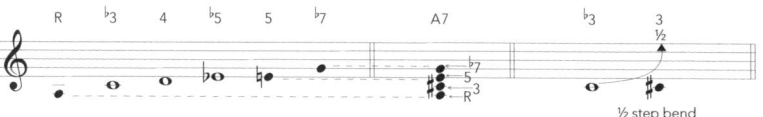

# The Harmonic and Melodic Minor Scales
## The Harmonic Minor Scale

The harmonic minor scale is a natural minor scale with a raised 7th.

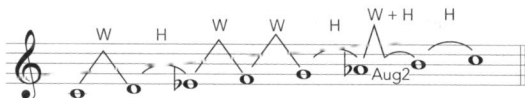

The harmonic minor scale formula is: R–2–♭3–4–5–♭6–7

Two factors make this scale sound distinctive: the half steps (between scale degrees 2–3, 5–6, and 7–R) and, most notably, the augmented second (a distance of three half steps) between scale degrees 6–7.

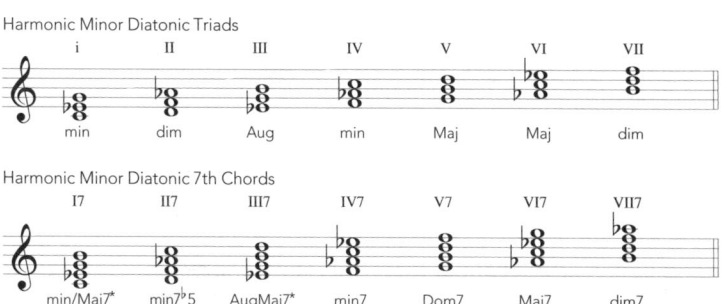

Let's harmonize the harmonic minor scale first in triads, then in 7th chords.

Harmonic Minor Diatonic Triads

| i | II | III | IV | V | VI | VII |
|---|----|-----|----|---|----|-----|
| min | dim | Aug | min | Maj | Maj | dim |

Harmonic Minor Diatonic 7th Chords

| I7 | II7 | III7 | IV7 | V7 | VI7 | VII7 |
|----|-----|------|-----|----|-----|------|
| min/Maj7* | min7♭5 | AugMaj7* | min7 | Dom7 | Maj7 | dim7 |

* This new chord quality is discussed on page 18.

Notice that two new chord qualities result from harmonizing the scale with 7th chords:

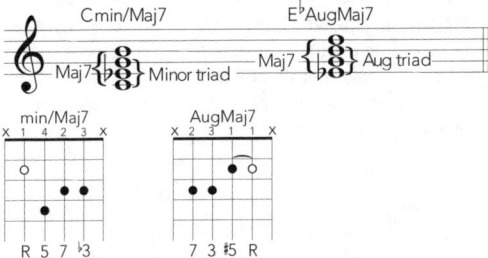

- a minor/major 7 chord (min/Maj7) on i (R–♭3–5–7).

and

- an augmented Maj7th chord (AugMaj7) on III7 (R–3–♯5–7),

## The Melodic Minor Scale

The melodic minor scale is a natural minor scale with raised 6th and raised 7th degrees. You can also think of it as a major scale with a ♭3.

> The melodic minor scale formula is: R–2–♭3–4–5–6–7

In classical music, the melodic minor scale ascends this way and descends in the natural minor form. In rock and jazz styles, however, the melodic minor scale is the same both ascending and descending. Some musicians call this scale "*jazz minor.*"

Here is a harmonization of the C Melodic Minor scale in triads, then in 7th chords. Notice the major triad on V and the dominant 7th chord on V7, as occurs in harmonic minor.

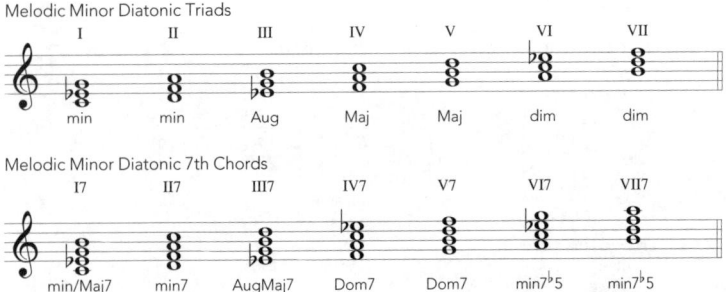

The consonant and dissonant degrees of the melodic minor scale are identical to those of the harmonic minor scale. For either scale, remember that the triad tones are consonant, and the remaining four scale tones are dissonant.

# Modes of Harmonic and Melodic Minor Scales

## The Modes of the Harmonic Minor Scale

The harmonic minor scale generates six modes. There is no modal name for the harmonic minor scale itself, as there is for the major scale (the major scale is also called the Ionian mode).

The harmonic minor modes are named as alterations of the major scale modes. These names imply a new kind of parallel approach for finding the modes. For instance, Dorian ♯4 is the Dorian mode with a raised 4th. Since most players are very familiar with the modes of the major scale, altering them to create new modes is a useful tool. Of course, just as with the modes of the major scale, you can take a derivative approach, and simply think in terms of reordering the harmonic minor scale.

Let's look at the modes of the C Harmonic Minor scale as an example. You will find the name of the mode, the mode, and its scale formula. You will also find the chord that results from stacking 3rds on the root of the mode. Taken together, all of these chords comprise the diatonic chords of the harmonic minor scale and its modes.

Of this group, the Phrygian major mode (also called Phrygian dominant) occurs most frequently (except for, of course, the harmonic minor scale itself). Learn this one first. Practice soloing with each mode by choosing a root from the notes of the harmonic minor scale, then playing that scale over the chord type that goes with that scale degree, such as F Dorian ♯4 over Fmin7.

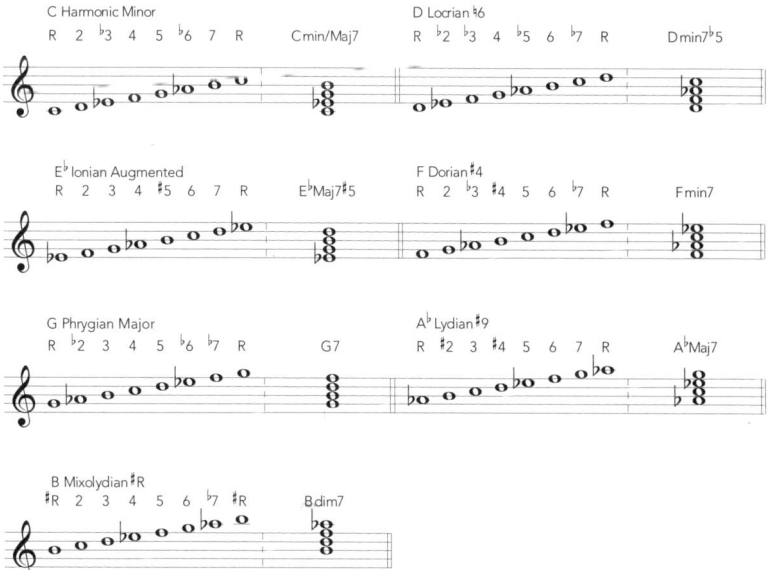

# The Modes of the Melodic Minor Scale

The melodic minor modes are in more common use than those of the harmonic minor scale. They are named as alterations of the major scale modes, except for the final mode, which is commonly called the altered dominant mode. They are used constantly in jazz and fusion, but much less so in other styles. Like the modes of the major and harmonic minor scales, each has a distinctive flavor.

Let's use the modes of C Melodic Minor as an example. Again, you will find the name of the mode, the mode, and its scale formula. You will also find the chord that results from stacking 3rds on the root of the mode. Taken together, all of these chords comprise the diatonic chords of the melodic minor scale and its modes.

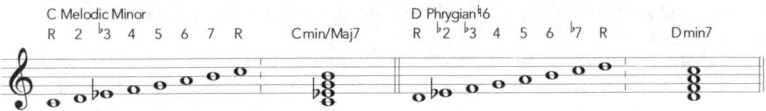

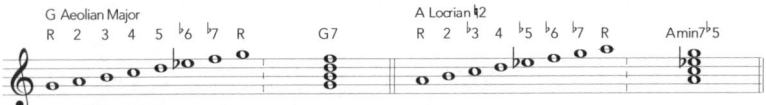

# Symmetrical Scales

A symmetrical scale is one that features a repeating interval or pattern of intervals.

## The Chromatic Scale

The chromatic scale is the most basic example of a symmetrical scale— the distance between every scale degree is a half step. Since the chromatic scale always contains all twelve notes of the octave, there is only one. In other words, no matter which note you start with, you will always get the same twelve notes. So the chromatic scale is never "in a key."

## The Whole Tone Scale

The whole tone scale is a six-tone scale with a whole step between each scale degree. Here are whole tone scales starting on C and C♯ (or D♭). Because of the missing scale step, it's okay to use enharmonic spellings and skip over a note name in the alphabet.

Whole Tone Scale formula is: R, 2, 3, ♯4/♭5, ♯5/♭6, ♭7

There are only two different whole tone scales. This scale repeats itself every major 2nd, (two frets). We have seen those beginning on C and C♯. Let's look at the whole tone scales on D and E♭. Notice that the C and D whole tone scales contain the same 6 pitches, allowing for enharmonic spellings. The C♯ and E♭ whole tone scales are also identical.

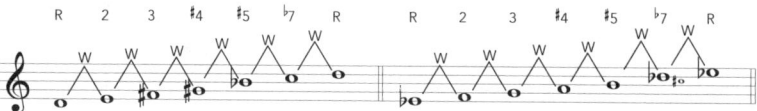

# The Half/Whole Diminished Scale

The half/whole diminished scale formula starts with a half step and then continues to alternate half and whole steps. As with the whole tone scale earlier, enharmonic spellings are expected. Here's the scale on C:

The half/whole diminished scale formula is:
R, ♭2, ♯2, 3, ♯4, 5, 6, ♭7

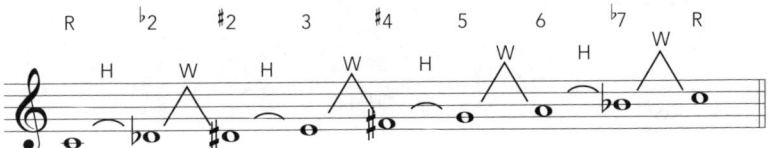

Just as the whole tone scale repeats itself every major 2nd, diminished scales repeat every minor third. In other words, there are half/whole diminished scales with roots on C, C♯/D♭ and D. All others are only enharmonic respellings of these three. Once you get to E♭, the notes from the C half/whole scale repeat themselves. This is true for the whole/half diminished scale, which is introduced on page 23, too. The half/whole scale is used with dominant chords with a ♭9 or ♯9. To sum it up:

The half/whole diminished scale contains two diminished 7th chords — one on the root of the scale, and one a half step higher. This is illustrated below. The upstemmed notes form a Cdim7 chord; the downstemmed notes form a C♯dim7 chord.

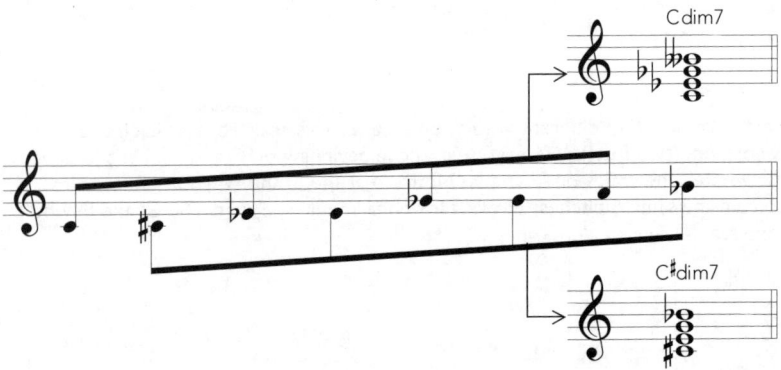

# The Whole/Half Diminished Scale

The whole/half diminished scale begins with a whole step, and then continues to alternate half and whole steps. Here's the C Whole/Half scale:

> The whole/half diminished scale formula is:
> R, 2, ♭3, 4, ♭5, ♭6, ♭♭7, 7

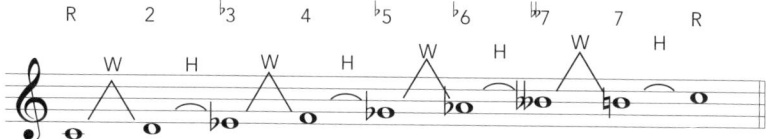

Starting any whole/half diminished scale three half steps higher results in an inversion of the scale. Just as with the half/whole scale, the whole/half scale has only three non-overlapping roots: on C, C#/D♭, and D. Notice that a whole/half scale contains the same notes as a half/whole scale whose root is one half step lower. For instance, D♭ whole/half contains the same notes as C half/whole. Play this to confirm it for yourself. This scale works well over diminished triads and diminished 7th chords.

This scale, like its half/whole sister, also contains two diminished 7th chords. Here, they occur on the root and whole step above, rather than the root and half step above.

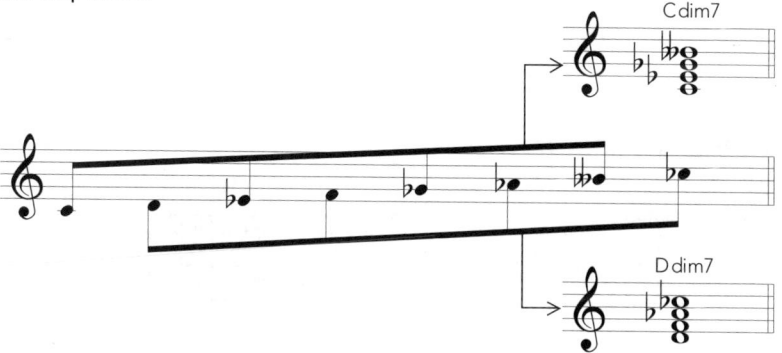

23

# A♭ Major and Dominant Scales

## Major/Ionian (1 2 3 4 5 6 7 8)

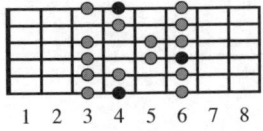
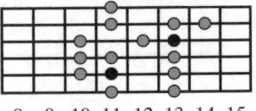
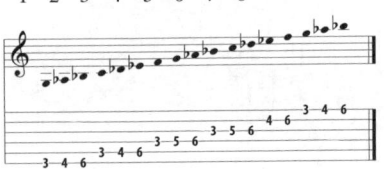
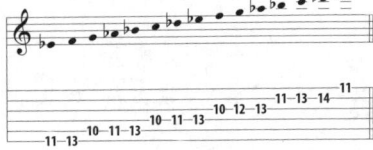

## Mixolydian (1 2 3 4 5 6 ♭7 8)
5th mode of the major scale

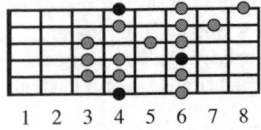
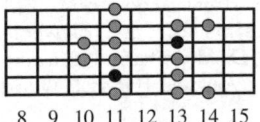

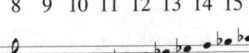
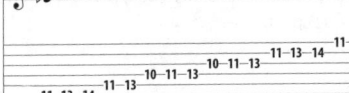

## Lydian (1 2 3 ♯4 5 6 7 8)
4th mode of the major scale

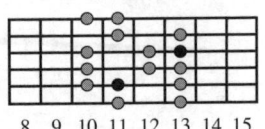
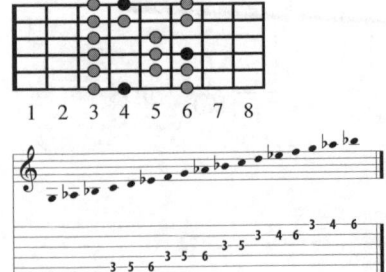
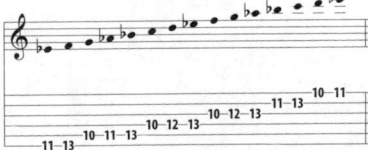

# Major Pentatonic (1 2 3 5 6 8)

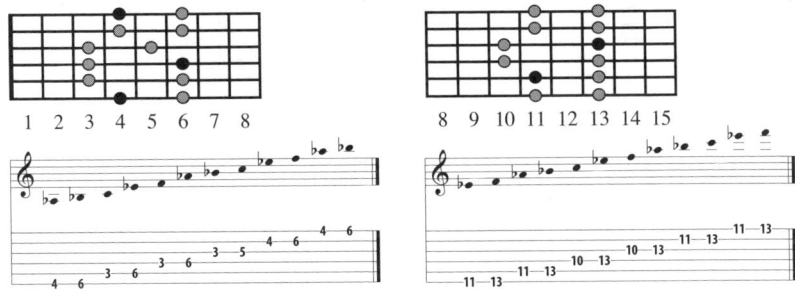

# Major 13 Pentatonic* (1 2 3 5 6 7 8)

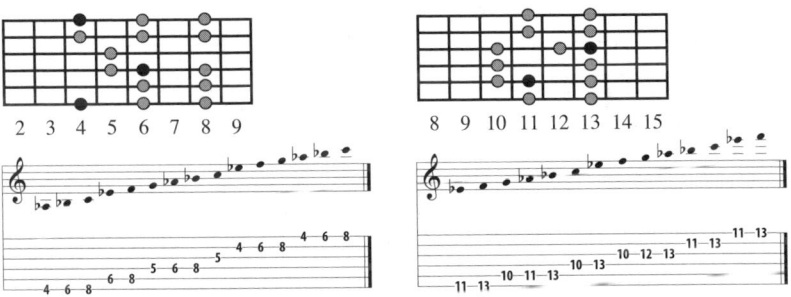

# Major Pentatonic Blues* (1 2 b3 3 5 6 8)

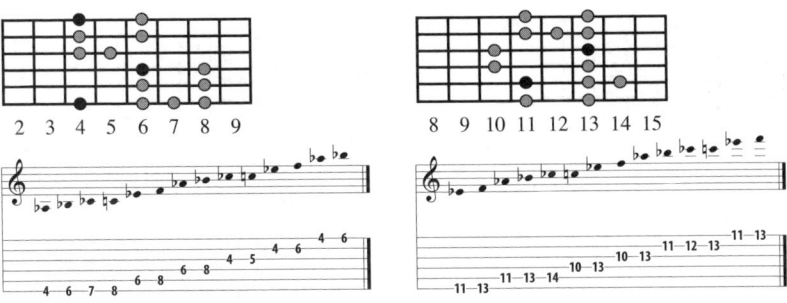

* While this scale has more than five notes, it is based on a five-note, pentatonic scale and it is best to think of it as a pentatonic scale.

# A♭

## Lydian Pentatonic (1 3 ♯4 5 7 8)

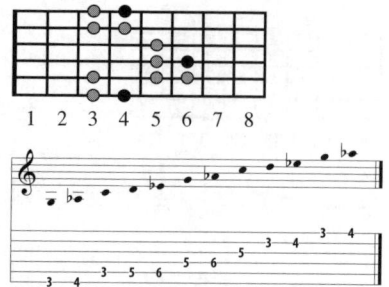
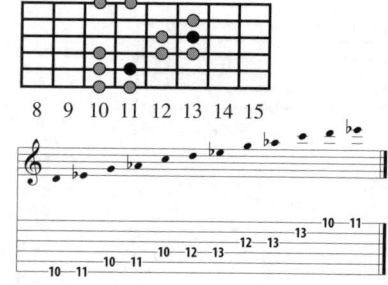

## Lydian ♭7 (1 2 3 ♯4 5 6 ♭7 8)
4th mode of the melodic minor scale

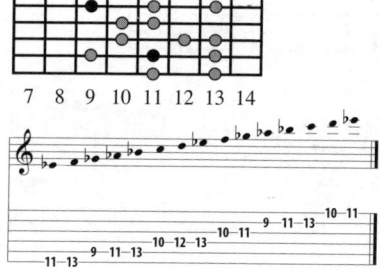

## Lydian ♯9 (1 ♯2 3 ♯4 5 6 7 8)
6th mode of the harmonic minor scale

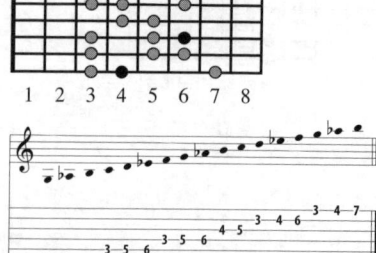
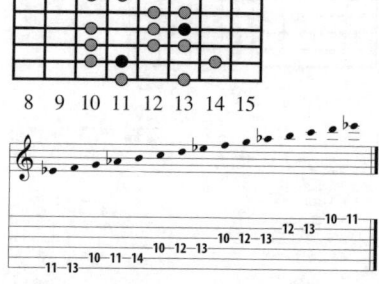

## Aeolian Major (1 2 3 4 5 ♭6 ♭7 8)
5th mode of the melodic minor scale

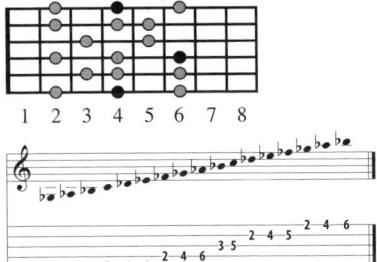
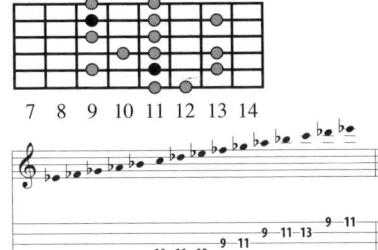

## Phrygian Major (1 ♭2 3 4 5 ♭6 ♭7 8)
5th mode of the harmonic minor scale

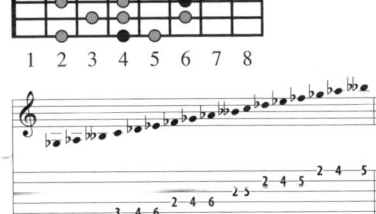
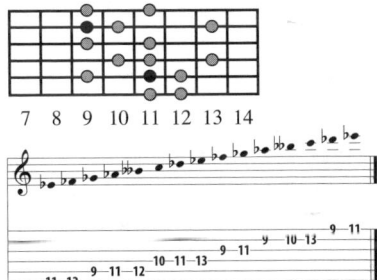

## Ionian Augmented (1 2 3 4 ♯5 6 7 8)
3rd mode of the harmonic minor scale

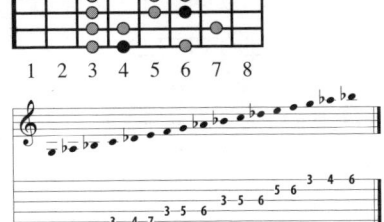
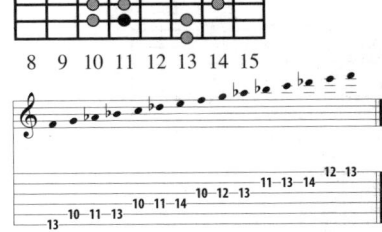

## Lydian Augmented (1 2 3 #4 #5 6 7 8)
3rd mode of the melodic minor scale

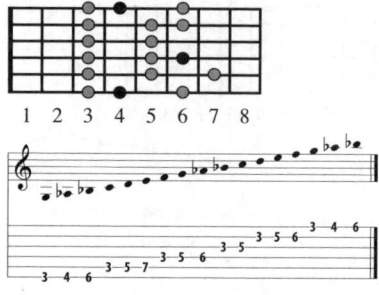
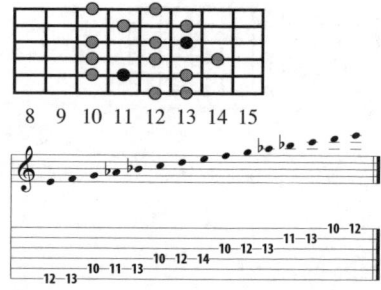

# Minor Scales

## Natural Minor/Aeolian (1 2 ♭3 4 5 ♭6 ♭7 8)
6th mode of the major scale

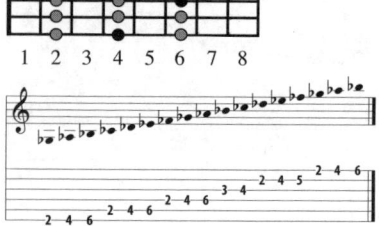
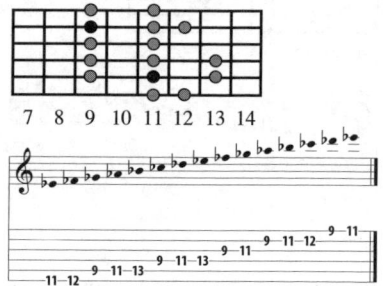

## Harmonic Minor (1 2 ♭3 4 5 ♭6 7 8)

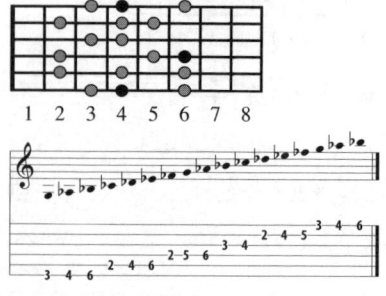
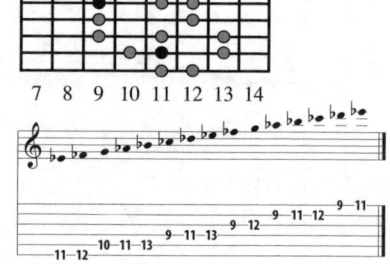

# Jazz Minor/Melodic Minor (1 2 ♭3 4 5 6 7 8)
Melodic Minor descends in Aeolian/Natural Minor

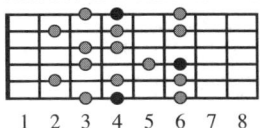

# Dorian (1 2 ♭3 4 5 6 ♭7 8)
2nd mode of the major scale

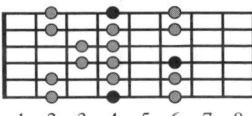
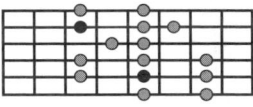

# Phrygian (1 ♭2 ♭3 4 5 ♭6 ♭7 8)
3rd mode of the major scale

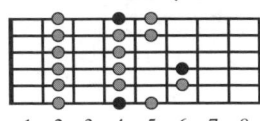
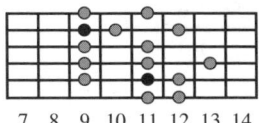

## Locrian (1 ♭2 ♭3 4 ♭5 ♭6 ♭7 8)
7th mode of the major scale

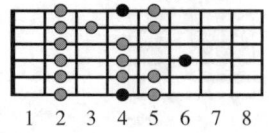
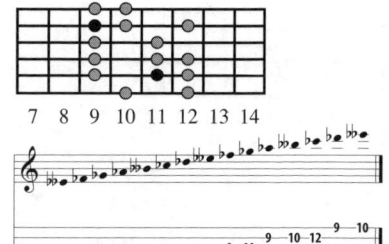

## Minor Pentatonic (1 ♭3 4 5 ♭7 8)

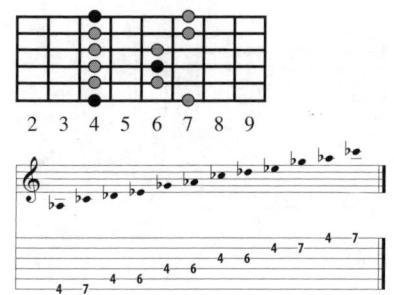
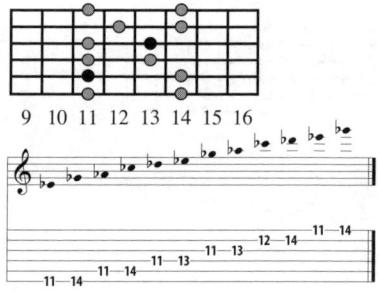

## Minor 13 Pentatonic* (1 ♭3 5 ♭6 ♭7 8)

\* While this scale has more than five notes, it is based on a five-note, pentatonic scale and it is best to think of it as a pentatonic scale.

## Minor Pentatonic Blues* (1 ♭3 4 ♭5 5 ♭7 8)

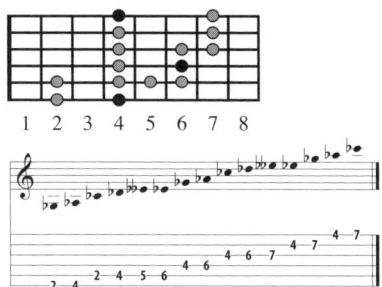
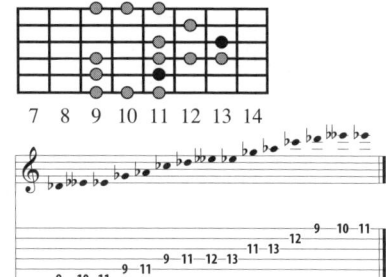

## Dorian Pentatonic (1 2 ♭3 5 ♭7 8)

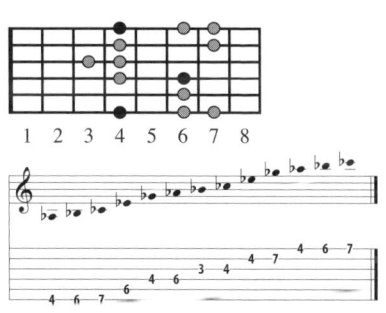
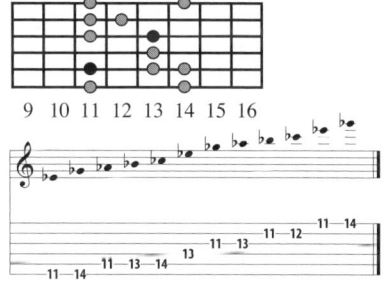

## Phrygian Pentatonic (1 ♭2 4 5 ♭7 8)

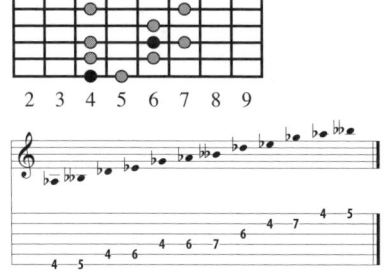
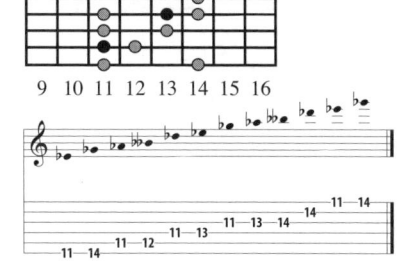

\* While this scale has more than five notes, it is based on a five-note, pentatonic scale and it is best to think of it as a pentatonic scale.

# A♭

## Phrygian ♮6 (1 ♭2 ♭3 4 5 6 ♭7 8)
2nd mode of the melodic minor scale

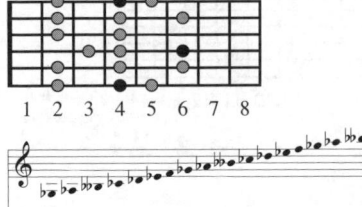
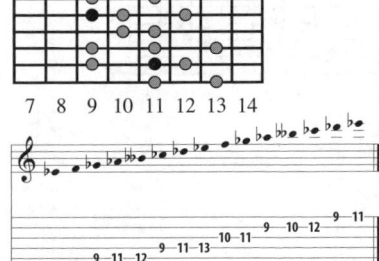

## Locrian ♮2 (1 2 ♭3 4 ♭5 6 ♭7 8)
6th mode of the melodic minor scale

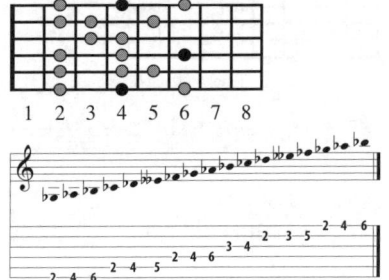
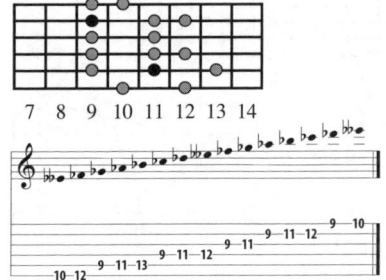

## Locrian ♮6 (1 ♭2 ♭3 4 ♭5 6 ♭7 8)
2nd mode of the harmonic minor scale

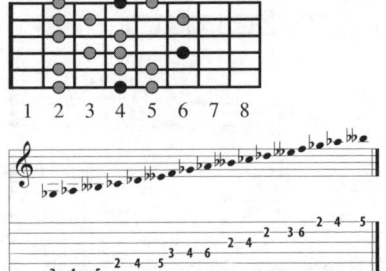
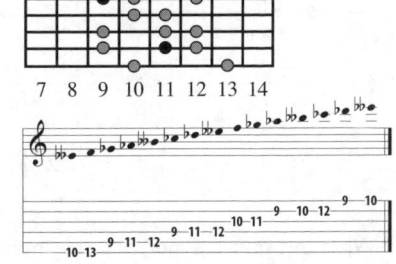

# Symmetrical Scales

## Chromatic (1 ♭2 2 ♭3 3 4 ♭5 5 ♭6 6 ♭7 7 8)

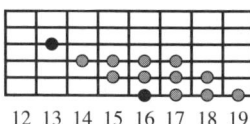

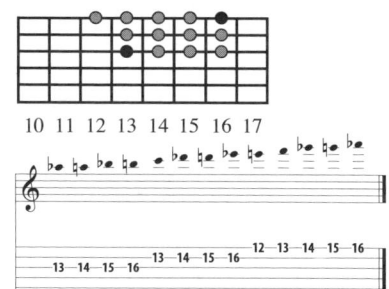

## Whole Tone (1 2 3 ♯4 ♯5 ♯6 8)

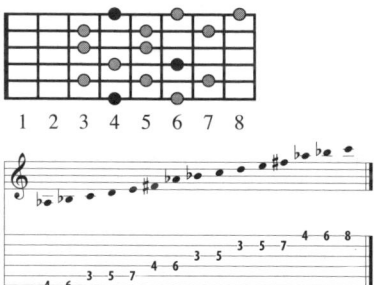
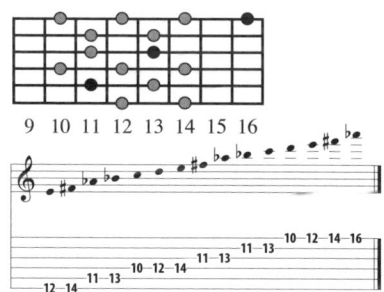

## Auxiliary, Whole/Half Diminished (1 2 ♭3 4 ♭5 ♭6 6 7 8)

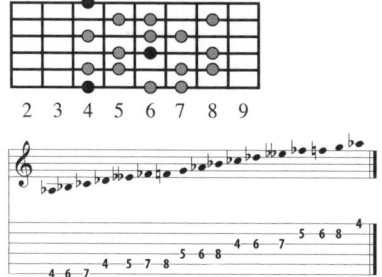
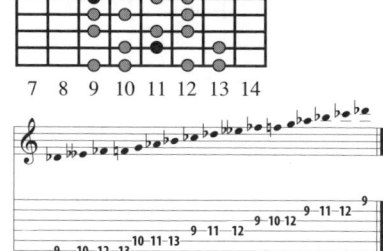

# A♭

## Symmetrical, Half/Whole Diminished (1 ♭2 ♭3 ♭4 ♭5 5 6 ♭7 8)

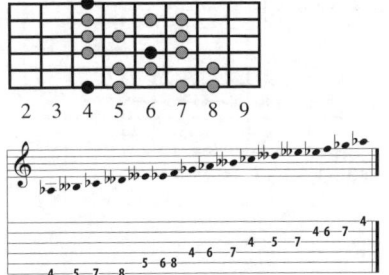
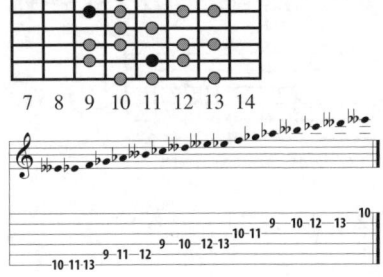

## Augmented (1 ♯2 3 5 ♯5 7 8)

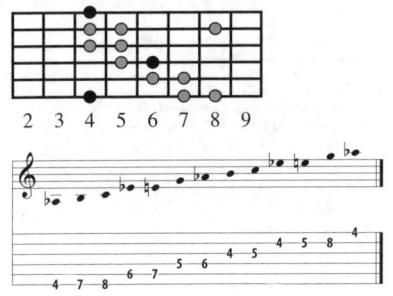
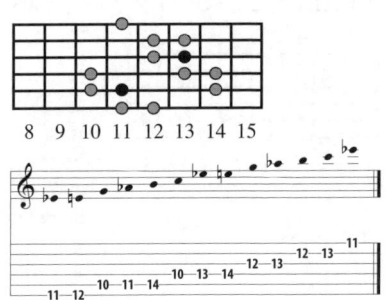

## Chromatic Augmented (1 ♭2 2 3 4 ♯4 ♯5 6 ♭7 8)

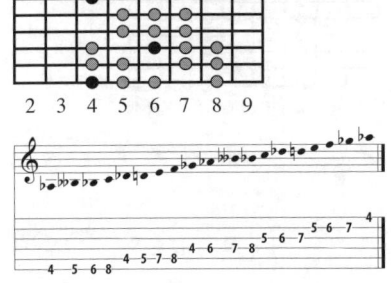
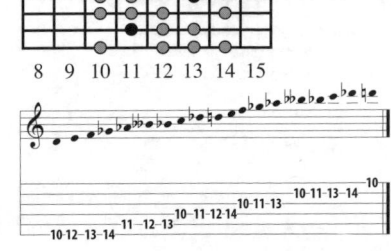

# Augmented ♭9 (1 ♭2 ♭3 3 4 5 ♭6 6 7 8)

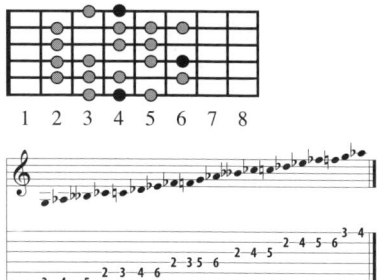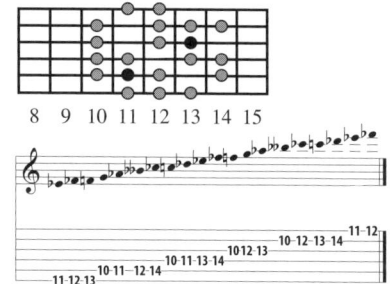

# Augmented 9 (1 2 ♭3 3 ♯4 5 ♭6 ♭7 7 8)

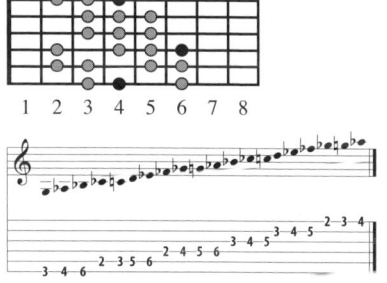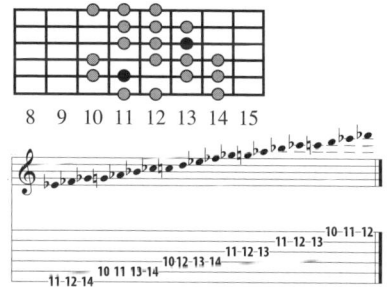

# Diminished Blues (1 ♭2 ♭3 3 ♯5 6 ♭7 8)

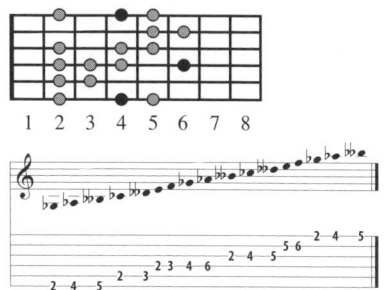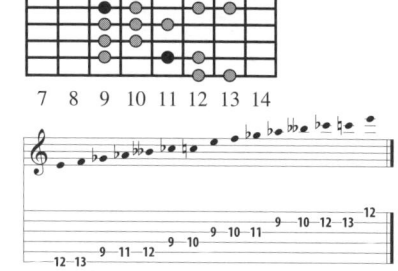

# Four Semitone Tritone (1 b2 2 b3 3 #4 5 b6 6 b7 8)

# Tetratonic (1 4 b5 7 8)

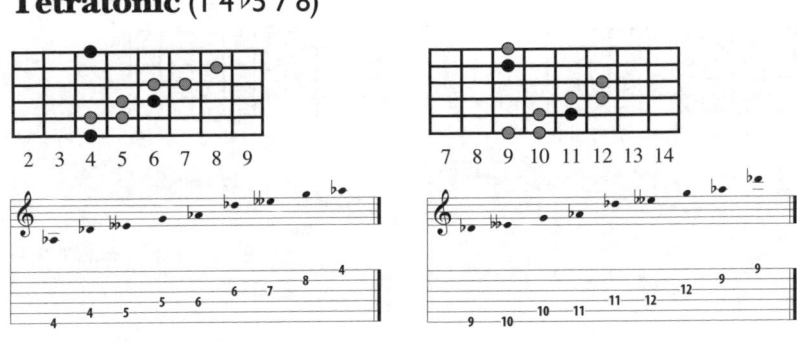

# Three Semitone Tritone (1 b2 2 b3 b5 5 b6 6 8)

## Tritone (1 ♭2 3 ♯4 5 ♭7 8)

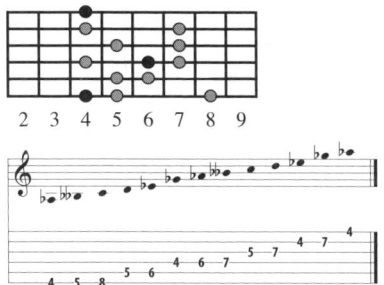
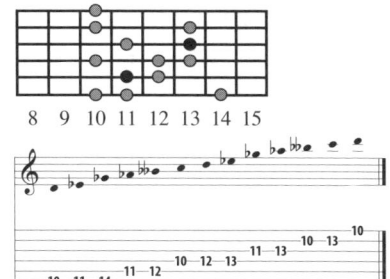

## Two-Semitone Tritone (1 ♭2 2 ♯4 5 ♭6 8)

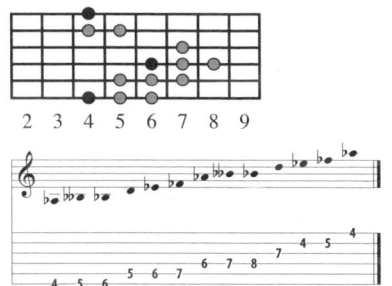
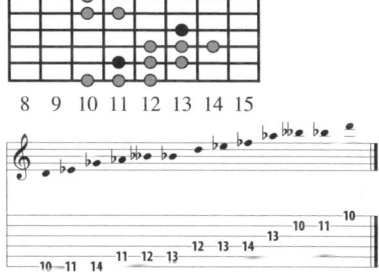

# Hybrid Scales

## Aeolian ♯11 (1 2 ♭3 ♯4 5 ♭6 ♭7 8)

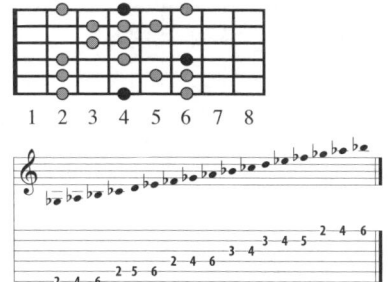
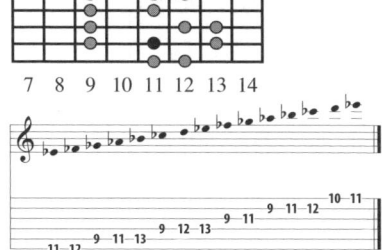

# Augmented Dominant (1 2 3 4 #5 6 b7 8)

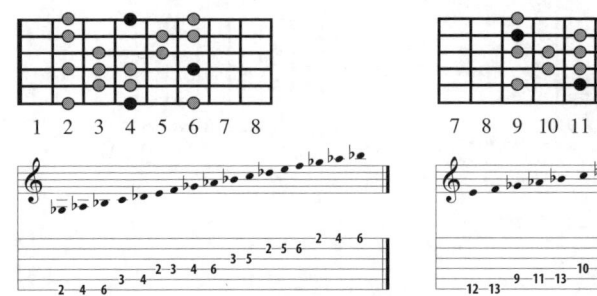

# Augmented Dominant b9 (1 b2 3 4 #5 6 b7 8)

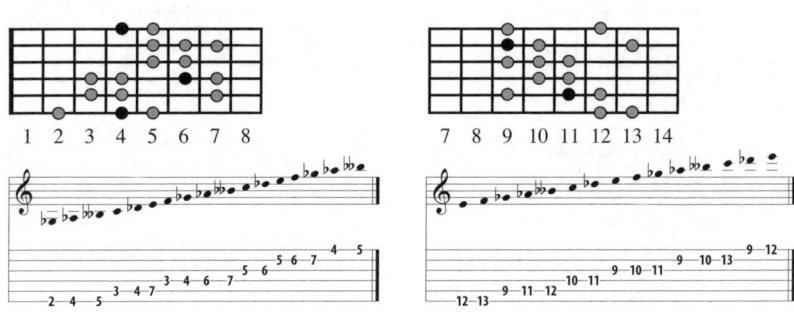

# Augmented Dominant #9 (1 #2 3 4 #5 6 b7 8)

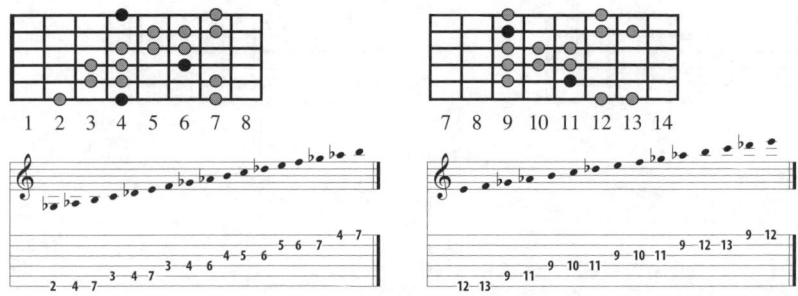

## Augmented #9 (1 #2 3 4 #5 6 7 8)

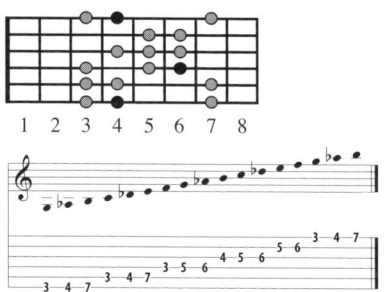
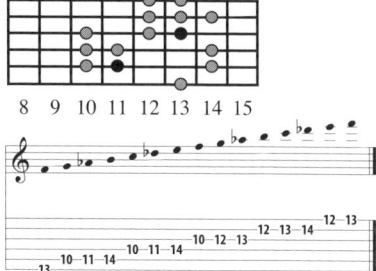

## Augmented Minor/Major 7 (1 2 ♭3 4 #5 6 7 8)

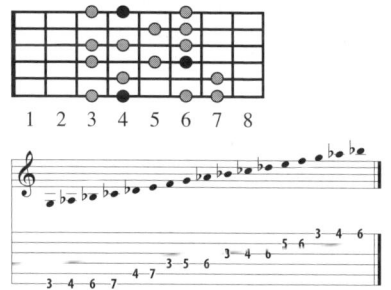
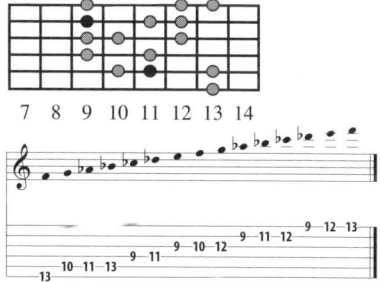

## Bebop Dominant (1 2 3 4 5 6 ♭7 7 8)

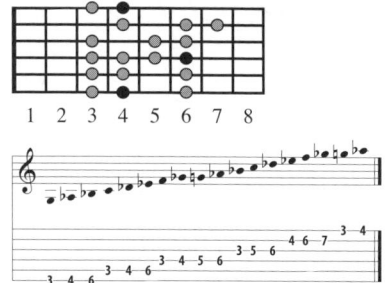
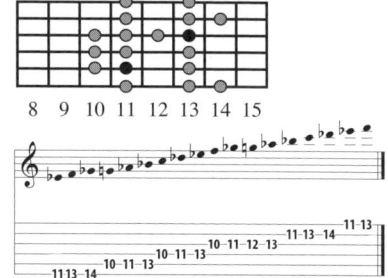

## Bebop Dorian (1 2 ♭3 3 4 5 6 ♭7 8)

## Bebop Major* (1 2 3 4 ♯4 5 6 7 8)

## Bebop Melodic Minor* (1 2 ♭3 4 ♯4 5 6 7 8)

\* Many musicians spell this scale with a ♯5 instead of a ♯4.

## Diminished Tritonic (1 ♭3 4 ♭5 8)

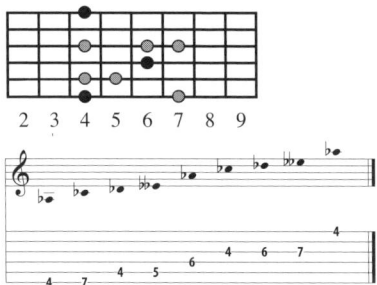
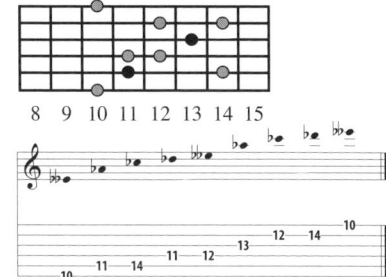

## Dominant ♭5 (1 2 3 4 ♭5 6 ♭7 8)

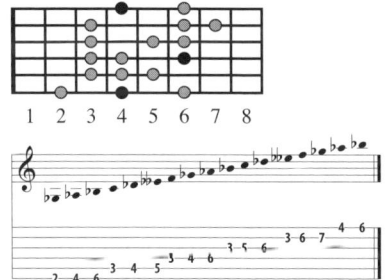
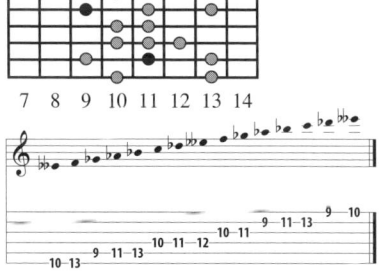

## Dominant ♭5 ♭9 #9 (1 ♭2 ♭3 ♭4 ♭5 6 ♭7 8)

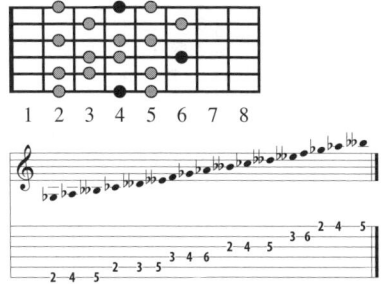
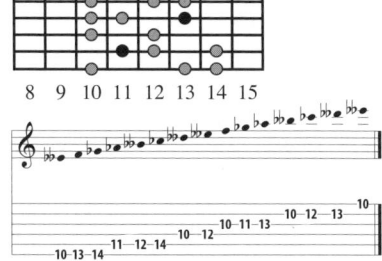

# A♭

## Dominant ♭9 ♯9 (1 ♭2 ♭3 ♭4 5 6 ♭7 8)

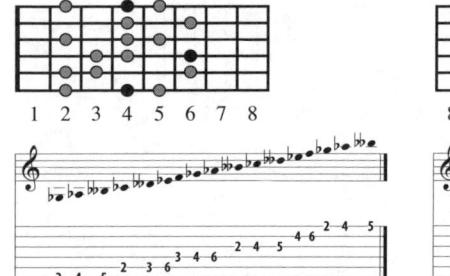
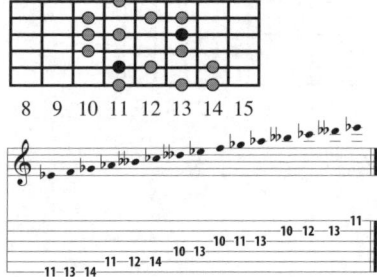

## Dominant ♭9 ♯9 ♭13 (1 ♭2 ♭3 ♭4 5 ♭6 ♭7 8)

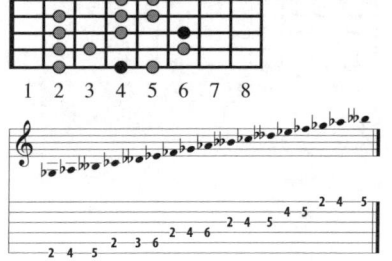
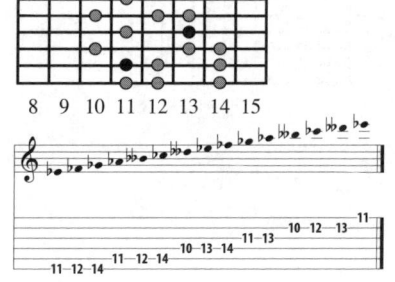

## Dominant ♯9 (1 ♯2 3 4 5 6 ♭7 8)

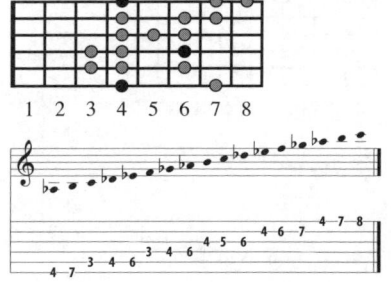
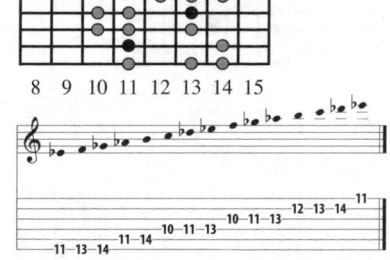

# Dominant ♭9 ♯11 (1 ♭2 3 ♯4 5 6 ♭7 8)

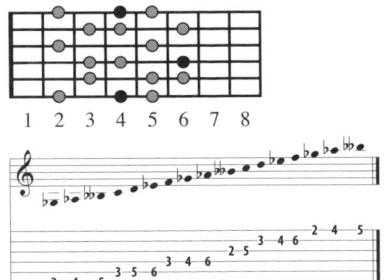
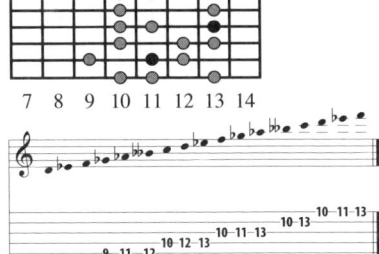

# Dominant ♭9 ♯11 ♭13 (1 ♭2 3 ♯4 5 ♭6 ♭7 8)

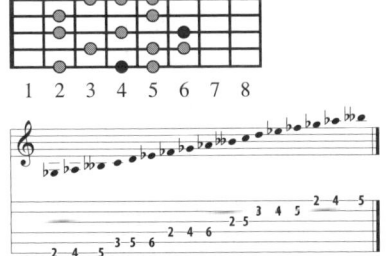
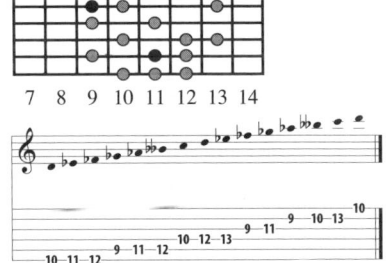

# Dominant 13 (1 2 3 5 6 ♭7 8)

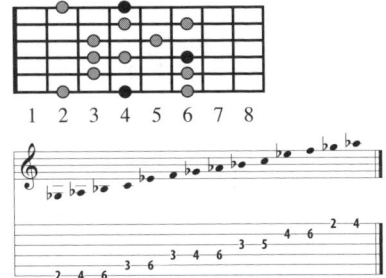
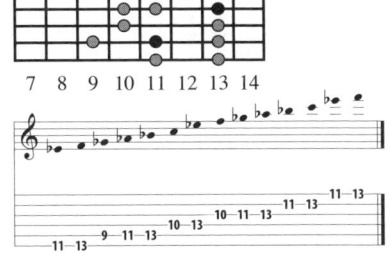

# Major and Dominant Scales

## Major/Ionian (1 2 3 4 5 6 7 8)

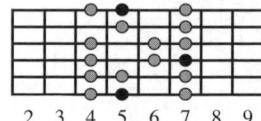
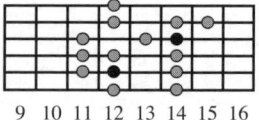
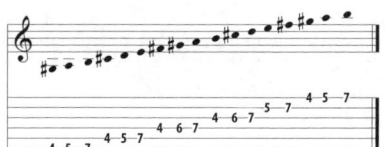
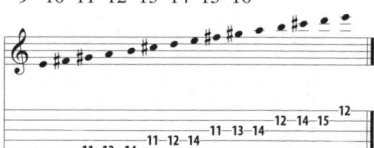

## Mixolydian (1 2 3 4 5 6 ♭7 8)
5th mode of the major scale

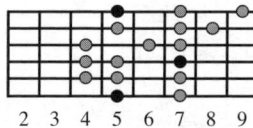
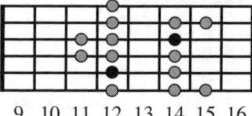
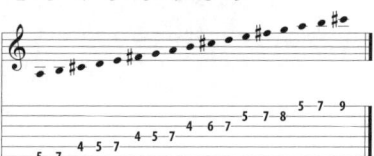
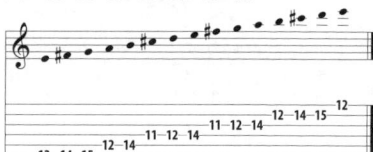

## Lydian (1 2 3 ♯4 5 6 7 8)
4th mode of the major scale

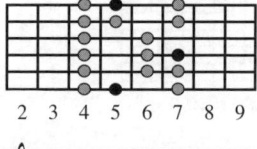
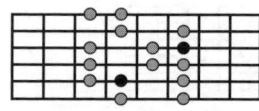
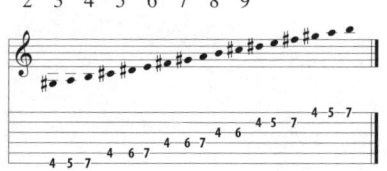

## **Major Pentatonic** (1 2 3 5 6 8)

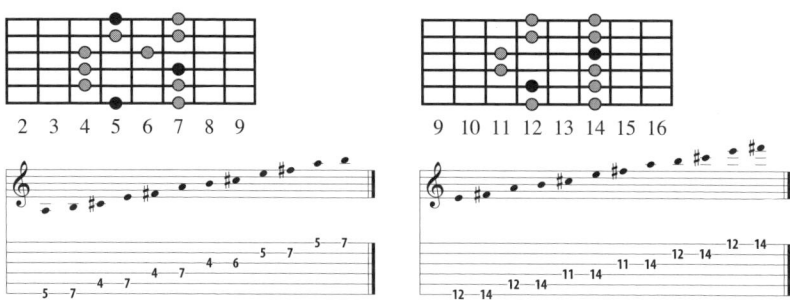

## **Major 13 Pentatonic**\* (1 2 3 5 6 7 8)

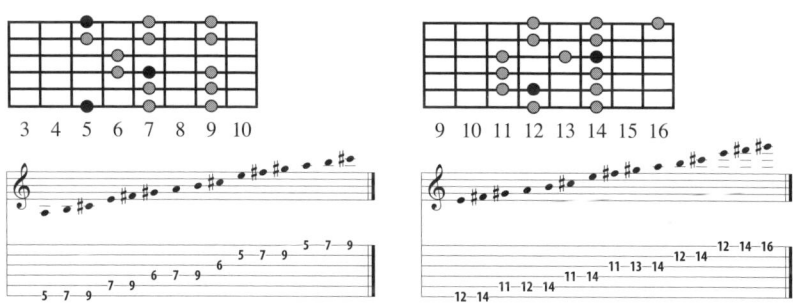

## **Major Pentatonic Blues**\* (1 2 ♭3 3 5 6 8)

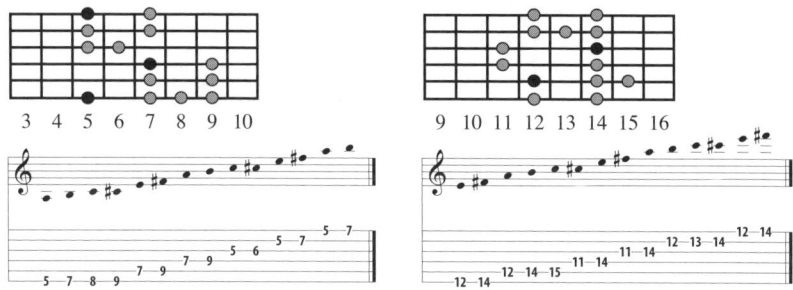

\* While this scale has more than five notes, it is based on a five-note, pentatonic scale and it is best to think of it as a pentatonic scale.

## Lydian Pentatonic (1 3 #4 5 7 8)

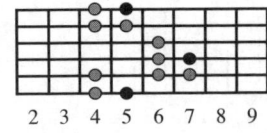
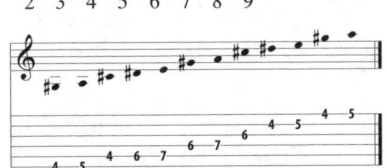
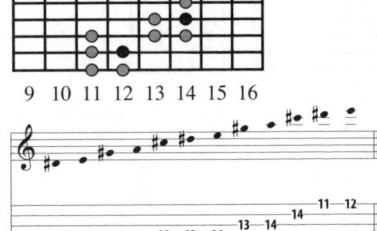

## Lydian ♭7 (1 2 3 #4 5 6 ♭7 8)
4th mode of the melodic minor scale

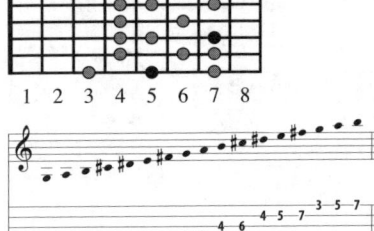
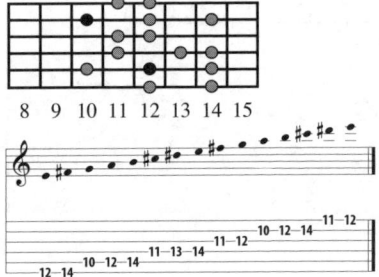

## Lydian #9 (1 #2 3 #4 5 6 7 8)
6th mode of the harmonic minor scale

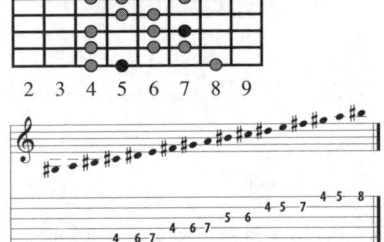
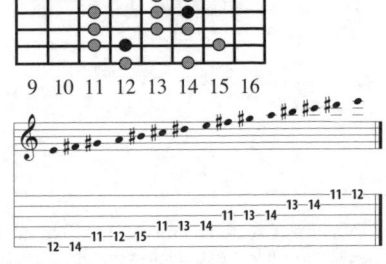

# Aeolian Major (1 2 3 4 5 ♭6 ♭7 8)

5th mode of the melodic minor scale

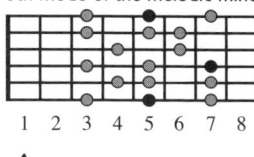
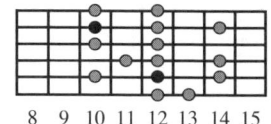

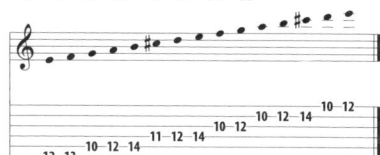

# Phrygian Major (1 ♭2 3 4 5 ♭6 ♭7 8)

5th mode of the harmonic minor scale

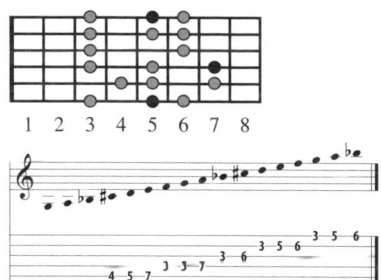
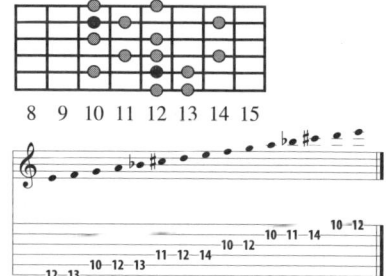

# Ionian Augmented (1 2 3 4 ♯5 6 7 8)

3rd mode of the harmonic minor scale

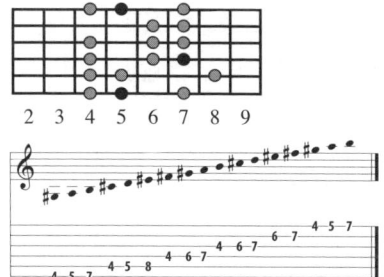
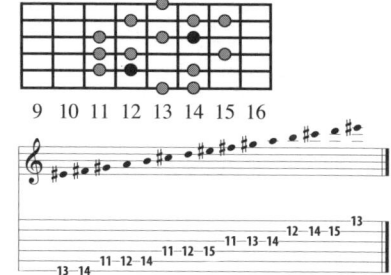

## Lydian Augmented (1 2 3 #4 #5 6 7 8)
3rd mode of the melodic minor scale

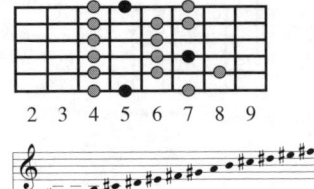
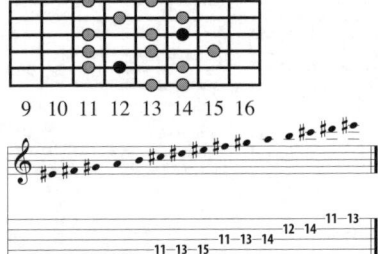

# Minor Scales

## Natural Minor/Aeolian (1 2 b3 4 5 b6 b7 8)
6th mode of the major scale

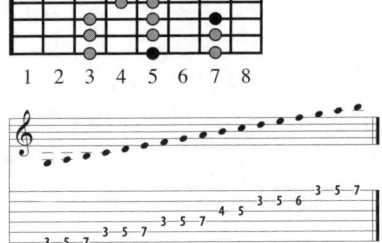
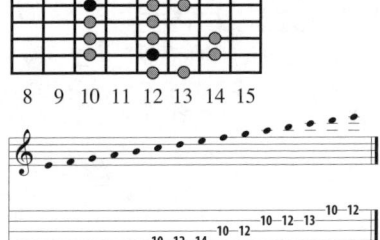

## Harmonic Minor (1 2 b3 4 5 b6 7 8)

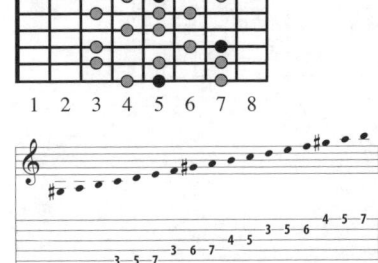
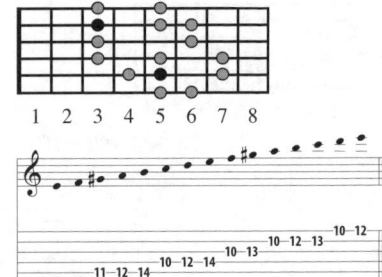

# Jazz Minor/Melodic Minor (1 2 ♭3 4 5 6 7 8)
Melodic Minor descends in Aeolian/Natural Minor

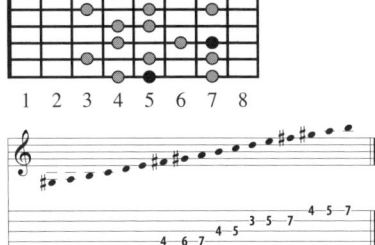
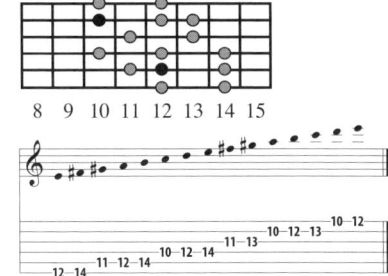

# Dorian (1 2 ♭3 4 5 6 ♭7 8)
2nd mode of the major scale

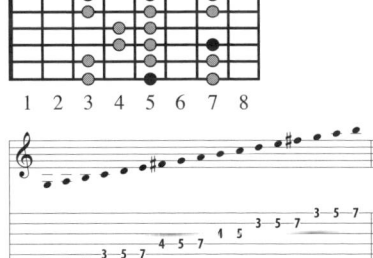
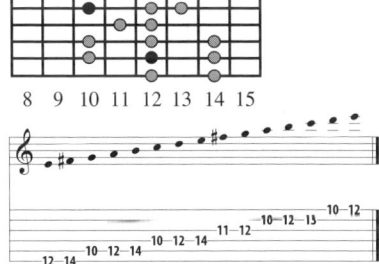

# Phrygian (1 ♭2 ♭3 4 5 ♭6 ♭7 8)
3rd mode of the major scale

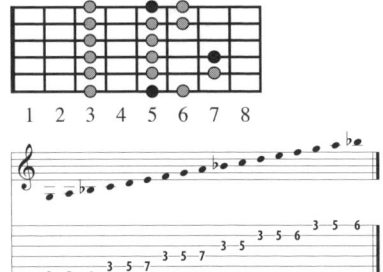
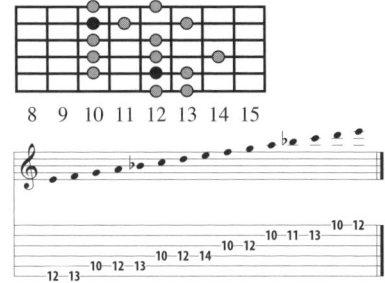

## **Locrian** (1 ♭2 ♭3 4 ♭5 ♭6 ♭7 8)
7th mode of the major scale

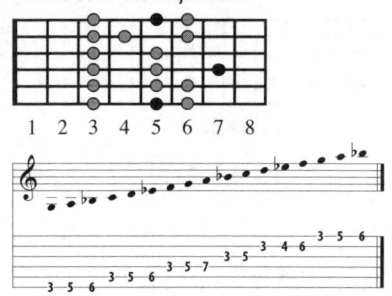

## **Minor Pentatonic** (1 ♭3 4 5 ♭7 8)

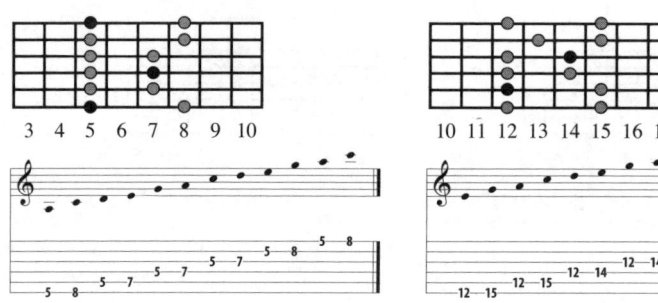

## **Minor 13 Pentatonic**\* (1 ♭3 5 ♭6 ♭7 8)

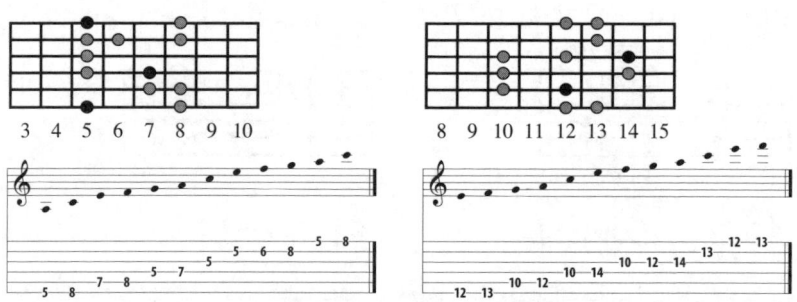

\* While this scale has more than five notes, it is based on a five-note, pentatonic scale and it is best to think of it as a pentatonic scale.

# Minor Pentatonic Blues* (1 ♭3 4 ♭5 5 ♭7 8)

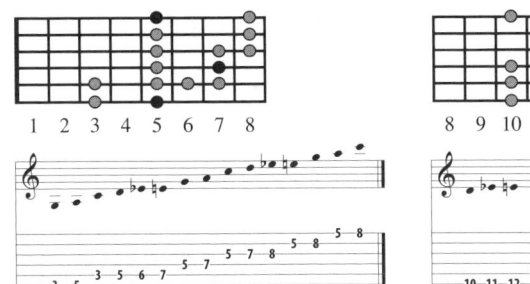
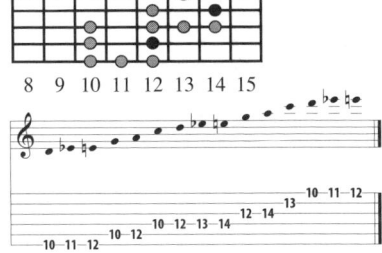

# Dorian Pentatonic (1 2 ♭3 5 ♭7 8)

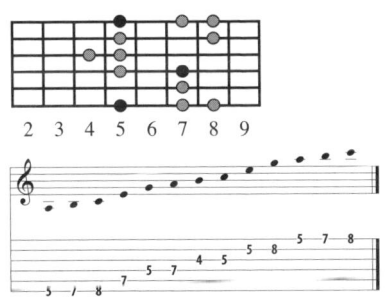
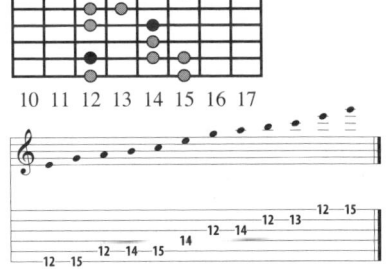

# Phrygian Pentatonic (1 ♭2 4 5 ♭7 8)

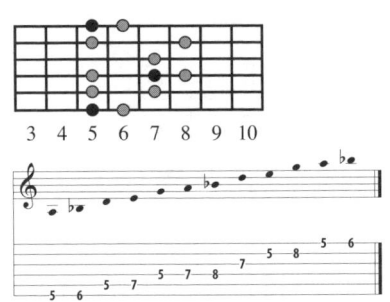
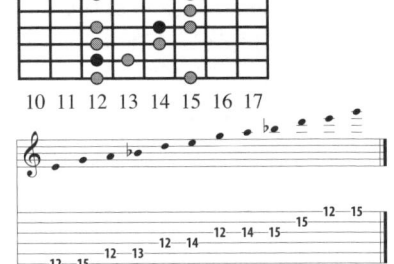

\* While this scale has more than five notes, it is based on a five-note, pentatonic scale and it is best to think of it as a pentatonic scale.

## Phrygian ♮6 (1 ♭2 ♭3 4 5 6 ♭7 8)
2nd mode of the melodic minor scale

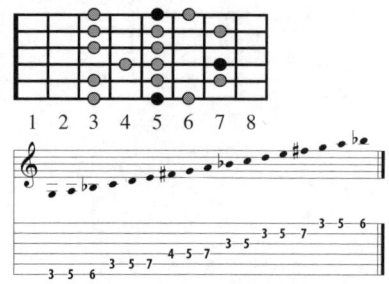
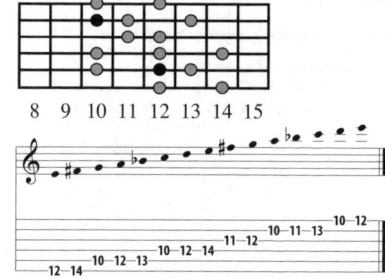

## Locrian ♮2 (1 2 ♭3 4 ♭5 ♭6 ♭7 8)
6th mode of the melodic minor scale

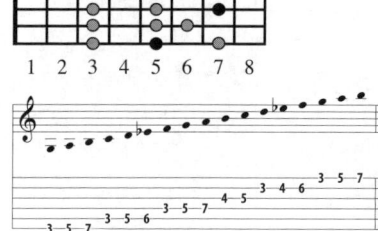
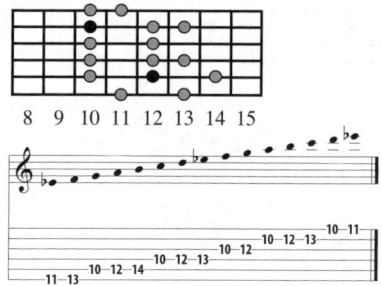

## Locrian ♮6 (1 ♭2 ♭3 4 ♭5 6 ♭7 8)
2nd mode of the harmonic minor scale

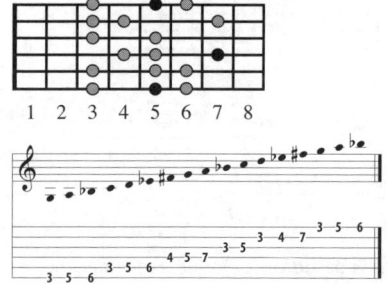
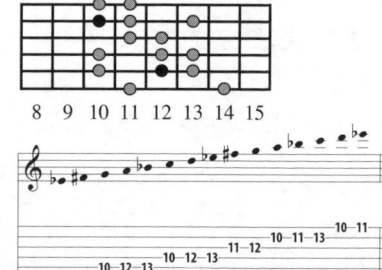

# Symmetrical Scales

## Chromatic (1 ♭2 2 ♭3 3 4 ♭5 5 ♭6 6 ♭7 7 8)

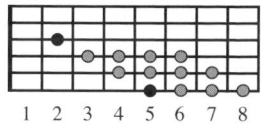
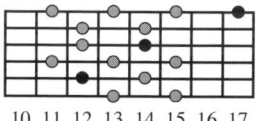

## Whole Tone (1 2 3 ♯4 ♯5 ♯6 8)

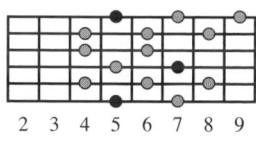

## Auxiliary, Whole/Half Diminished (1 2 ♭3 4 ♭5 ♭6 6 7 8)

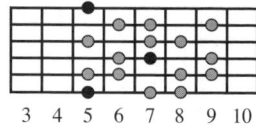
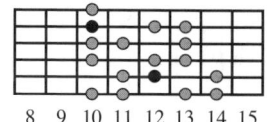

# Symmetrical, Half/Whole Diminished (1 ♭2 ♭3 ♭4 ♭5 5 6 ♭7 8)

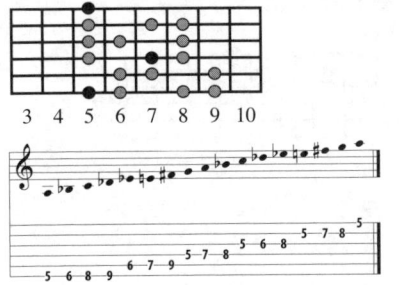
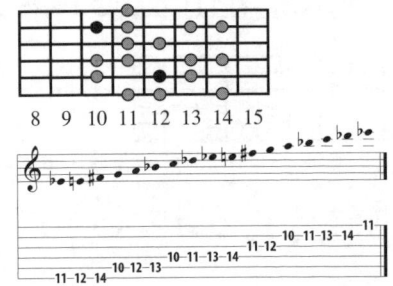

# Augmented (1 #2 3 5 #5 7 8)

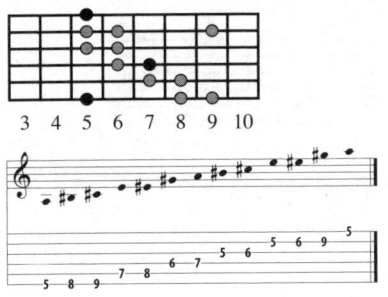
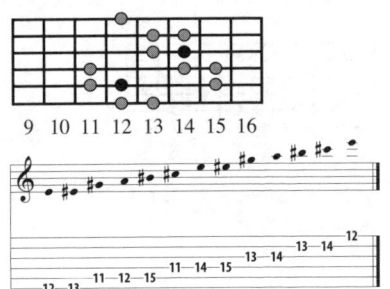

# Chromatic Augmented (1 ♭2 2 3 4 #4 #5 6 ♭7 8)

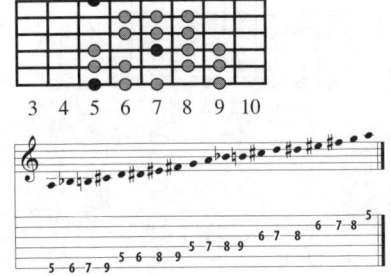
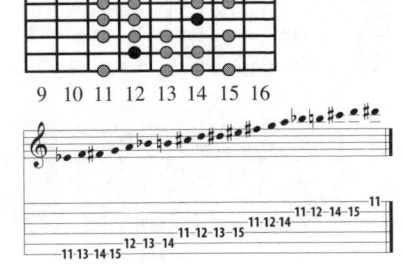

## Augmented ♭9 (1 ♭2 ♭3 3 4 5 ♭6 6 7 8)

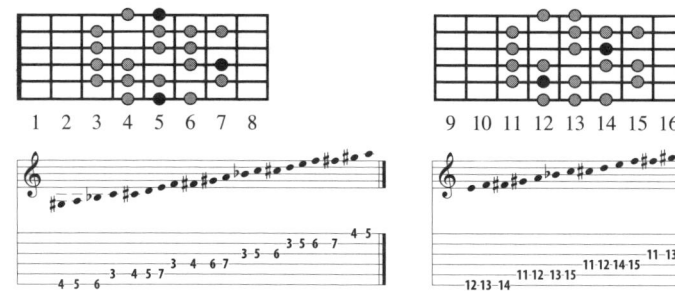

## Augmented 9 (1 2 ♭3 3 ♯4 5 ♭6 ♭7 7 8)

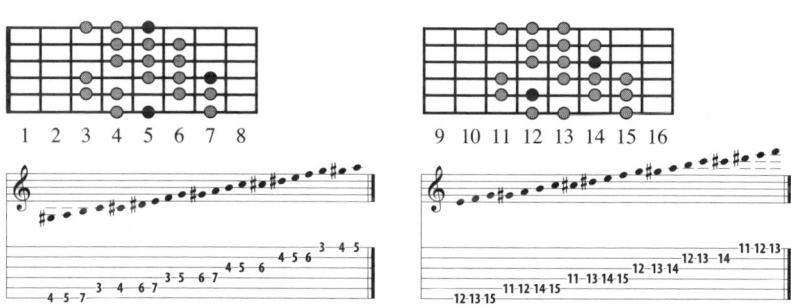

## Diminished Blues (1 ♭2 ♭3 3 ♯5 6 ♭7 8)

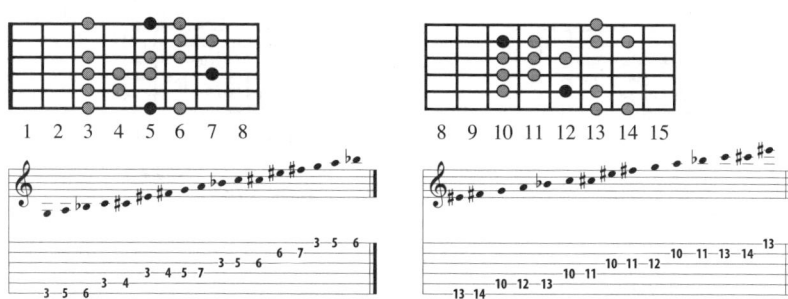

# Four Semitone Tritone (1 ♭2 2 ♭3 3 ♯4 5 ♭6 6 ♭7 8)

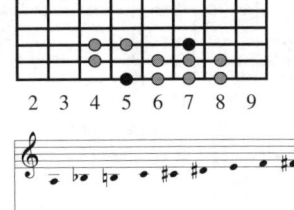

# Tetratonic (1 4 ♭5 7 8)

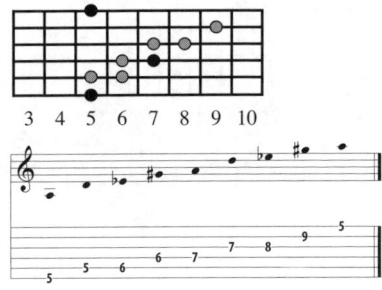
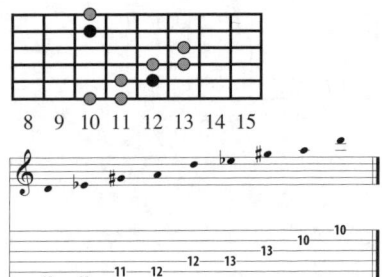

# Three Semitone Tritone (1 ♭2 2 ♭3 ♭5 5 ♭6 6 8)

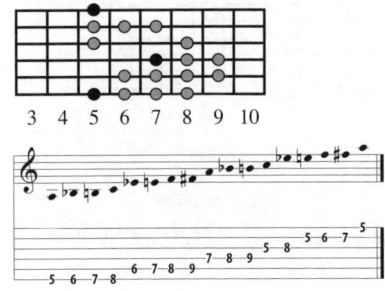
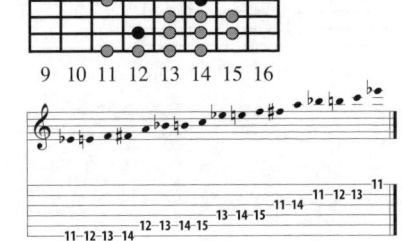

## Tritone (1 ♭2 3 ♯4 5 ♭7 8)

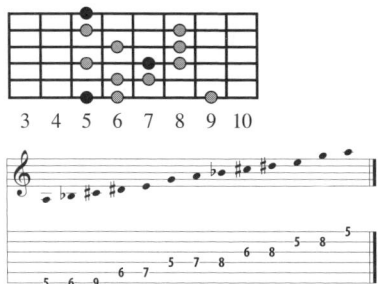 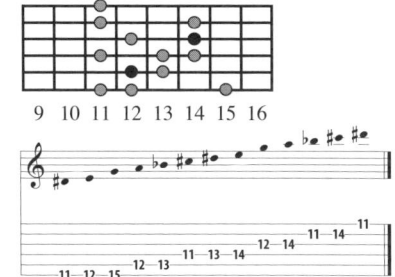

## Two-Semitone Tritone (1 ♭2 2 ♯4 5 ♭6 8)

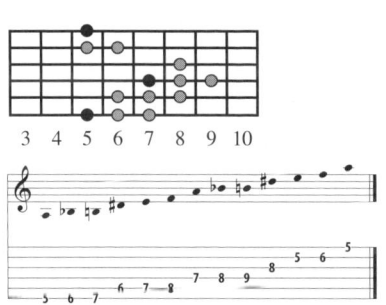 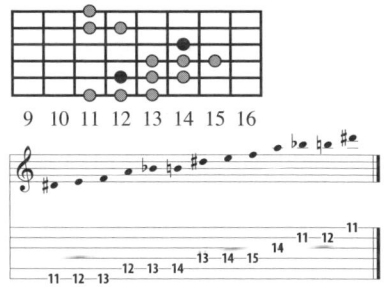

# Hybrid Scales

## Aeolian ♯11 (1 2 ♭3 ♯4 5 ♭6 ♭7 8)

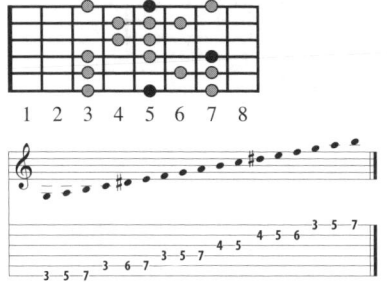 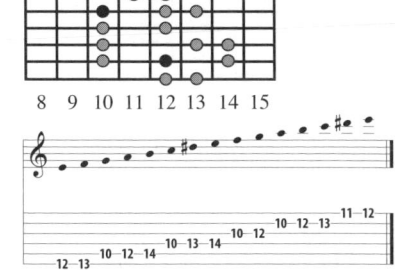

## Augmented Dominant (1 2 3 4 #5 6 b7 8)

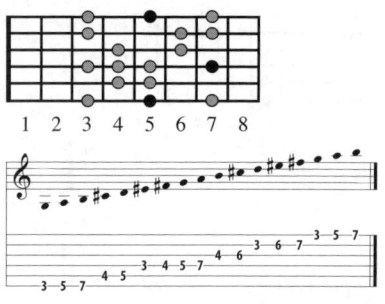
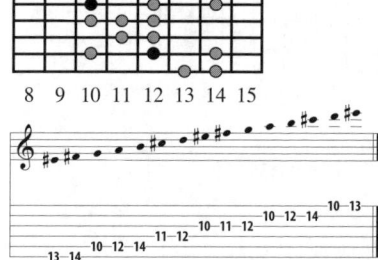

## Augmented Dominant b9 (1 b2 3 4 #5 6 b7 8)

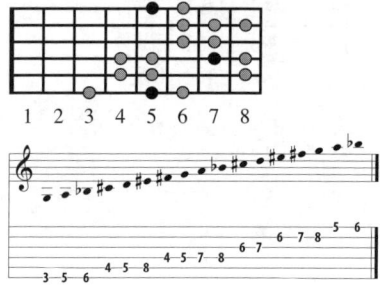
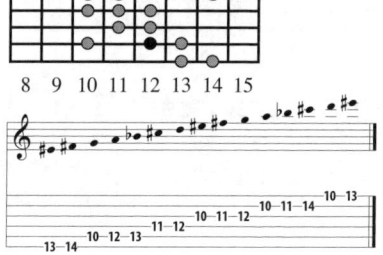

## Augmented Dominant #9 (1 #2 3 4 #5 6 b7 8)

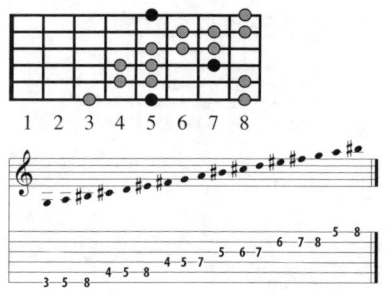
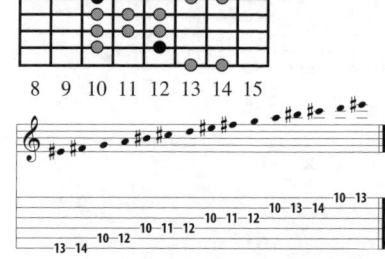

## Augmented ♯9 (1 ♯2 3 4 ♯5 6 7 8)

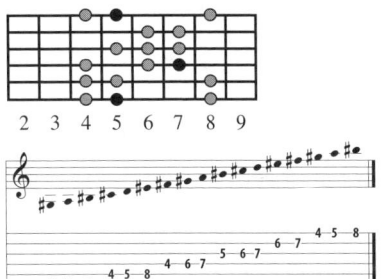
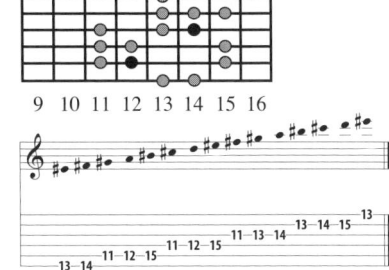

## Augmented Minor/Major 7 (1 2 ♭3 4 ♯5 6 7 8)

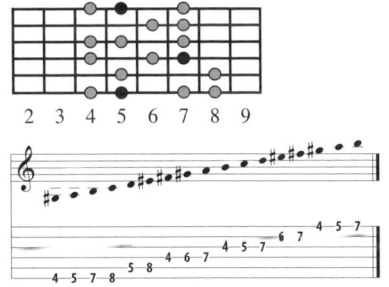
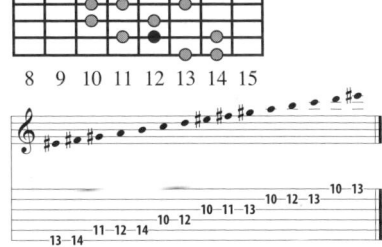

## Bebop Dominant (1 2 3 4 5 6 ♭7 7 8)

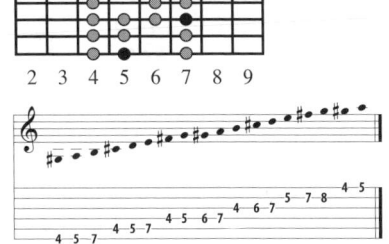
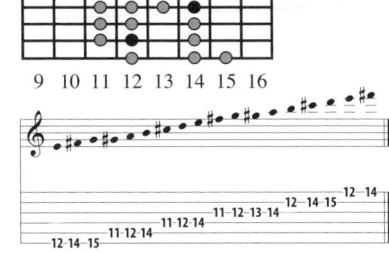

## Bebop Dorian (1 2 ♭3 3 4 5 6 ♭7 8)

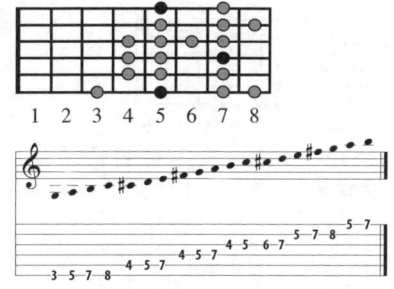
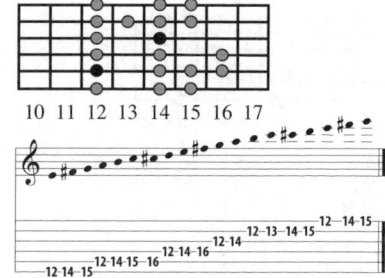

## Bebop Major* (1 2 3 4 ♯4 5 6 7 8)

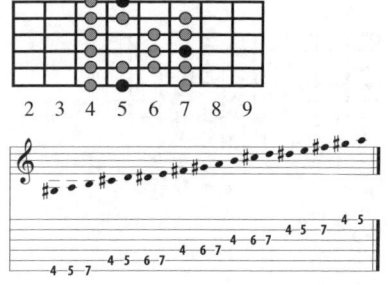
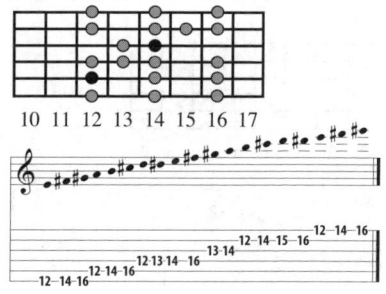

## Bebop Melodic Minor* (1 2 ♭3 4 ♯4 5 6 7 8)

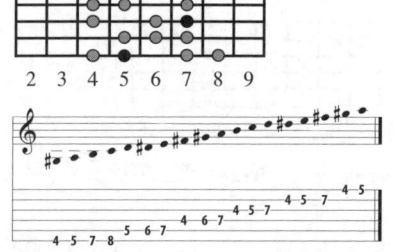
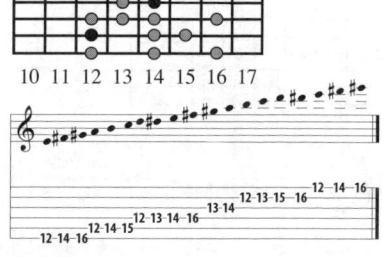

* Many musicians spell this scale with a ♯5 instead of a ♯4.

## Diminished Tritonic (1 ♭3 4 ♭5 8)

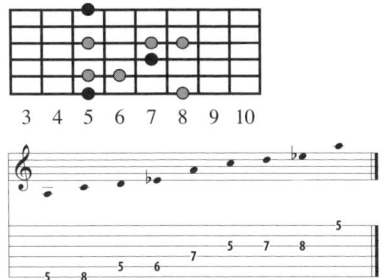

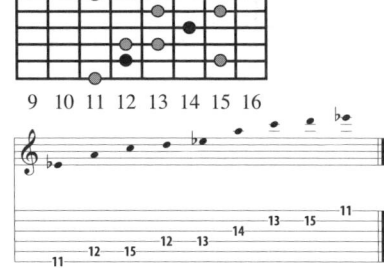

## Dominant ♭5 (1 2 3 4 ♭5 6 ♭7 8)

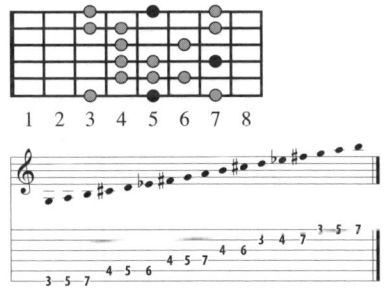

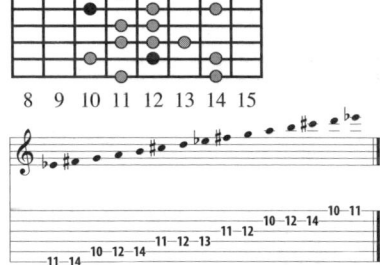

## Dominant ♭5 ♭9 #9 (1 ♭2 ♭3 ♭4 ♭5 6 ♭7 8)

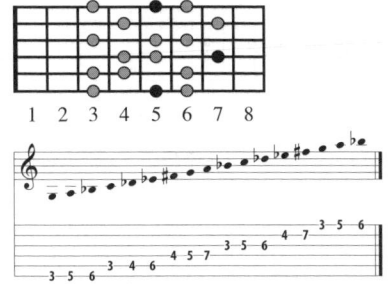

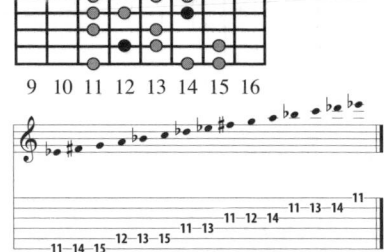

## Dominant ♭9 ♯9 (1 ♭2 ♯3 ♭4 5 6 ♭7 8)

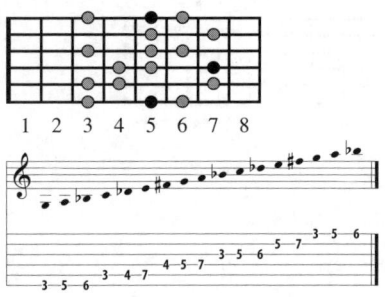
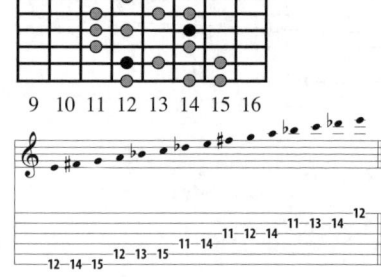

## Dominant ♭9 ♯9 ♭13 (1 ♭2 ♯3 ♭4 5 ♭6 ♭7 8)

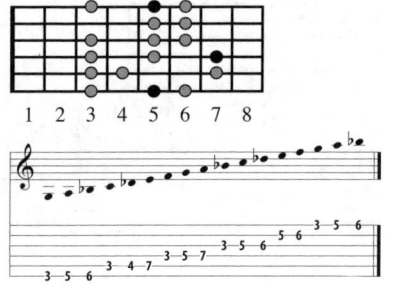
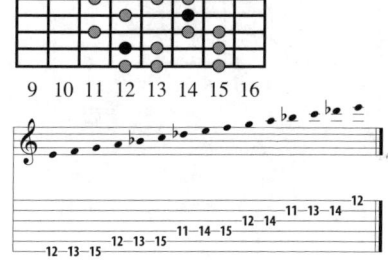

## Dominant ♯9 (1 ♯2 3 4 5 6 ♭7 8)

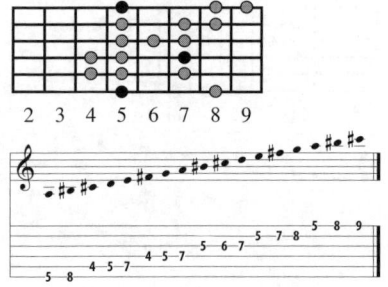
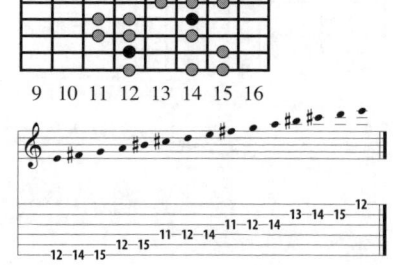

## Dominant ♭9 ♯11 (1 ♭2 3 ♯4 5 6 ♭7 8)

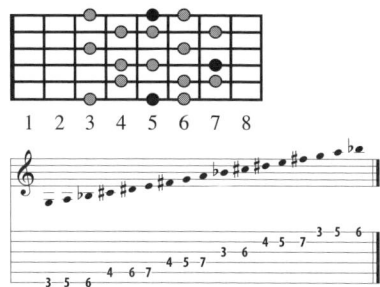
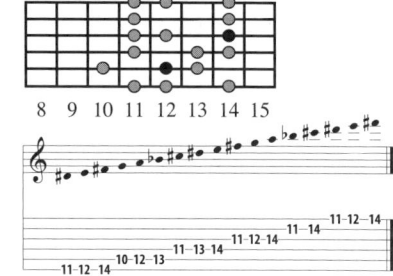

## Dominant ♭9 ♯11 ♭13 (1 ♭2 3 ♯4 5 ♭6 ♭7 8)

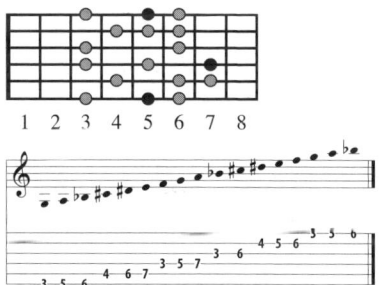
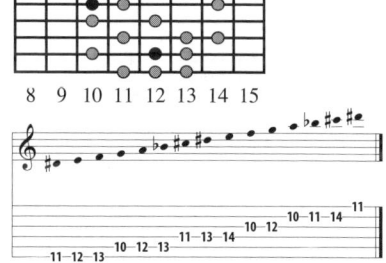

## Dominant 13 (1 2 3 5 6 ♭7 8)

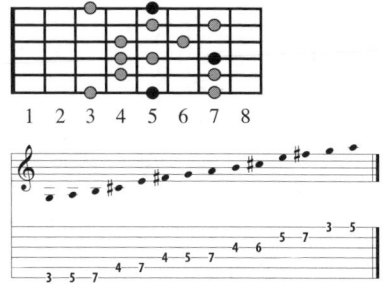
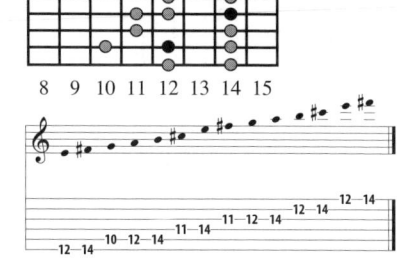

# Major and Dominant Scales

## Major/Ionian (1 2 3 4 5 6 7 8)

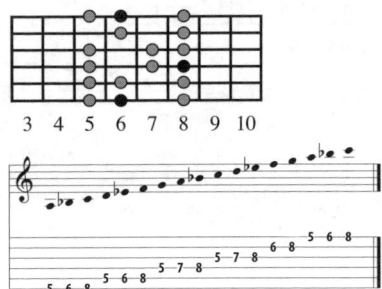
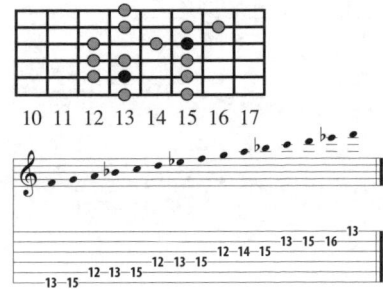

## Mixolydian (1 2 3 4 5 6 ♭7 8)
5th mode of the major scale

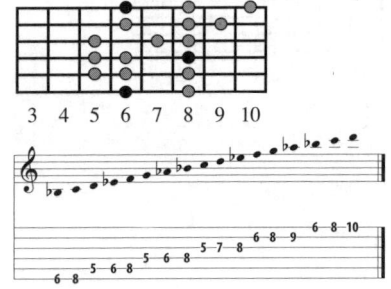
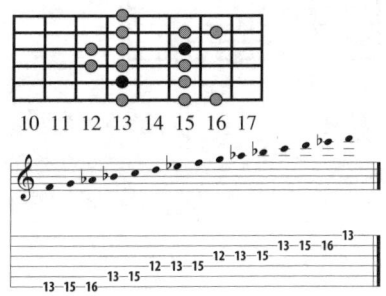

## Lydian (1 2 3 ♯4 5 6 7 8)
4th mode of the major scale

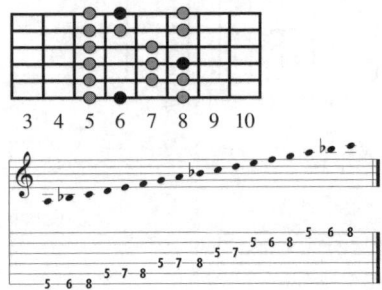
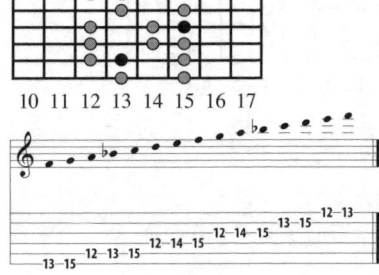

## Major Pentatonic (1 2 3 5 6 8)

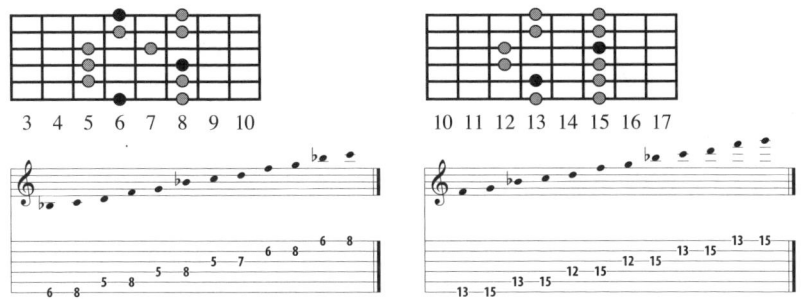

## Major 13 Pentatonic* (1 2 3 5 6 7 8)

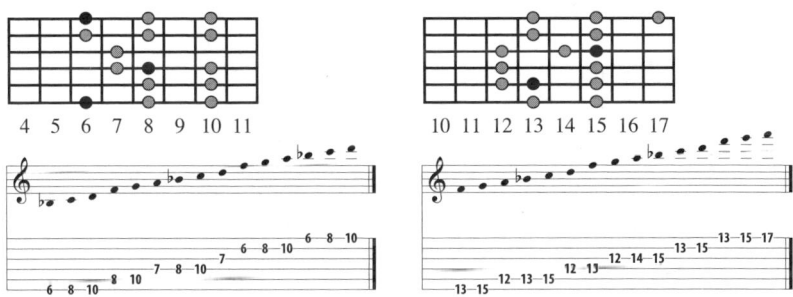

## Major Pentatonic Blues* (1 2 b3 3 5 6 8)

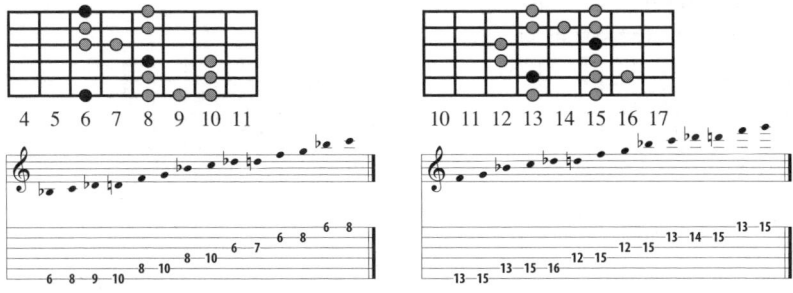

* While this scale has more than five notes, it is based on a five-note, pentatonic scale and it is best to think of it as a pentatonic scale.

# Lydian Pentatonic (1 3 #4 5 7 8)

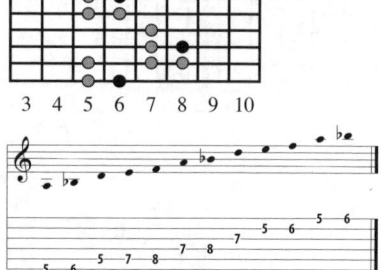
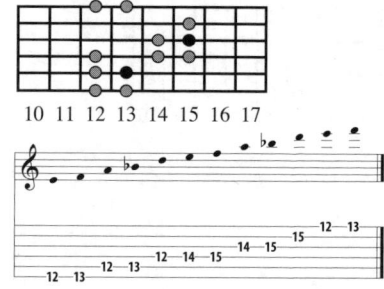

# Lydian ♭7 (1 2 3 #4 5 6 ♭7 8)
4th mode of the melodic minor scale

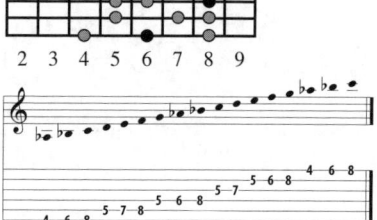
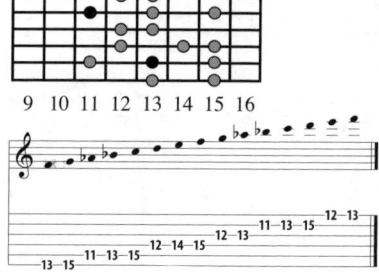

# Lydian #9 (1 #2 3 #4 5 6 7 8)
6th mode of the harmonic minor scale

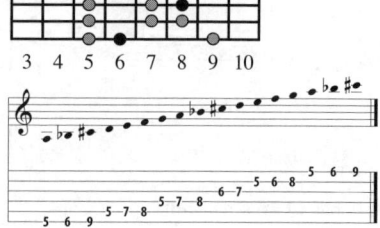
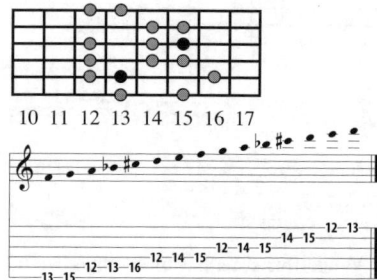

## Aeolian Major (1 2 3 4 5 ♭6 ♭7 8)
5th mode of the melodic minor scale

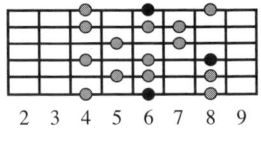
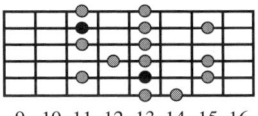

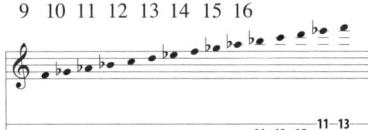

## Phrygian Major (1 ♭2 3 4 5 ♭6 ♭7 8)
5th mode of the harmonic minor scale

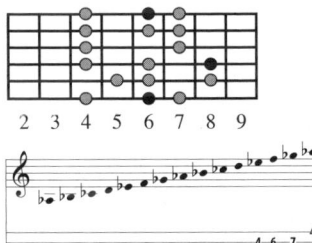
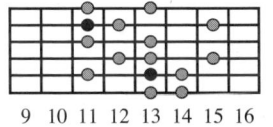

## Ionian Augmented (1 2 3 4 ♯5 6 7 8)
3rd mode of the harmonic minor scale

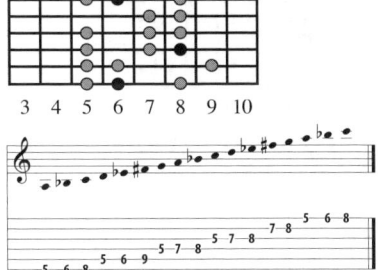
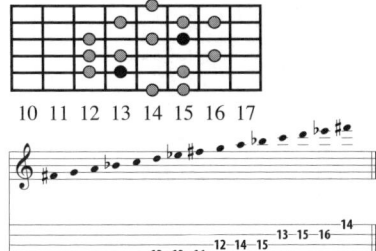

## Lydian Augmented (1 2 3 #4 #5 6 7 8)
3rd mode of the melodic minor scale

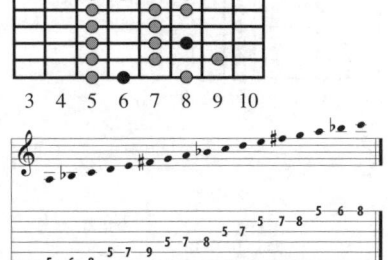
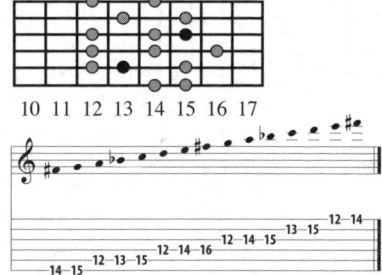

# Minor Scales

## Natural Minor/Aeolian (1 2 ♭3 4 5 ♭6 ♭7 8)
6th mode of the major scale

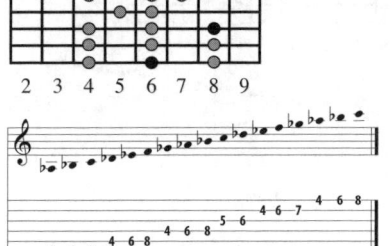
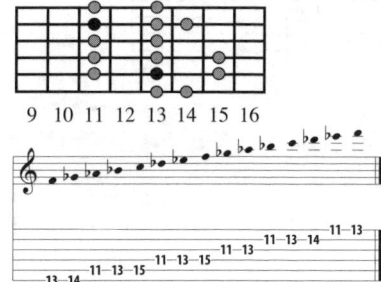

## Harmonic Minor (1 2 ♭3 4 5 ♭6 7 8)

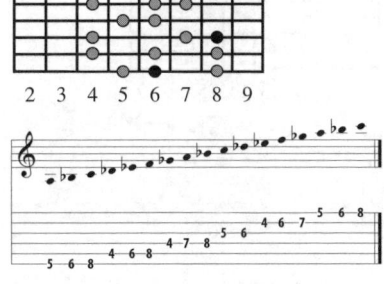
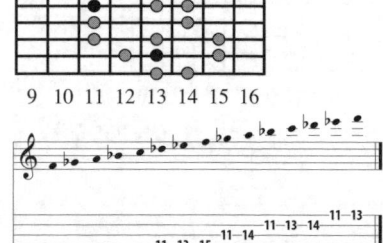

# Jazz Minor/Melodic Minor (1 2 ♭3 4 5 6 7 8)
Melodic Minor descends in Aeolian/Natural Minor

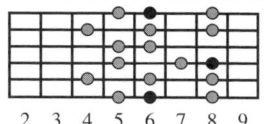

# Dorian (1 2 ♭3 4 5 6 ♭7 8)
2nd mode of the major scale

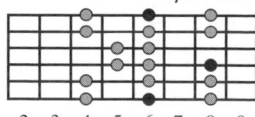
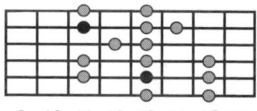

# Phrygian (1 ♭2 ♭3 4 5 ♭6 ♭7 8)
3rd mode of the major scale

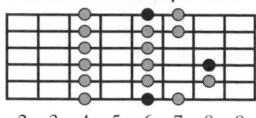
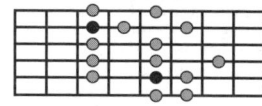

## Locrian (1 ♭2 ♭3 4 ♭5 ♭6 ♭7 8)
7th mode of the major scale

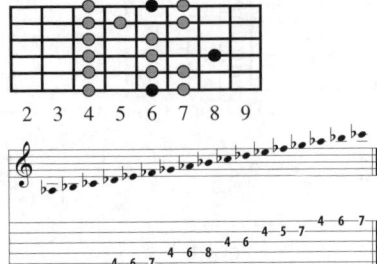
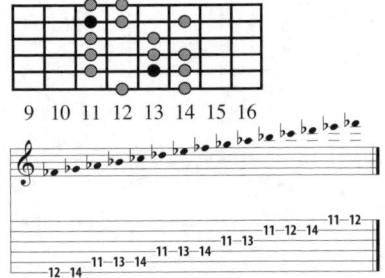

## Minor Pentatonic (1 ♭3 4 5 ♭7 8)

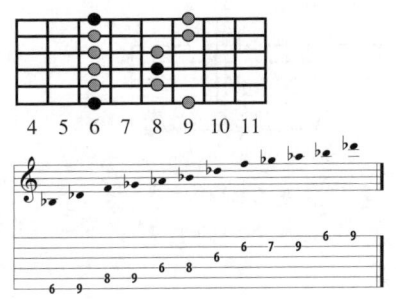
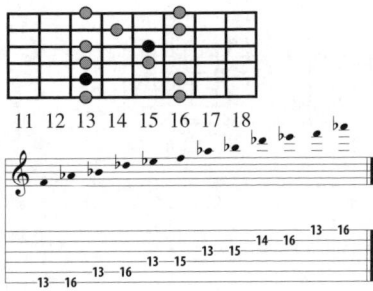

## Minor 13 Pentatonic* (1 ♭3 5 ♭6 ♭7 8)

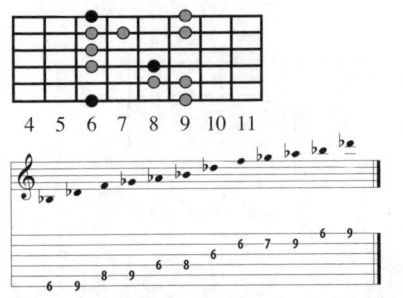
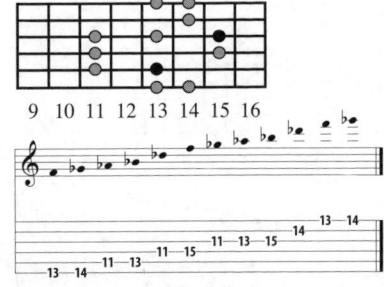

* While this scale has more than five notes, it is based on a five-note, pentatonic scale and it is best to think of it as a pentatonic scale.

## Minor Pentatonic Blues* (1 ♭3 4 ♭5 5 ♭7 8)

## Dorian Pentatonic (1 2 ♭3 5 ♭7 8)

## Phrygian Pentatonic (1 ♭2 4 5 ♭7 8)

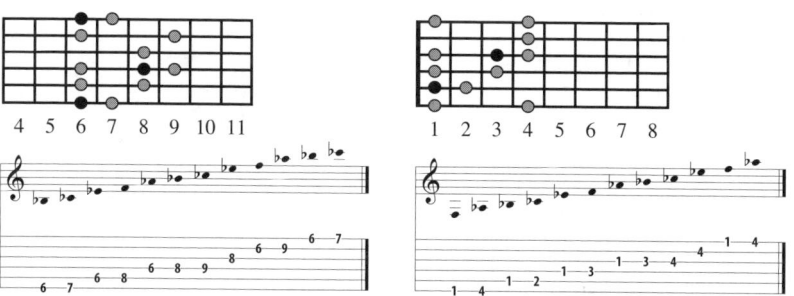

* While this scale has more than five notes, it is based on a five-note, pentatonic scale and it is best to think of it as a pentatonic scale.

# Phrygian ♮6 (1 ♭2 ♭3 4 5 6 ♭7 8)
2nd mode of the melodic minor scale

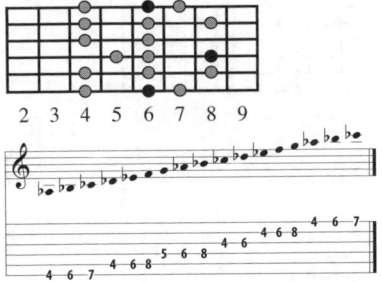
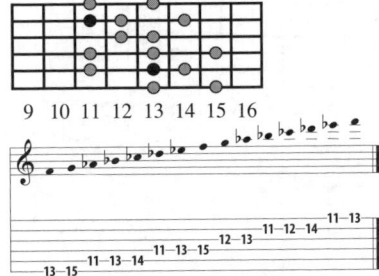

# Locrian ♮2 (1 2 ♭3 4 ♭5 ♭6 ♭7 8)
6th mode of the melodic minor scale

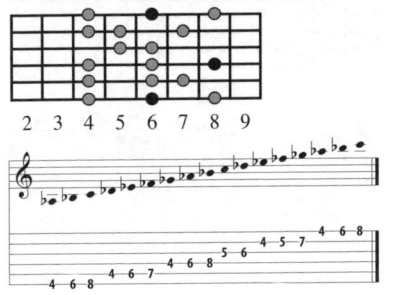
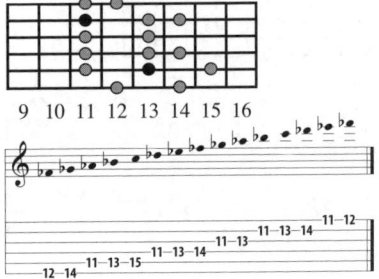

# Locrian ♮6 (1 ♭2 ♭3 4 ♭5 6 ♭7 8)
2nd mode of the harmonic minor scale

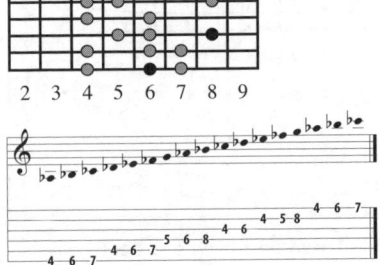
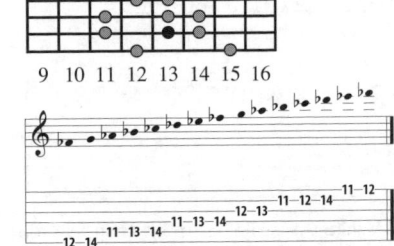

# Symmetrical Scales

## Chromatic (1 ♭2 2 ♭3 3 4 ♭5 5 ♭6 6 ♭7 7 8)

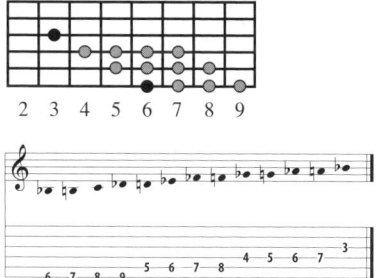
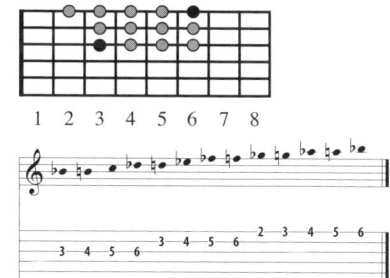

## Whole Tone (1 2 3 ♯4 ♯5 ♯6 8)

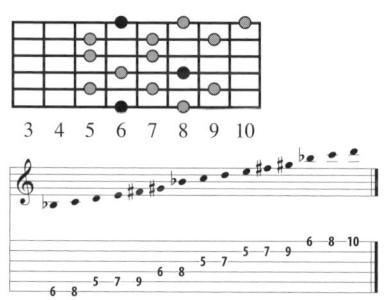
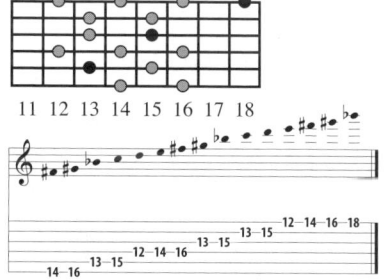

## Auxiliary, Whole/Half Diminished (1 2 ♭3 4 ♭5 ♭6 6 7 8)

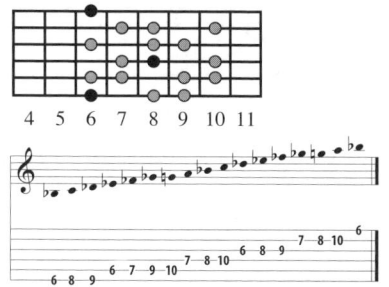
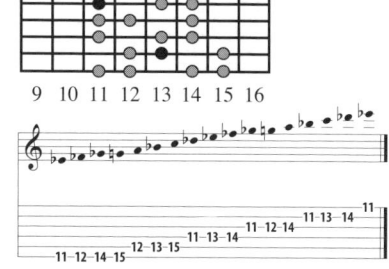

# Symmetrical, Half/Whole Diminished (1 ♭2 ♭3 ♭4 ♭5 5 6 ♭7 8)

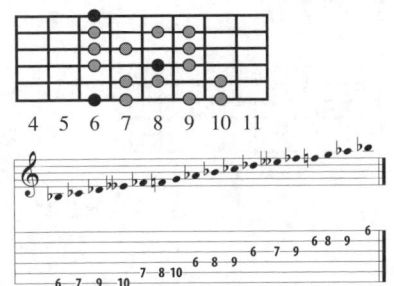
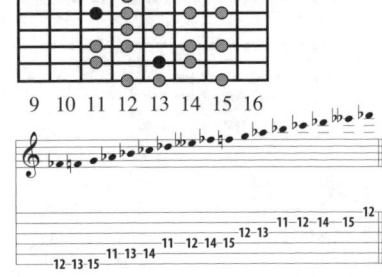

# Augmented (1 #2 3 5 #5 7 8)

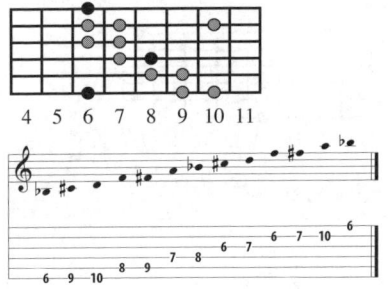
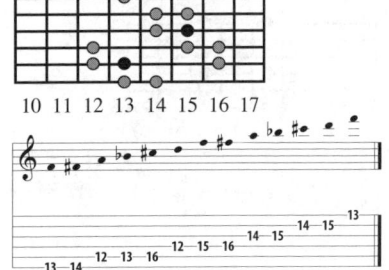

# Chromatic Augmented (1 ♭2 2 3 4 #4 #5 6 ♭7 8)

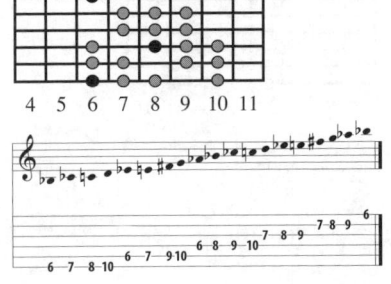
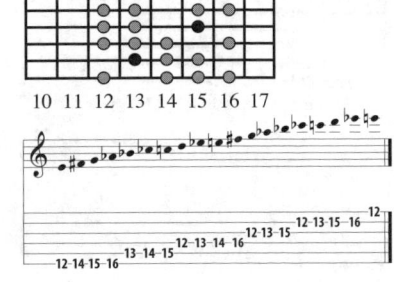

## Augmented ♭9 (1 ♭2 ♭3 3 4 5 ♭6 6 7 8)

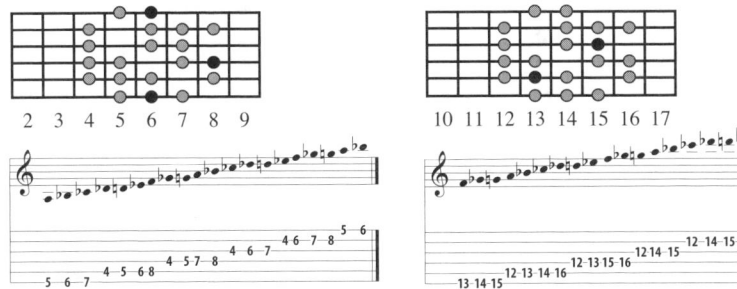

## Augmented 9 (1 2 ♭3 3 ♯4 5 ♭6 ♭7 7 8)

## Diminished Blues (1 ♭2 ♭3 3 ♯5 6 ♭7 8)

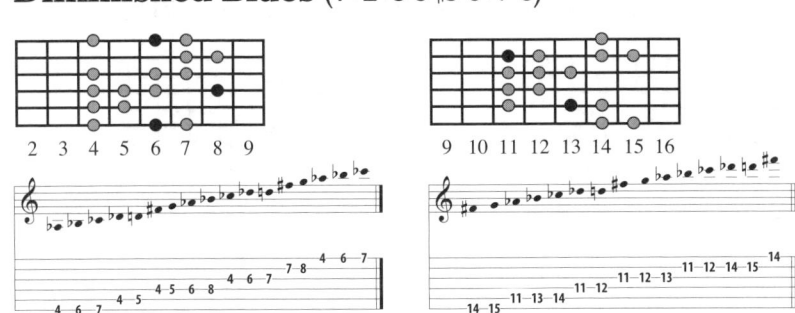

## Four Semitone Tritone (1 ♭2 2 ♭3 3 ♯4 5 ♭6 6 ♭7 8)

## Tetratonic (1 4 ♭5 7 8)

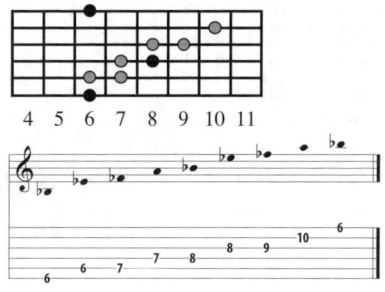
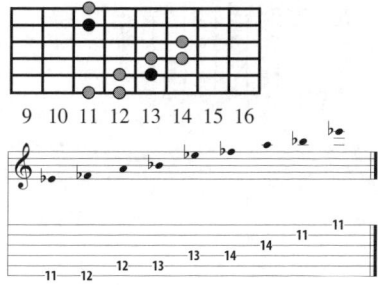

## Three Semitone Tritone (1 ♭2 2 ♭3 ♭5 5 ♭6 6 8)

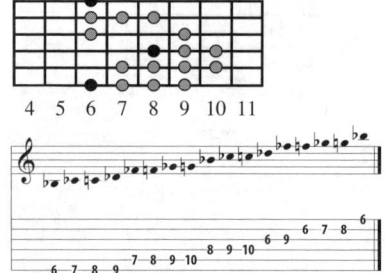

## Tritone (1 ♭2 3 ♯4 5 ♭7 8)

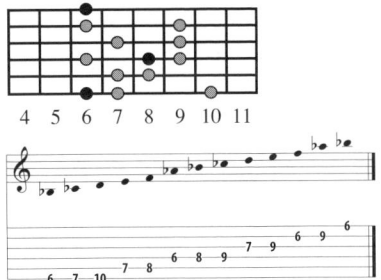
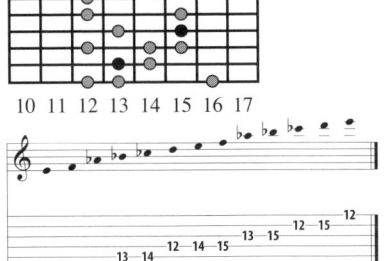

## Two-Semitone Tritone (1 ♭2 2 ♯4 5 ♭6 8)

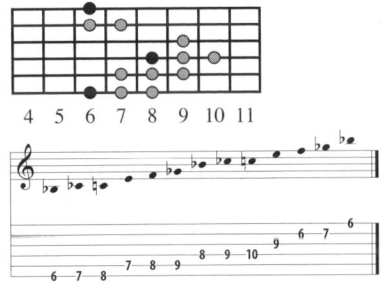
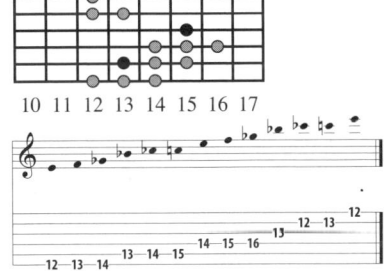

# Hybrid Scales

## Aeolian ♯11 (1 2 ♭3 ♯4 5 ♭6 ♭7 8)

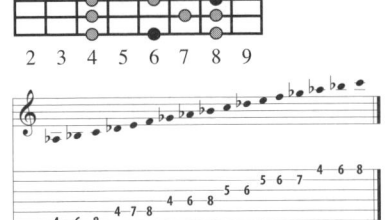
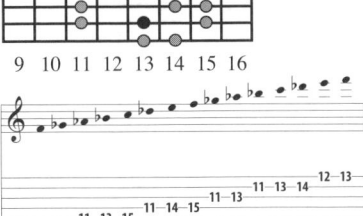

## Augmented Dominant (1 2 3 4 ♯5 6 ♭7 8)

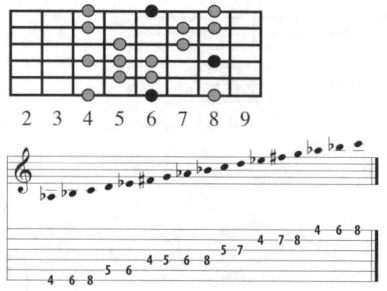
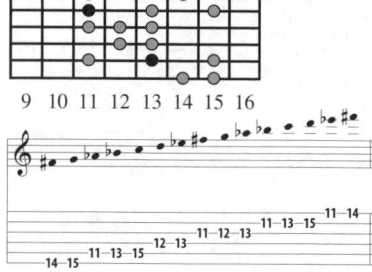

## Augmented Dominant ♭9 (1 ♭2 3 4 ♯5 6 ♭7 8)

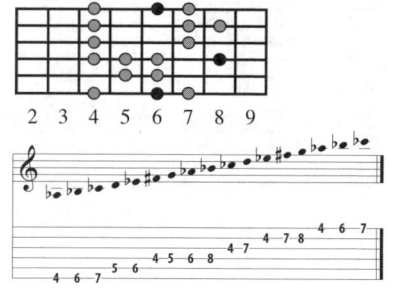
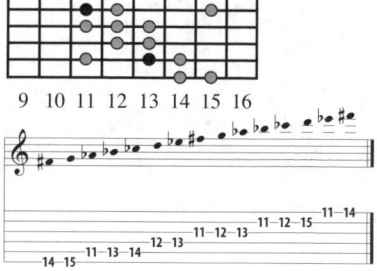

## Augmented Dominant ♯9 (1 ♯2 3 4 ♯5 6 ♭7 8)

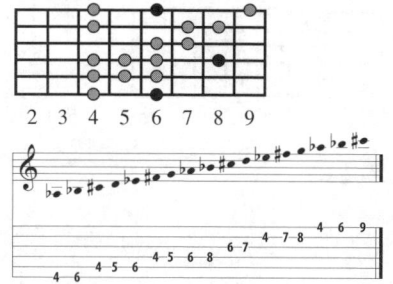
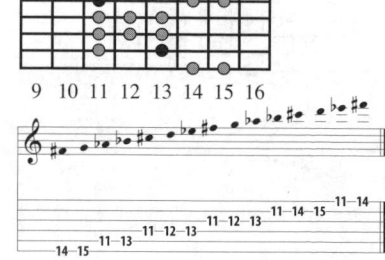

## Augmented #9 (1 #2 3 4 #5 6 7 8)

## Augmented Minor/Major 7 (1 2 ♭3 4 #5 6 7 8)

## Bebop Dominant (1 2 3 4 5 6 ♭7 7 8)

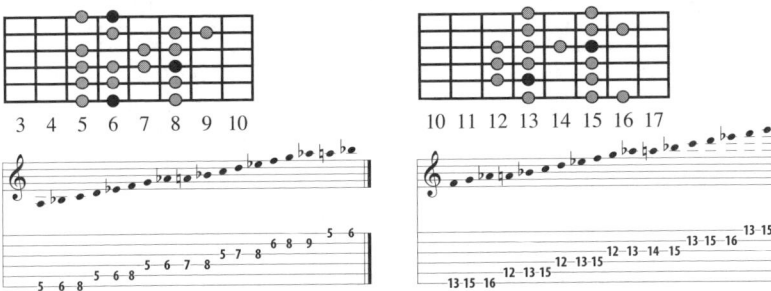

## Bebop Dorian (1 2 ♭3 3 4 5 6 ♭7 8)

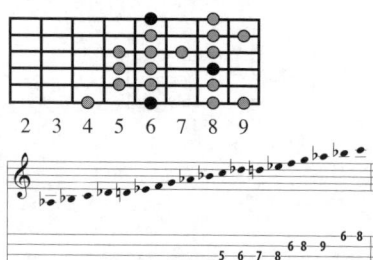
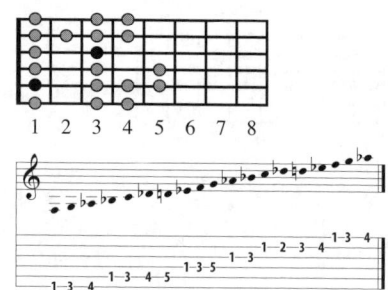

## Bebop Major* (1 2 3 4 ♯4 5 6 7 8)

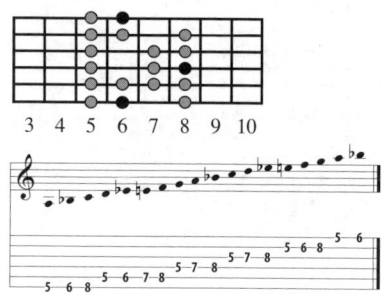
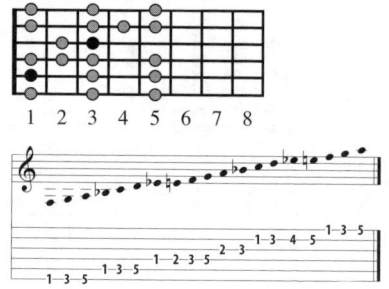

## Bebop Melodic Minor* (1 2 ♭3 4 ♯4 5 6 7 8)

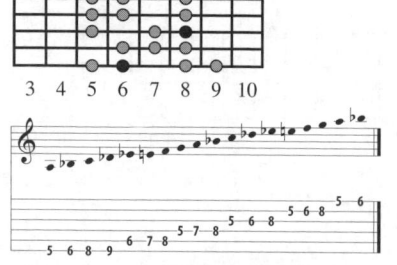
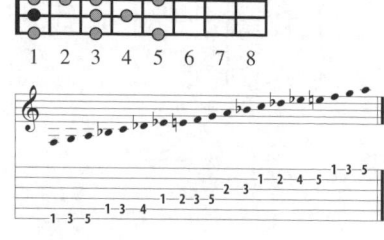

* Many musicians spell this scale with a ♯5 instead of a ♯4.

## Diminished Tritonic (1 ♭3 4 ♭5 8)

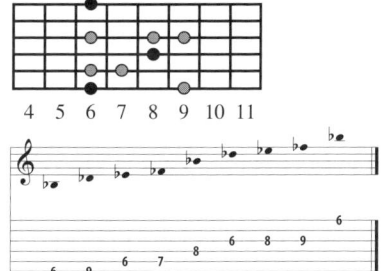
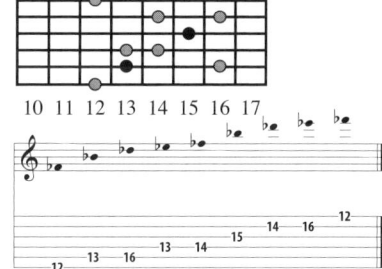

## Dominant ♭5 (1 2 3 4 ♭5 6 ♭7 8)

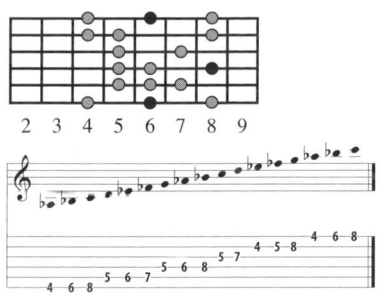
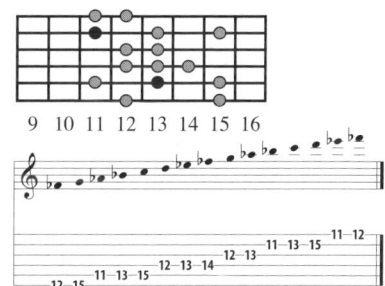

## Dominant ♭5 ♭9 ♯9 (1 ♭2 ♭3 ♭4 ♭5 6 ♭7 8)

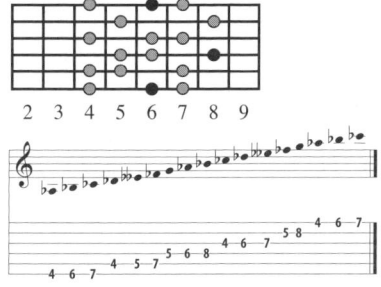
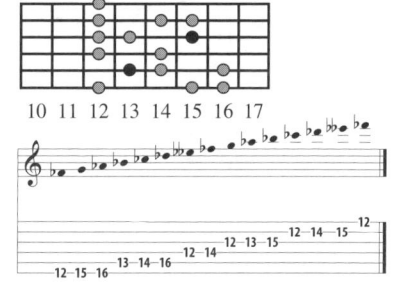

## Dominant ♭9 ♯9 (1 ♭2 ♭3 ♭4 5 6 ♭7 8)

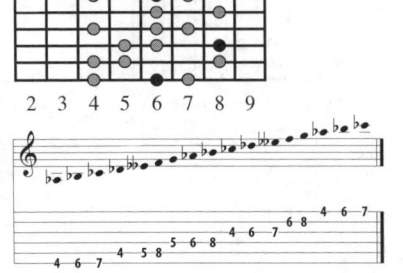
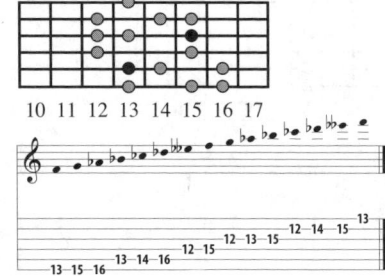

## Dominant ♭9 ♯9 ♭13 (1 ♭2 ♭3 ♭4 5 ♭6 ♭7 8)

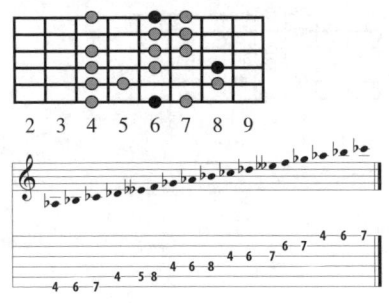
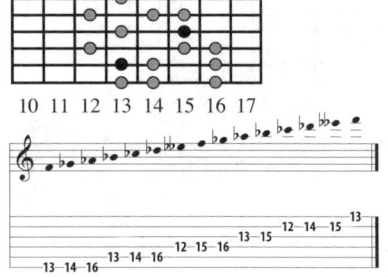

## Dominant ♯9 (1 ♯2 3 4 5 6 ♭7 8)

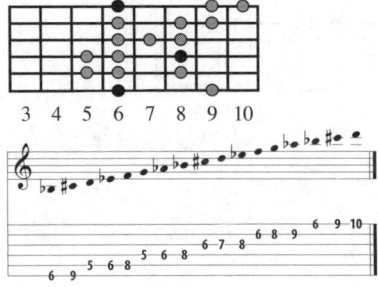
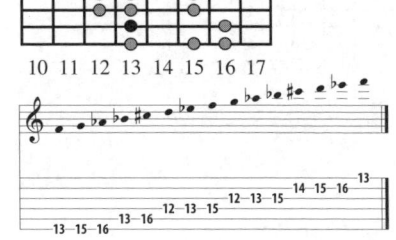

## Dominant ♭9 ♯11 (1 ♭2 3 ♯4 5 6 ♭7 8)

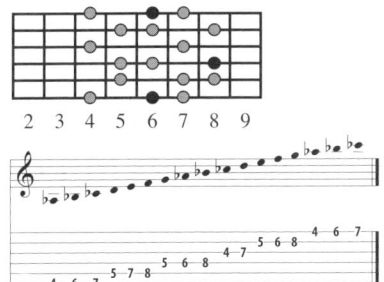
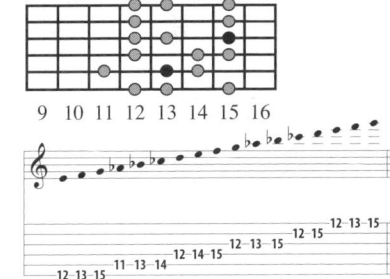

## Dominant ♭9 ♯11 ♭13 (1 ♭2 3 ♯4 5 ♭6 ♭7 8)

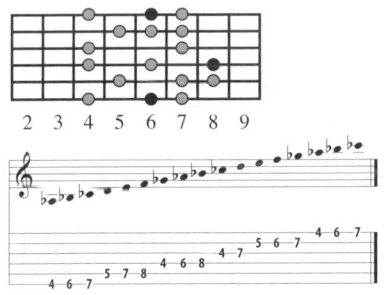
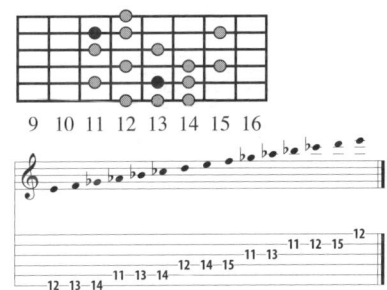

## Dominant 13 (1 2 3 5 6 ♭7 8)

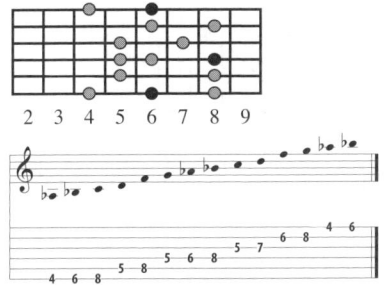
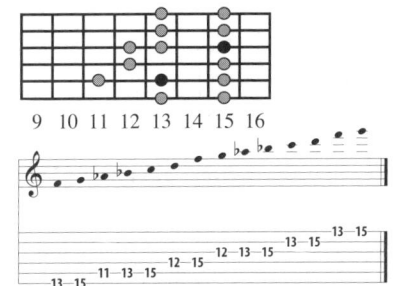

# Major and Dominant Scales

## Major/Ionian (1 2 3 4 5 6 7 8)

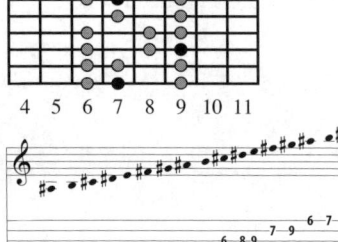
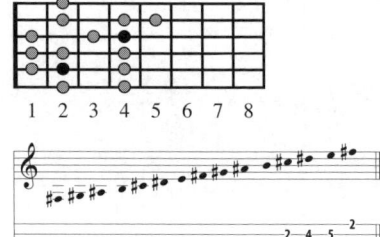

## Mixolydian (1 2 3 4 5 6 ♭7 8)
5th mode of the major scale

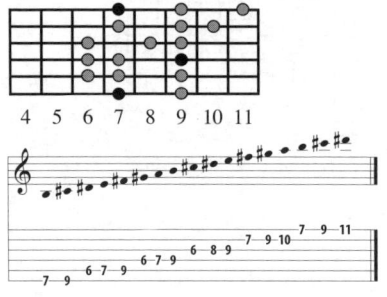
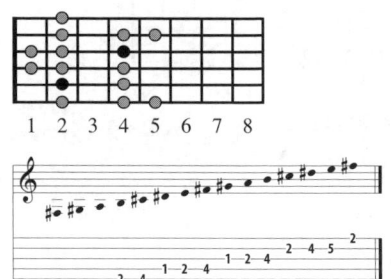

## Lydian (1 2 3 ♯4 5 6 7 8)
4th mode of the major scale

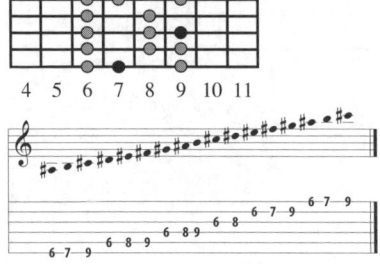
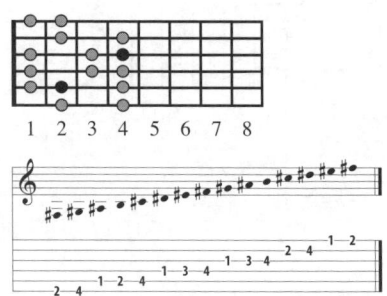

## Major Pentatonic (1 2 3 5 6 8)

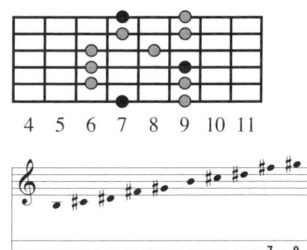
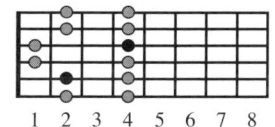

## Major 13 Pentatonic* (1 2 3 5 6 7 8)

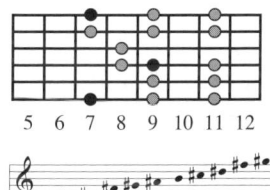
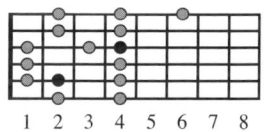
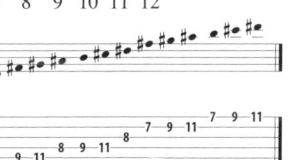

## Major Pentatonic Blues* (1 2 ♭3 3 5 6 8)

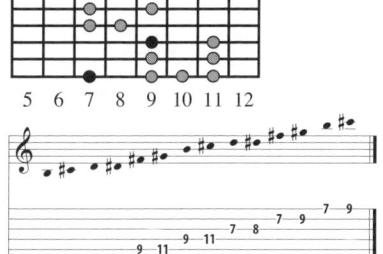
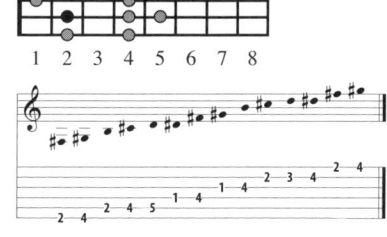

* While this scale has more than five notes, it is based on a five-note, pentatonic scale and it is best to think of it as a pentatonic scale.

# Lydian Pentatonic (1 3 #4 5 7 8)

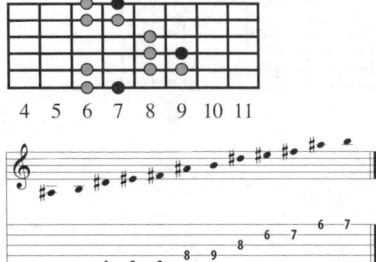
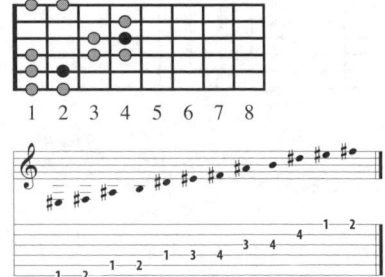

# Lydian ♭7 (1 2 3 #4 5 6 ♭7 8)
4th mode of the melodic minor scale

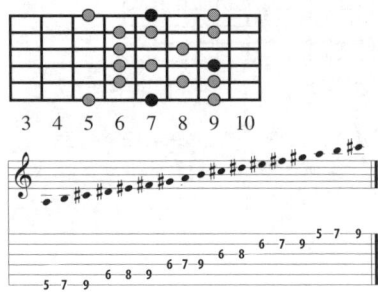
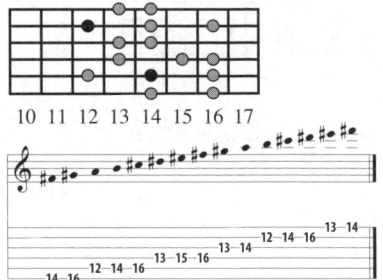

# Lydian #9 (1 #2 3 #4 5 6 7 8)
6th mode of the harmonic minor scale

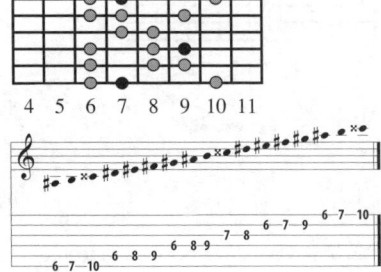
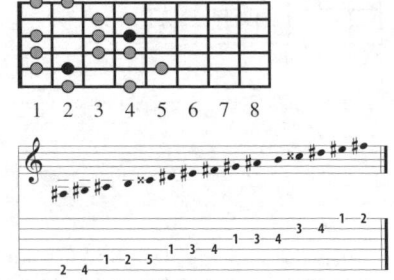

## Aeolian Major (1 2 3 4 5 ♭6 ♭7 8)
5th mode of the melodic minor scale

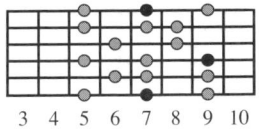
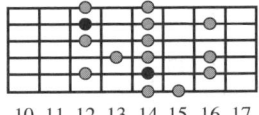

## Phrygian Major (1 ♭2 3 4 5 ♭6 ♭7 8)
5th mode of the harmonic minor scale

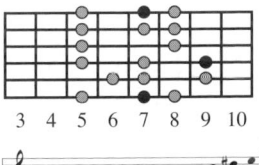
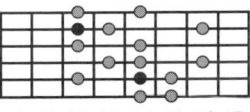

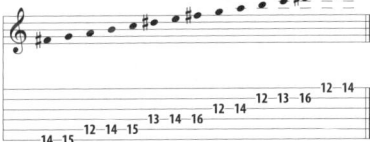

## Ionian Augmented (1 2 3 4 ♯5 6 7 8)
3rd mode of the harmonic minor scale

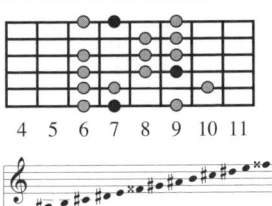
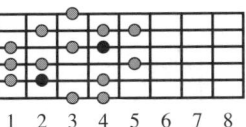

## Lydian Augmented (1 2 3 #4 #5 6 7 8)
3rd mode of the melodic minor scale

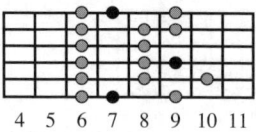
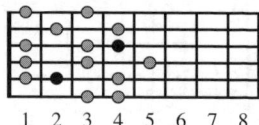
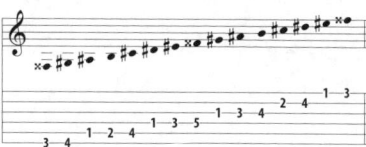

# Minor Scales

## Natural Minor/Aeolian (1 2 b3 4 5 b6 b7 8)
6th mode of the major scale

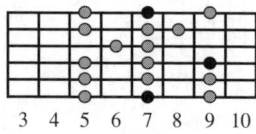
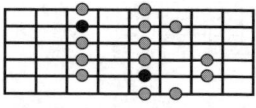

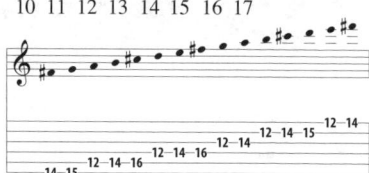

## Harmonic Minor (1 2 b3 4 5 b6 7 8)

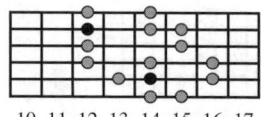
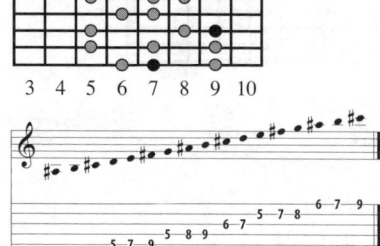
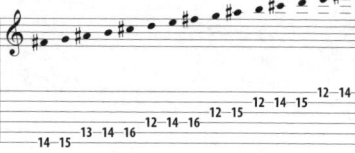

## Jazz Minor/Melodic Minor (1 2 ♭3 4 5 6 7 8)
Melodic Minor descends in Aeolian/Natural Minor

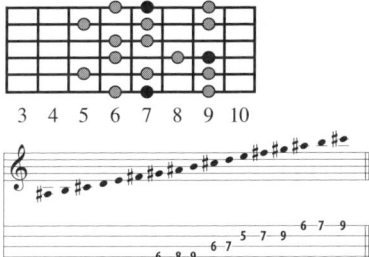
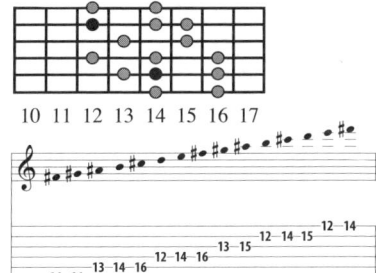

## Dorian (1 2 ♭3 4 5 6 ♭7 8)
2nd mode of the major scale

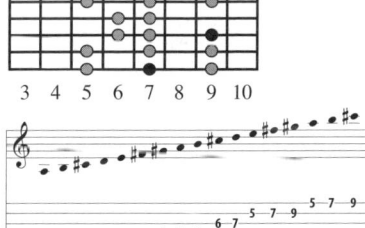
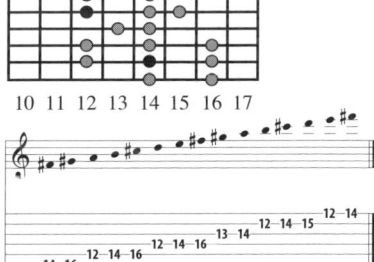

## Phrygian (1 ♭2 ♭3 4 5 ♭6 ♭7 8)
3rd mode of the major scale

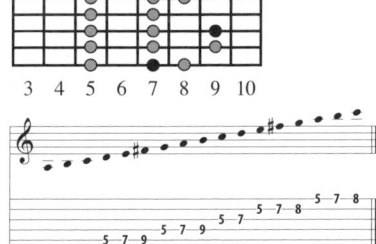
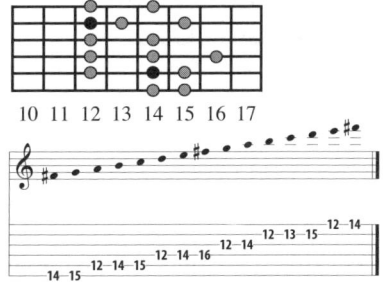

## Locrian (1 ♭2 ♭3 4 ♭5 ♭6 ♭7 8)
7th mode of the major scale

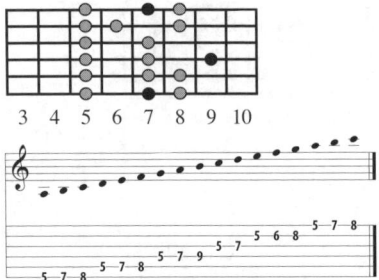
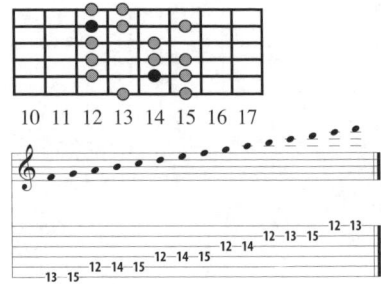

## Minor Pentatonic (1 ♭3 4 5 ♭7 8)

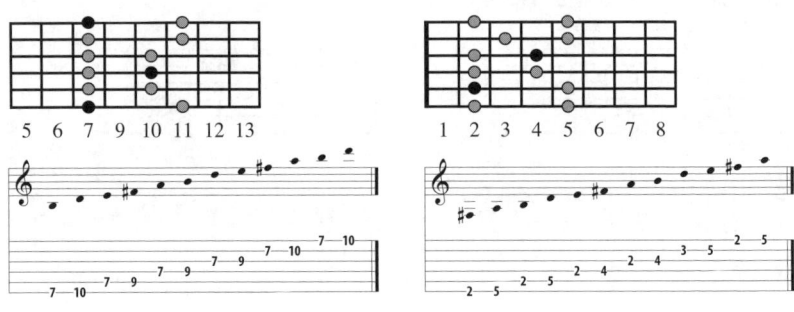

## Minor 13 Pentatonic* (1 ♭3 5 ♭6 ♭7 8)

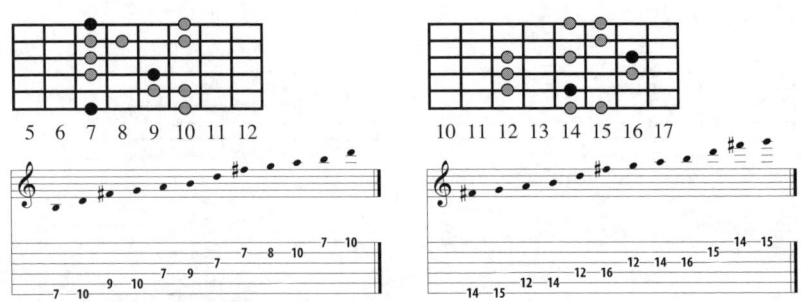

* While this scale has more than five notes, it is based on a five-note, pentatonic scale and it is best to think of it as a pentatonic scale.

## Minor Pentatonic Blues* (1 ♭3 4 ♭5 5 ♭7 8)

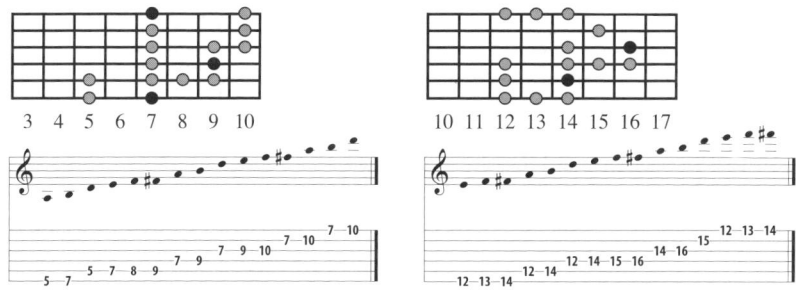

## Dorian Pentatonic (1 2 ♭3 5 ♭7 8)

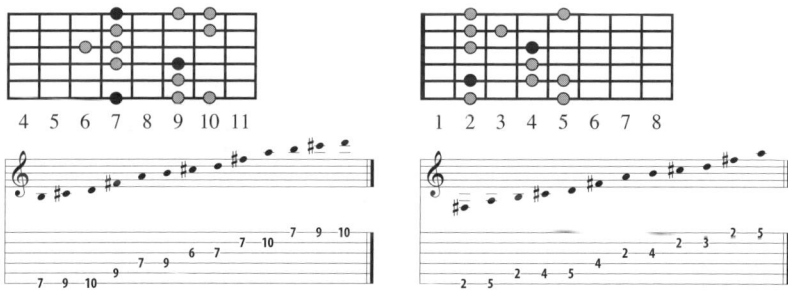

## Phrygian Pentatonic (1 ♭2 4 5 ♭7 8)

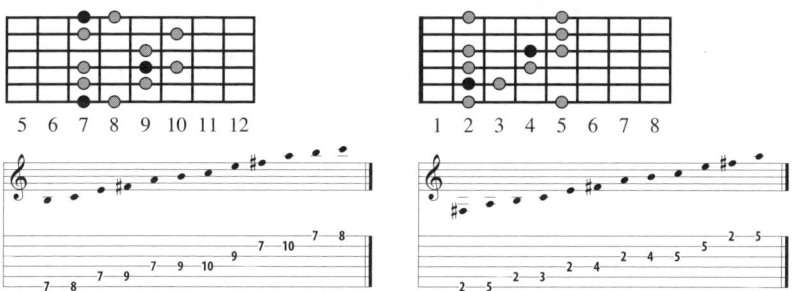

* While this scale has more than five notes, it is based on a five-note, pentatonic scale and it is best to think of it as a pentatonic scale.

# Phrygian ♮6 (1 ♭2 ♭3 4 5 6 ♭7 8)
2nd mode of the melodic minor scale

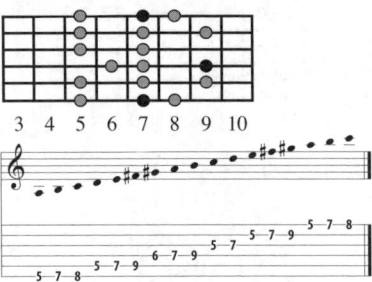
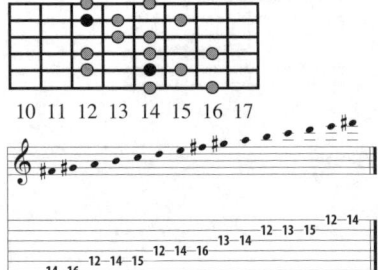

# Locrian ♮2 (1 2 ♭3 4 ♭5 ♭6 ♭7 8)
6th mode of the melodic minor scale

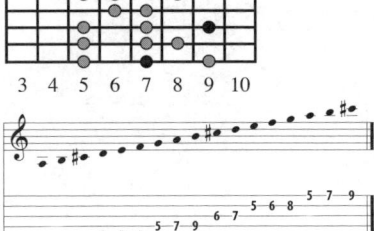
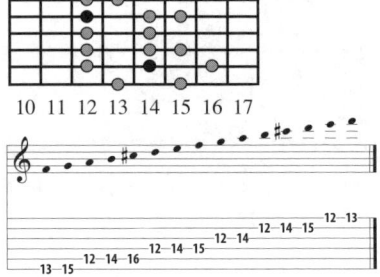

# Locrian ♮6 (1 ♭2 ♭3 4 ♭5 6 ♭7 8)
2nd mode of the harmonic minor scale

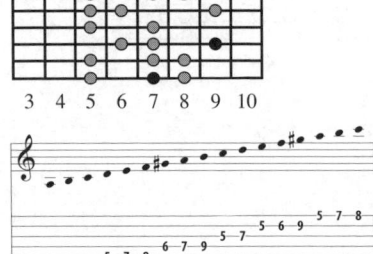
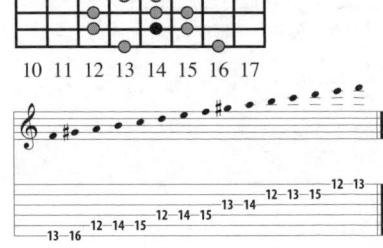

# Symmetrical Scales

## Chromatic (1 ♭2 2 ♭3 3 4 ♭5 5 ♭6 6 ♭7 7 8)

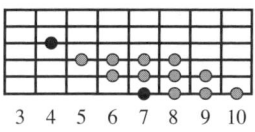

## Whole Tone (1 2 3 ♯4 ♯5 ♯6 8)

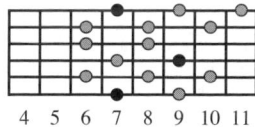
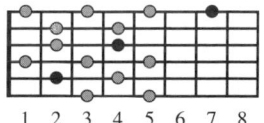

## Auxiliary, Whole/Half Diminished (1 2 ♭3 4 ♭5 ♭6 6 7 8)

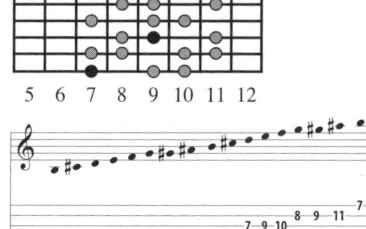
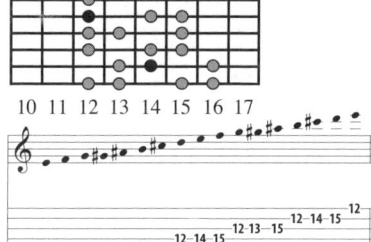

# Symmetrical, Half/Whole Diminished (1 ♭2 ♭3 ♭4 ♭5 5 6 ♭7 8)

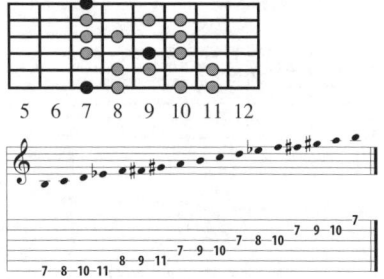
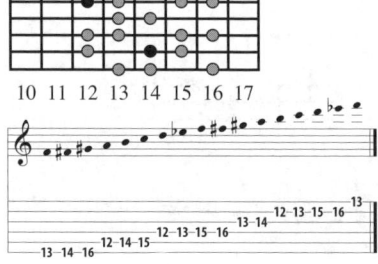

# Augmented (1 #2 3 5 #5 7 8)

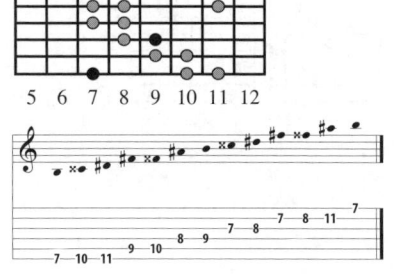
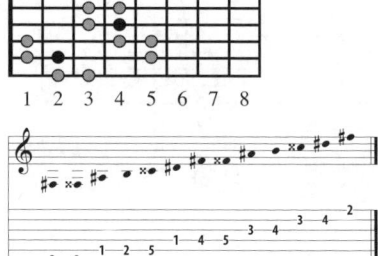

# Chromatic Augmented (1 ♭2 2 3 4 #4 #5 6 ♭7 8)

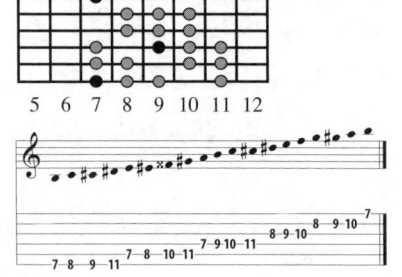
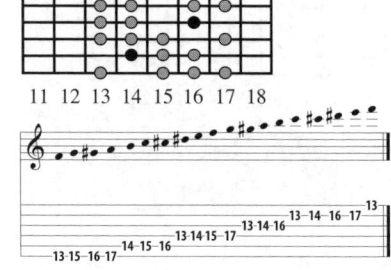

## Augmented ♭9 (1 ♭2 ♭3 3 4 5 ♭6 6 7 8)

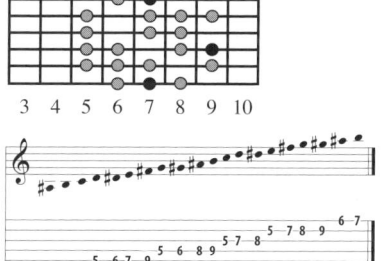
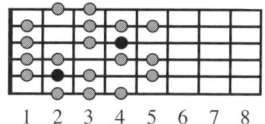

## Augmented 9 (1 2 ♭3 3 ♯4 5 ♭6 ♭7 7 8)

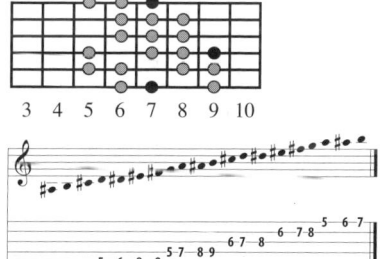
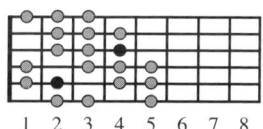

## Diminished Blues (1 ♭2 ♭3 3 ♯5 6 ♭7 8)

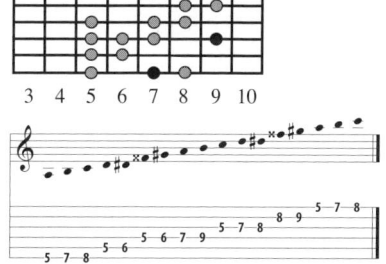
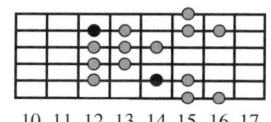

# Four Semitone Tritone (1 b2 2 b3 3 #4 5 b6 6 b7 8)

# Tetratonic (1 4 b5 7 8)

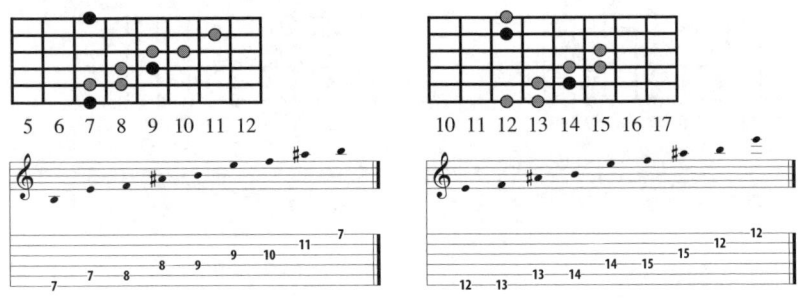

# Three Semitone Tritone (1 b2 2 b3 b5 5 b6 6 8)

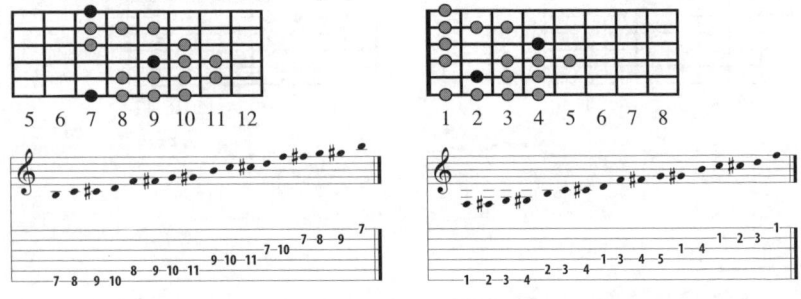

# Tritone (1 ♭2 3 ♯4 5 ♭7 8)

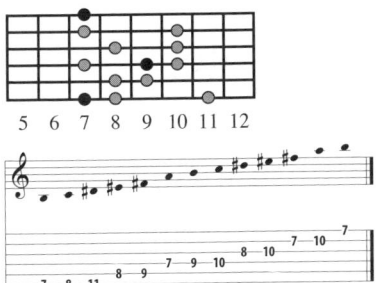
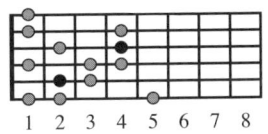

## Two-Semitone Tritone (1 ♭2 2 ♯4 5 ♭6 8)

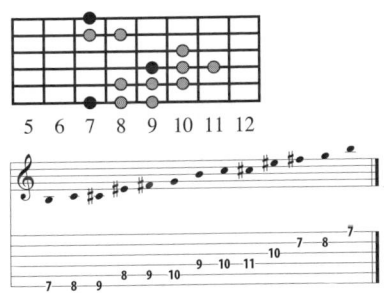
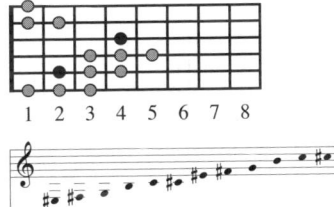

# Hybrid Scales

## Aeolian ♯11 (1 2 ♭3 ♯4 5 ♭6 ♭7 8)

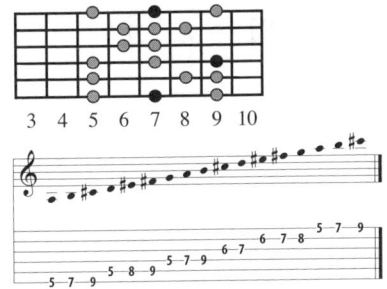
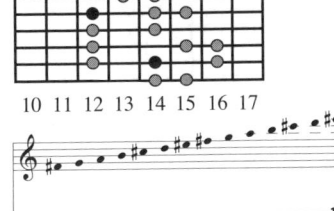

## Augmented Dominant (1 2 3 4 #5 6 b7 8)

## Augmented Dominant b9 (1 b2 3 4 #5 6 b7 8)

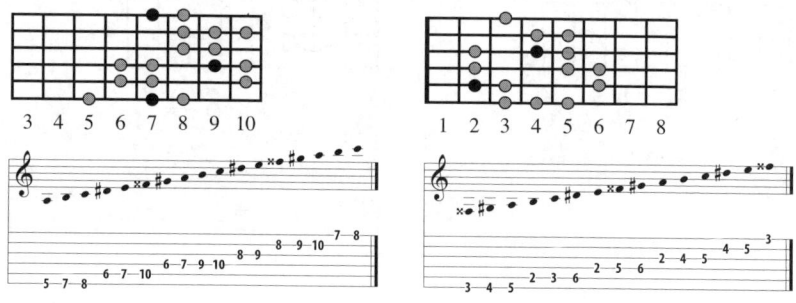

## Augmented Dominant #9 (1 #2 3 4 #5 6 b7 8)

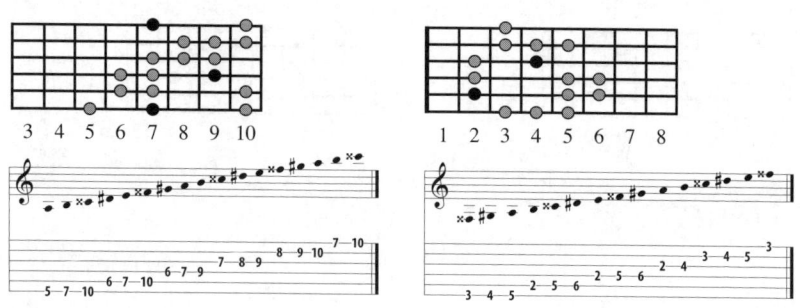

# Augmented ♯9 (1 ♯2 3 4 ♯5 6 7 8)

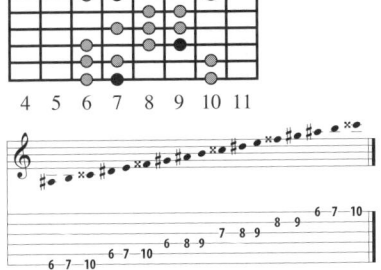
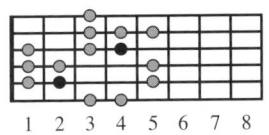

# Augmented Minor/Major 7 (1 2 ♭3 4 ♯5 6 7 8)

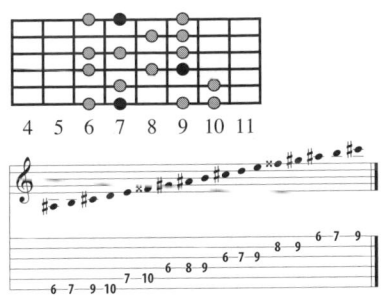
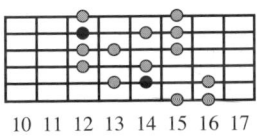

# Bebop Dominant (1 2 3 4 5 6 ♭7 7 8)

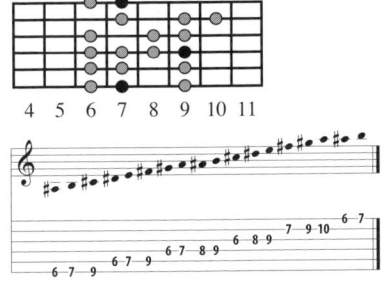
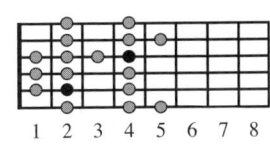

## Bebop Dorian (1 2 ♭3 3 4 5 6 ♭7 8)

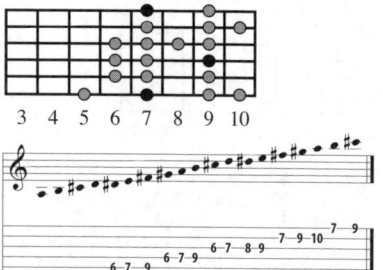

## Bebop Major* (1 2 3 4 ♯4 5 6 7 8)

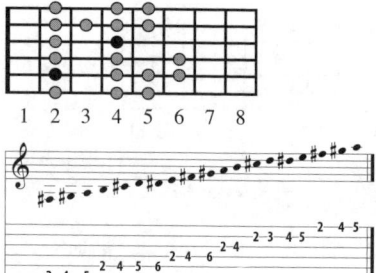
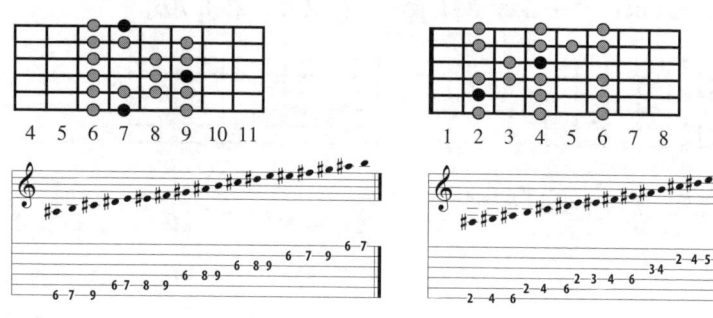

## Bebop Melodic Minor* (1 2 ♭3 4 ♯4 5 6 7 8)

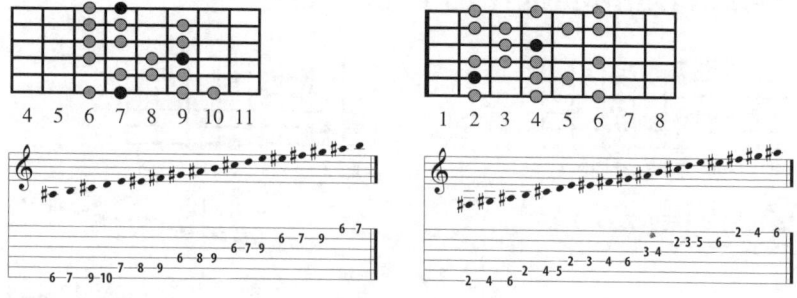

* Many musicians spell this scale with a ♯5 instead of a ♯4.

# Diminished Tritonic (1 ♭3 4 ♭5 8)

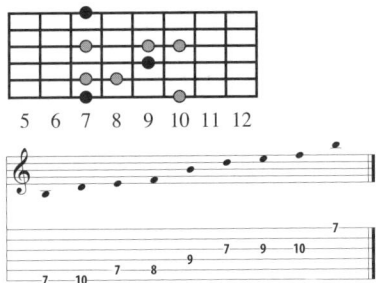

# Dominant ♭5 (1 2 3 4 ♭5 6 ♭7 8)

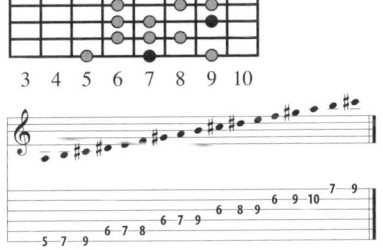
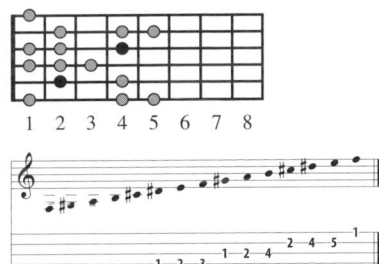

# Dominant ♭5 ♭9 ♯9 (1 ♭2 ♭3 ♭4 ♭5 6 ♭7 8)

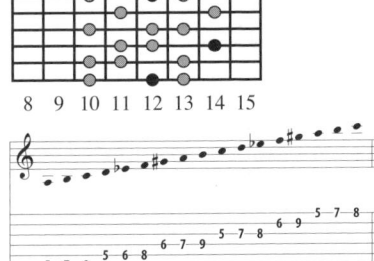
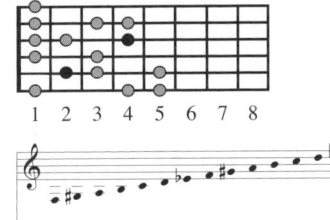

## Dominant ♭9 ♯9 (1 ♭2 ♭3 ♭4 5 6 ♭7 8)

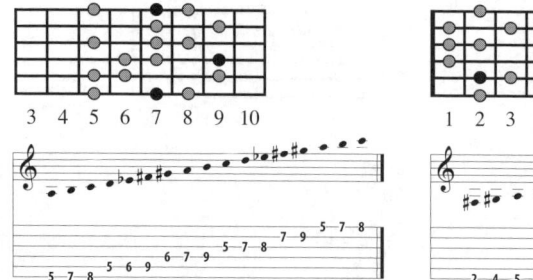
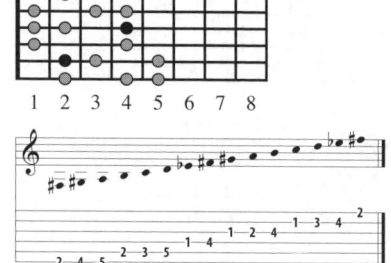

## Dominant ♭9 ♯9 ♭13 (1 ♭2 ♭3 ♭4 5 ♭6 ♭7 8)

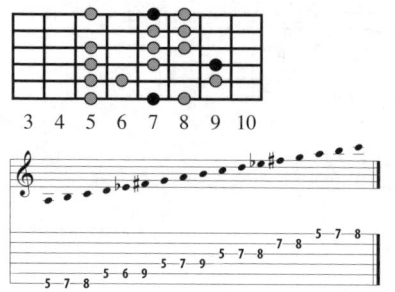
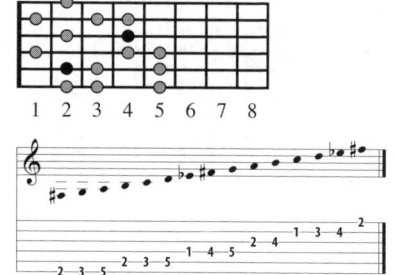

## Dominant ♯9 (1 ♯2 3 4 5 6 ♭7 8)

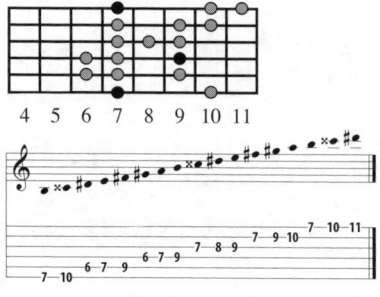
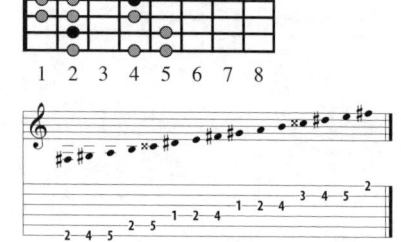

## Dominant ♭9 ♯11 (1 ♭2 3 ♯4 5 6 ♭7 8)

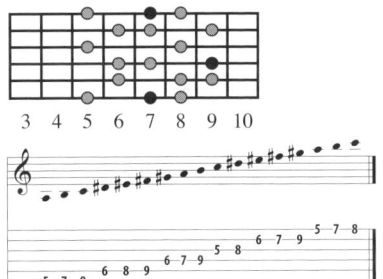 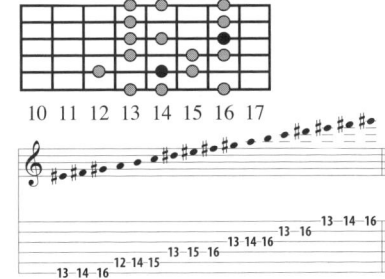

## Dominant ♭9 ♯11 ♭13 (1 ♭2 3 ♯4 5 ♭6 ♭7 8)

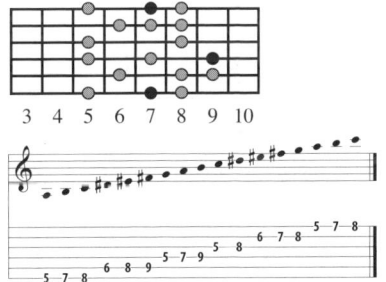 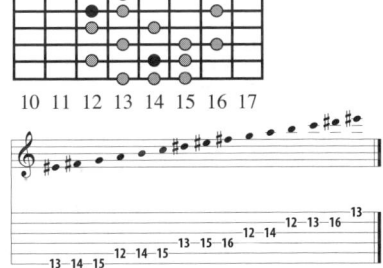

## Dominant 13 (1 2 3 5 6 ♭7 8)

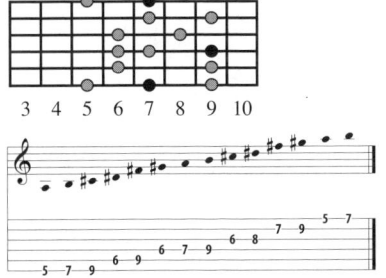 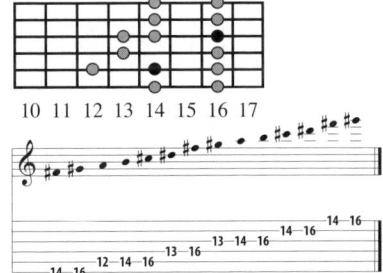

# Major and Dominant Scales

## Major/Ionian (1 2 3 4 5 6 7 8)

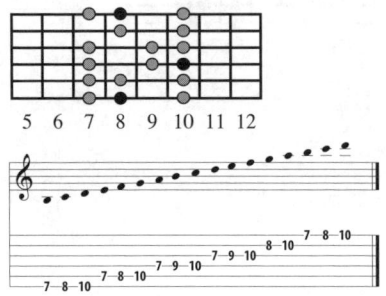
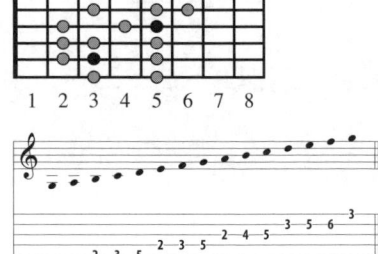

## Mixolydian (1 2 3 4 5 6 ♭7 8)
5th mode of the major scale

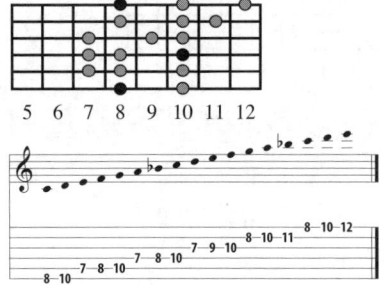
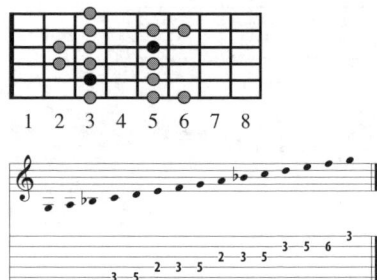

## Lydian (1 2 3 ♯4 5 6 7 8)
4th mode of the major scale

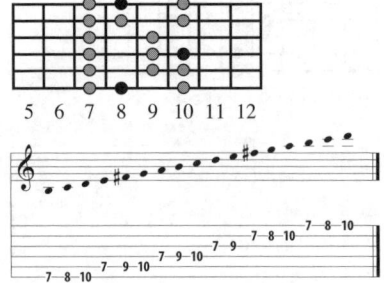
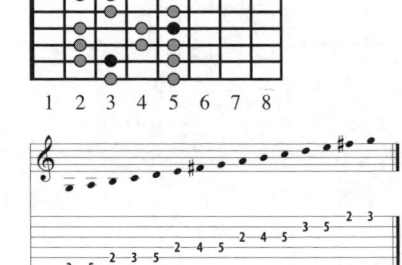

## Major Pentatonic (1 2 3 5 6 8)

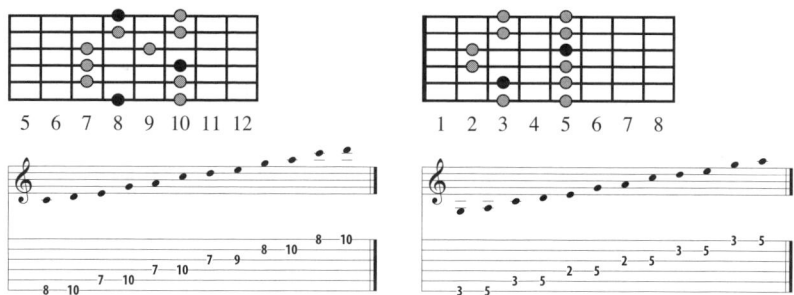

## Major 13 Pentatonic* (1 2 3 5 6 7 8)

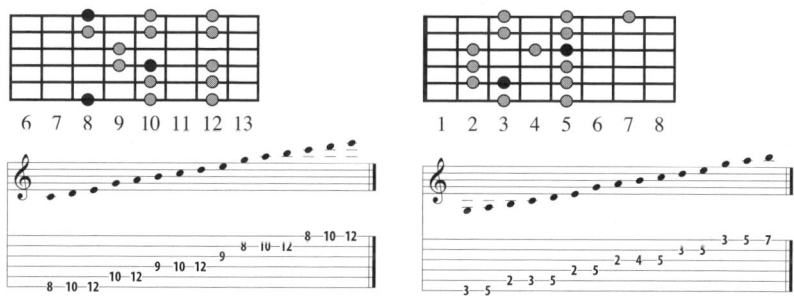

## Major Pentatonic Blues* (1 2 ♭3 3 5 6 8)

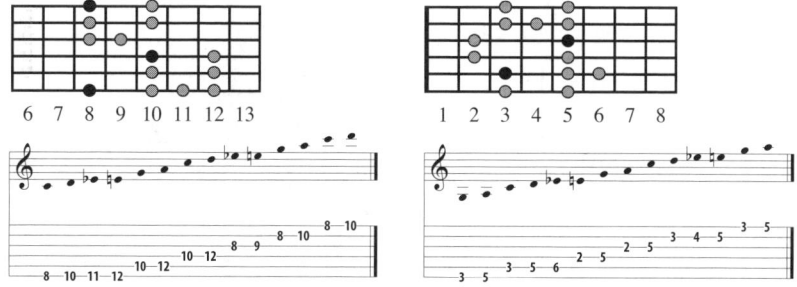

* While this scale has more than five notes, it is based on a five-note, pentatonic scale and it is best to think of it as a pentatonic scale.

# Lydian Pentatonic (1 3 #4 5 7 8)

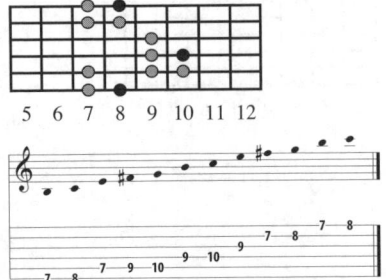
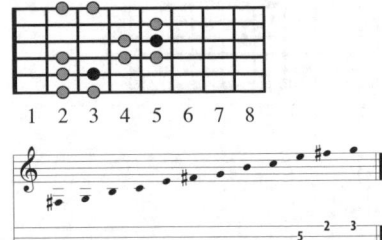

# Lydian ♭7 (1 2 3 #4 5 6 ♭7 8)
4th mode of the melodic minor scale

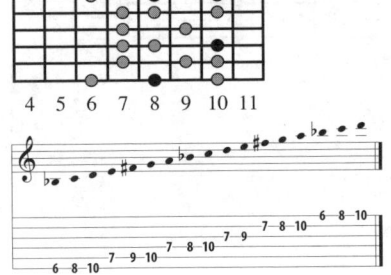
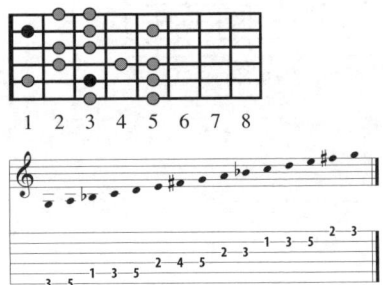

# Lydian #9 (1 #2 3 #4 5 6 7 8)
6th mode of the harmonic minor scale

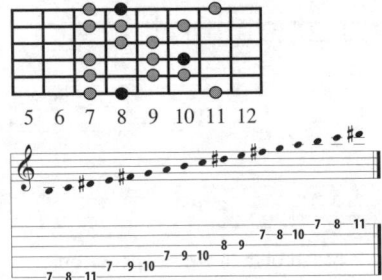
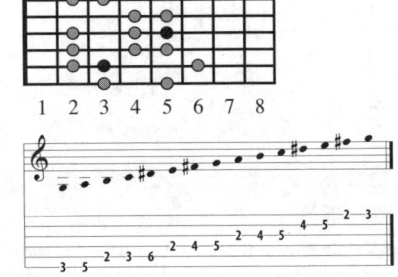

## Aeolian Major (1 2 3 4 5 ♭6 ♭7 8)
5th mode of the melodic minor scale

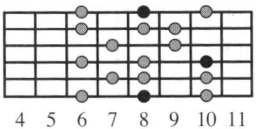
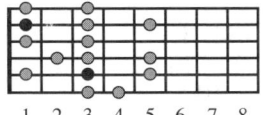
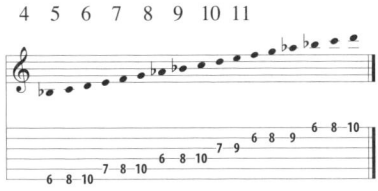

## Phrygian Major (1 ♭2 3 4 5 ♭6 ♭7 8)
5th mode of the harmonic minor scale

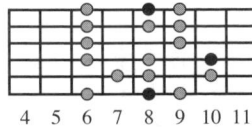
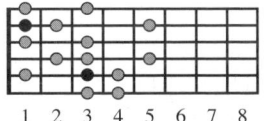
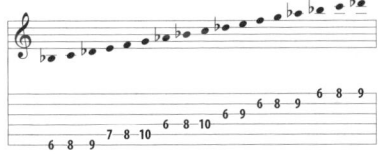

## Ionian Augmented (1 2 3 4 ♯5 6 7 8)
3rd mode of the harmonic minor scale

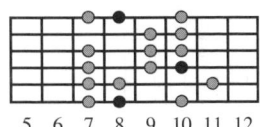
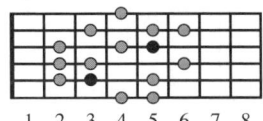
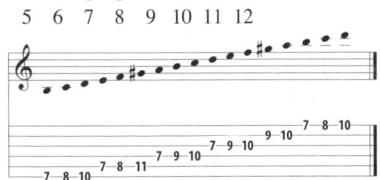

## Lydian Augmented (1 2 3 #4 #5 6 7 8)
3rd mode of the melodic minor scale

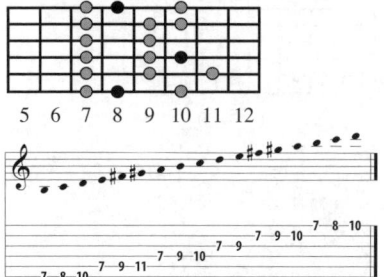
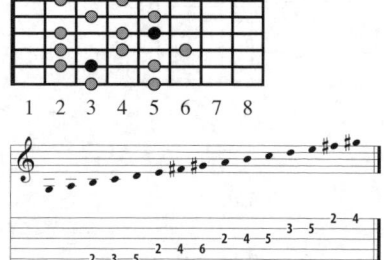

# Minor Scales

## Natural Minor/Aeolian (1 2 ♭3 4 5 ♭6 ♭7 8)
6th mode of the major scale

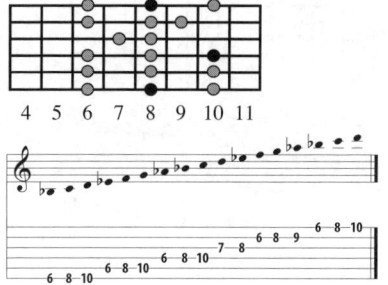
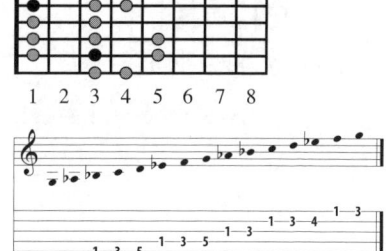

## Harmonic Minor (1 2 ♭3 4 5 ♭6 7 8)

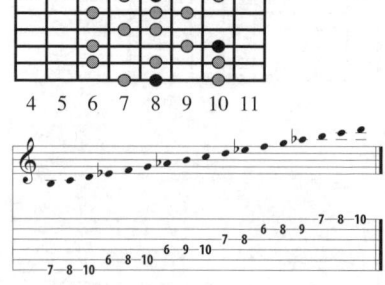

## Jazz Minor/Melodic Minor (1 2 ♭3 4 5 6 7 8)
Melodic Minor descends in Aeolian/Natural Minor

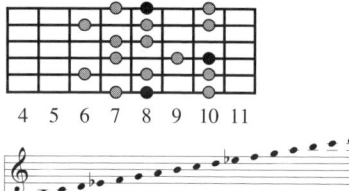
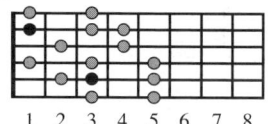

## Dorian (1 2 ♭3 4 5 6 ♭7 8)
2nd mode of the major scale

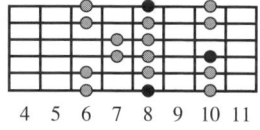
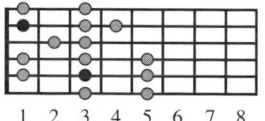
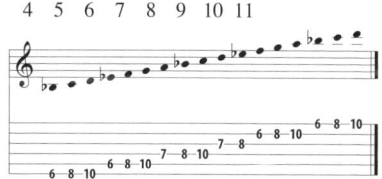

## Phrygian (1 ♭2 ♭3 4 5 ♭6 ♭7 8)
3rd mode of the major scale

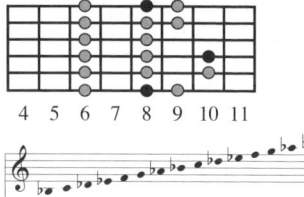
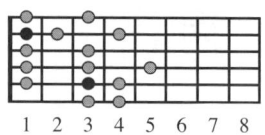

## Locrian (1 ♭2 ♭3 4 ♭5 ♭6 ♭7 8)
7th mode of the major scale

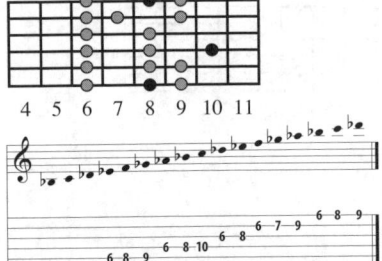
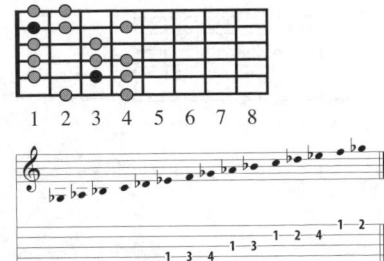

## Minor Pentatonic (1 ♭3 4 5 ♭7 8)

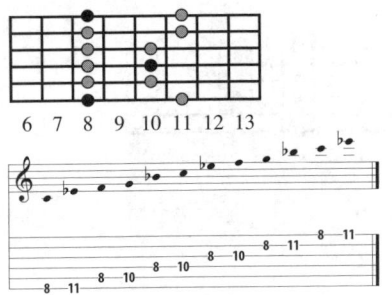
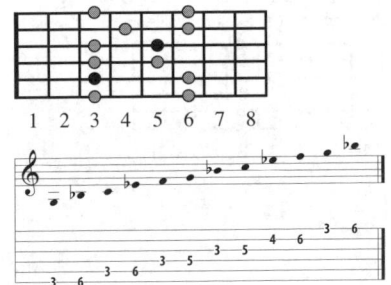

## Minor 13 Pentatonic* (1 ♭3 5 ♭6 ♭7 8)

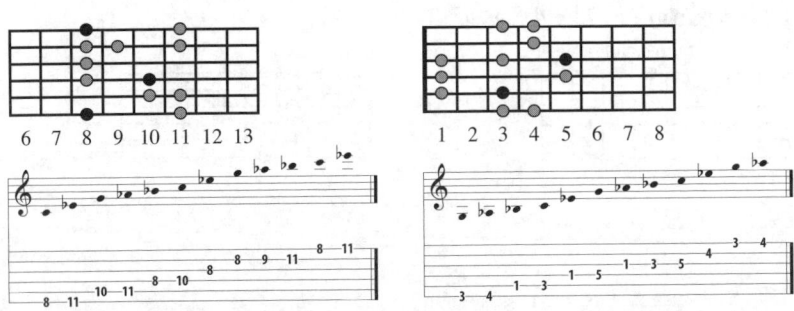

\* While this scale has more than five notes, it is based on a five-note, pentatonic scale and it is best to think of it as a pentatonic scale.

## Minor Pentatonic Blues* (1 ♭3 4 ♭5 5 ♭7 8)

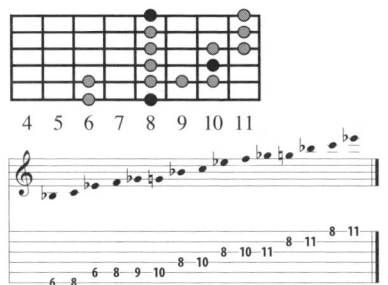
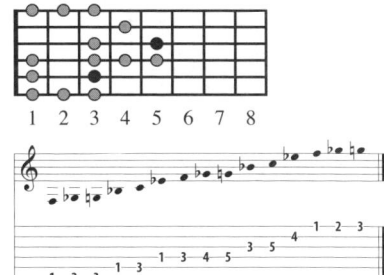

## Dorian Pentatonic (1 2 ♭3 5 ♭7 8)

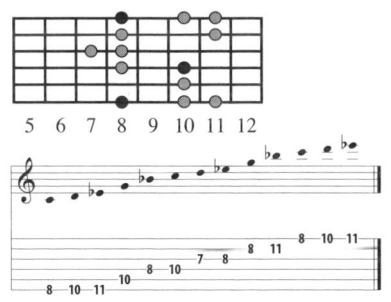
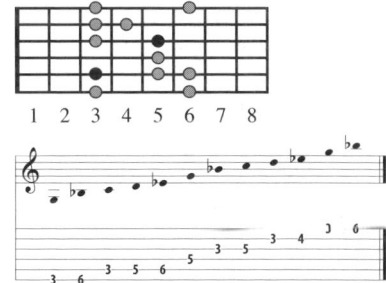

## Phrygian Pentatonic (1 ♭2 4 5 ♭7 8)

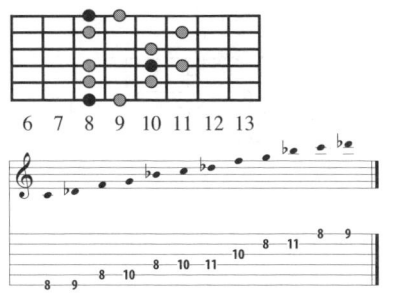

* While this scale has more than five notes, it is based on a five-note, pentatonic scale and it is best to think of it as a pentatonic scale.

## Phrygian ♮6 (1 ♭2 ♭3 4 5 6 ♭7 8)
2nd mode of the melodic minor scale

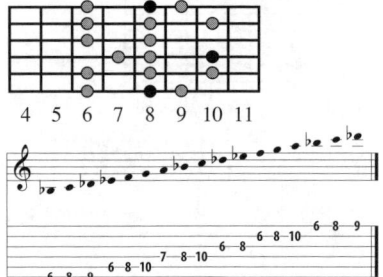
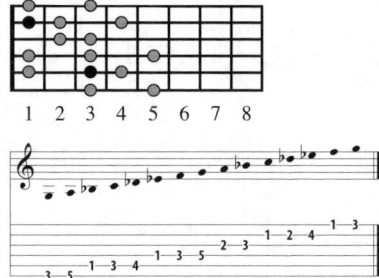

## Locrian ♮2 (1 2 ♭3 4 ♭5 ♭6 ♭7 8)
6th mode of the melodic minor scale

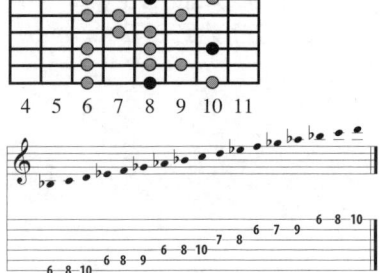
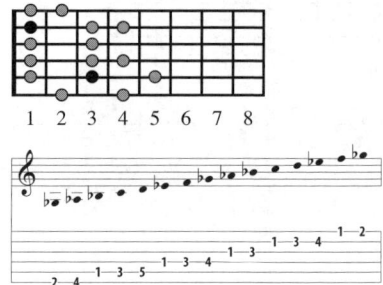

## Locrian ♮6 (1 ♭2 ♭3 4 ♭5 6 ♭7 8)
2nd mode of the harmonic minor scale

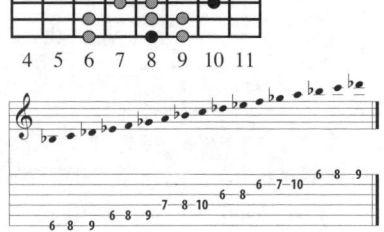
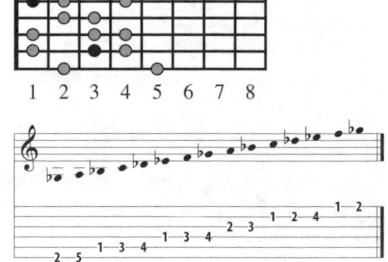

# Symmetrical Scales

## Chromatic (1 ♭2 2 ♭3 3 4 ♭5 5 ♭6 6 ♭7 7 8)

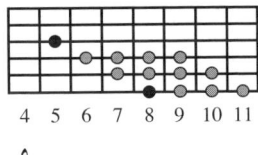
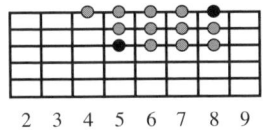

## Whole Tone (1 2 3 ♯4 ♯5 ♯6 8)

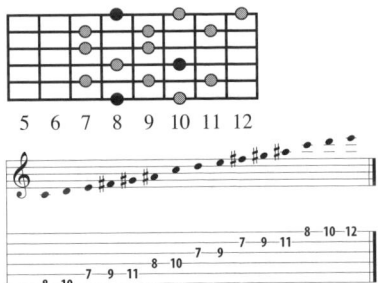
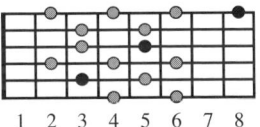

## Auxiliary, Whole/Half Diminished (1 2 ♭3 4 ♭5 ♭6 6 7 8)

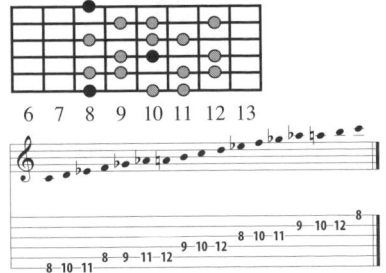
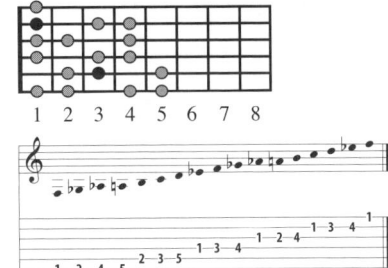

# Symmetrical, Half/Whole Diminished (1 ♭2 ♭3 ♭4 ♭5 5 6 ♭7 8)

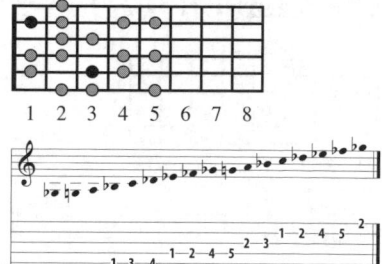

# Augmented (1 ♯2 3 5 ♯5 7 8)

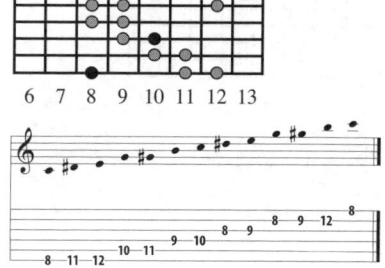

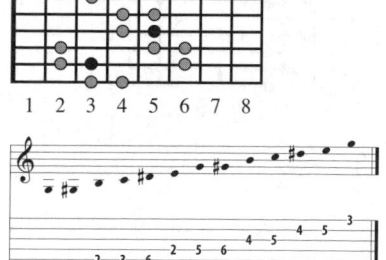

# Chromatic Augmented (1 ♭2 2 3 4 ♯4 ♯5 6 ♭7 8)

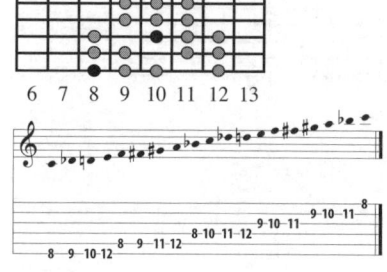

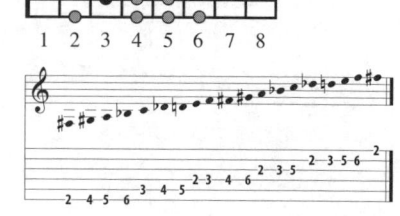

## Augmented ♭9 (1 ♭2 ♭3 3 4 5 ♭6 6 7 8)

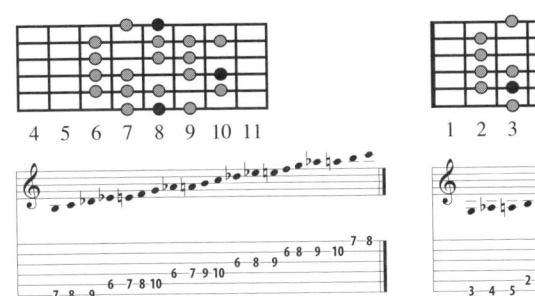
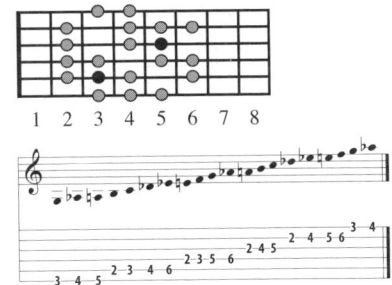

## Augmented 9 (1 2 ♭3 3 ♯4 5 ♭6 ♭7 7 8)

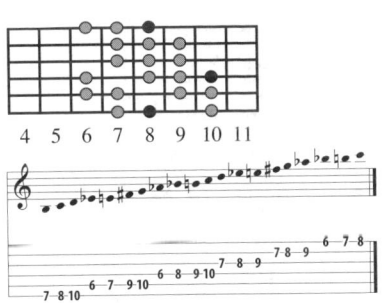
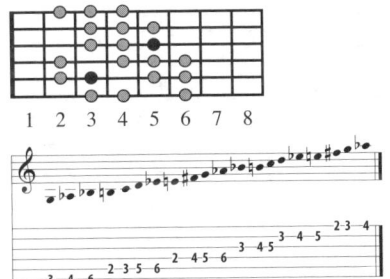

## Diminished Blues (1 ♭2 ♭3 3 ♯5 6 ♭7 8)

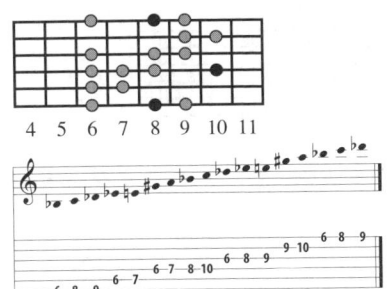
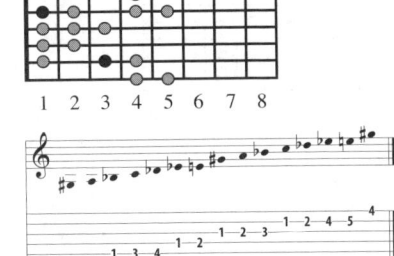

# Four Semitone Tritone (1 ♭2 2 ♭3 3 ♯4 5 ♭6 6 ♭7 8)

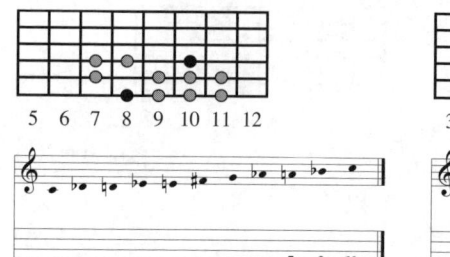

# Tetratonic (1 4 ♭5 7 8)

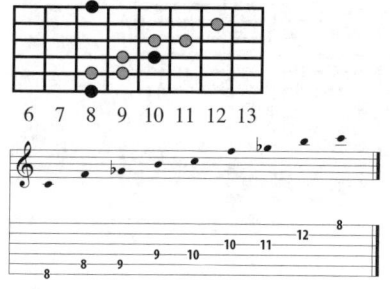

# Three Semitone Tritone (1 ♭2 2 ♭3 ♭5 5 ♭6 6 8)

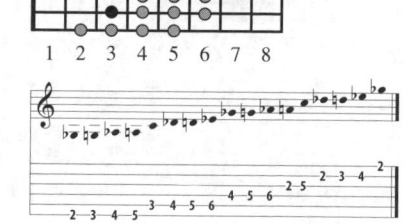

## Tritone (1 ♭2 3 ♯4 5 ♭7 8)

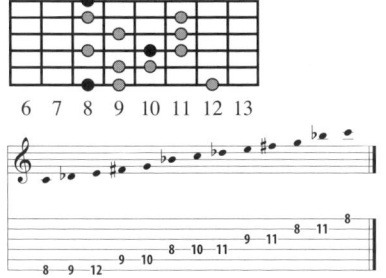
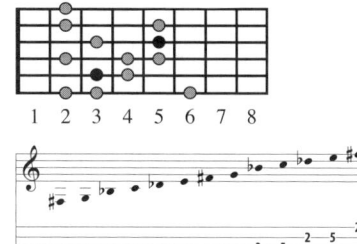

## Two-Semitone Tritone (1 ♭2 2 ♯4 5 ♭6 8)

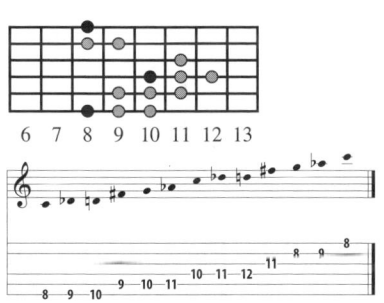
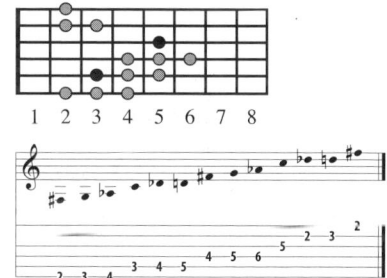

# Hybrid Scales

## Aeolian ♯11 (1 2 ♭3 ♯4 5 ♭6 ♭7 8)

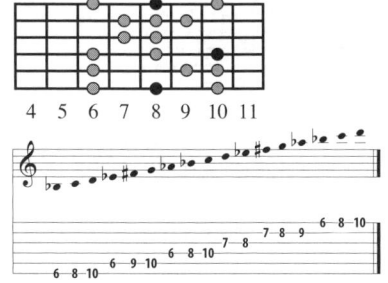
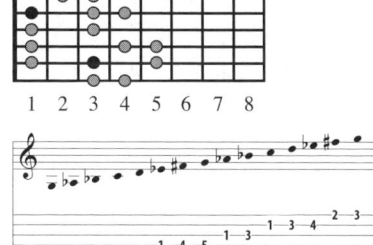

## Augmented Dominant (1 2 3 4 #5 6 b7 8)

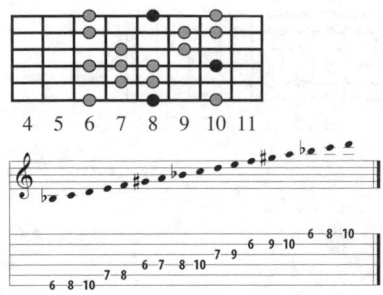
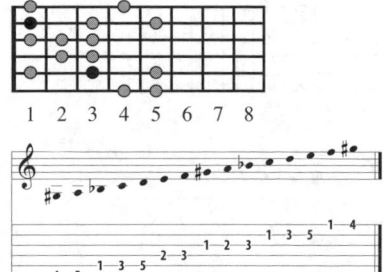

## Augmented Dominant b9 (1 b2 3 4 #5 6 b7 8)

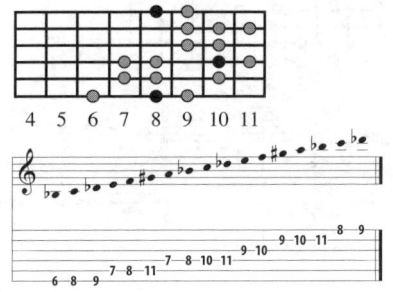
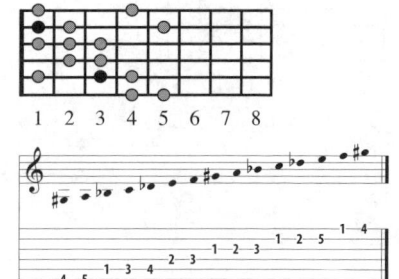

## Augmented Dominant #9 (1 #2 3 4 #5 6 b7 8)

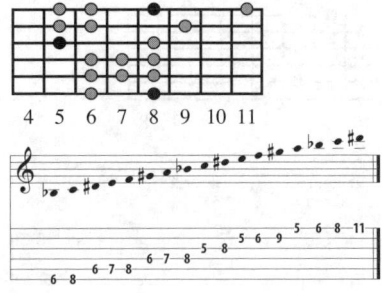

## Augmented #9 (1 #2 3 4 #5 6 7 8)

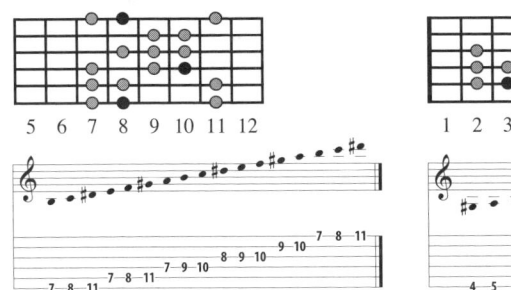
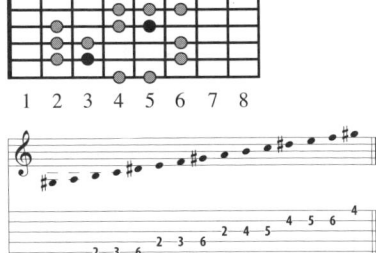

## Augmented Minor/Major 7 (1 2 ♭3 4 #5 6 7 8)

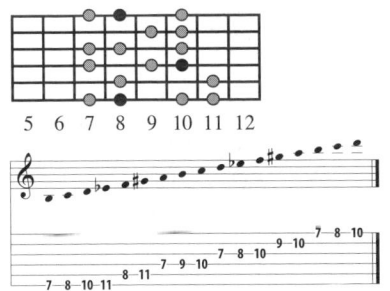
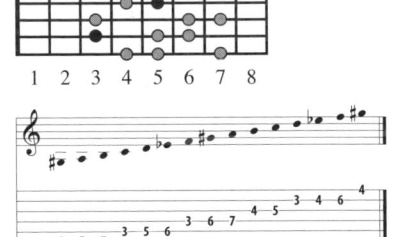

## Bebop Dominant (1 2 3 4 5 6 ♭7 7 8)

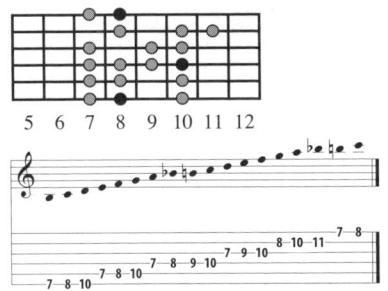
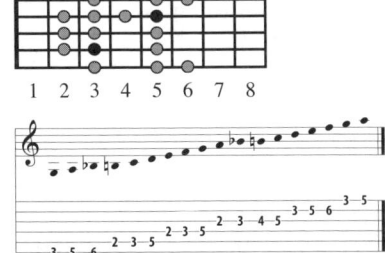

## Bebop Dorian (1 2 ♭3 3 4 5 6 ♭7 8)

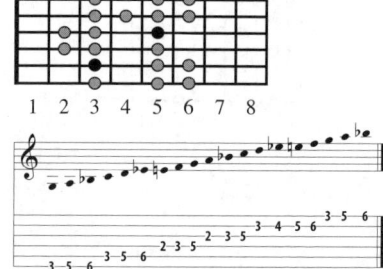

## Bebop Major* (1 2 3 4 ♯4 5 6 7 8)

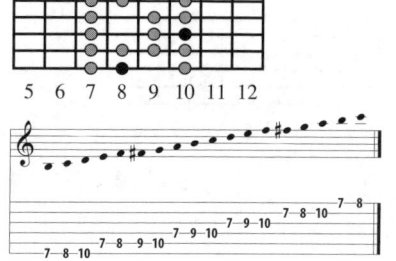
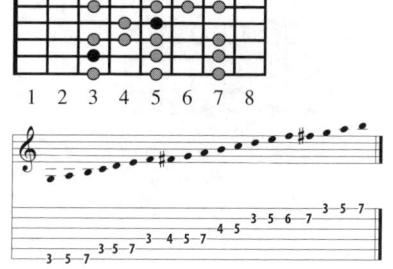

## Bebop Melodic Minor* (1 2 ♭3 4 ♯4 5 6 7 8)

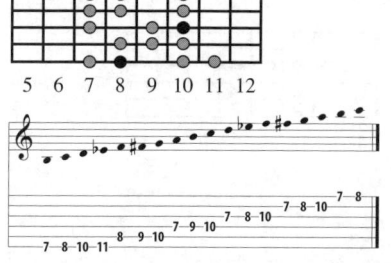
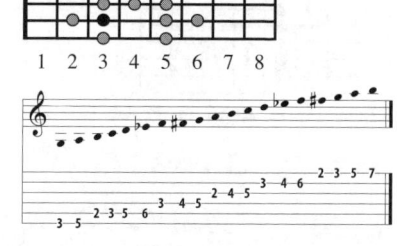

\* Many musicians spell this scale with a ♯5 instead of a ♯4.

## Diminished Tritonic (1 ♭3 4 ♭5 8)

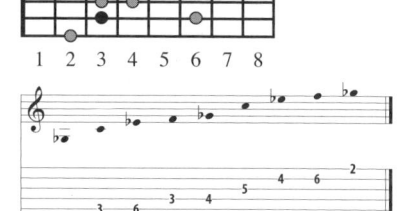

## Dominant ♭5 (1 2 3 4 ♭5 6 ♭7 8)

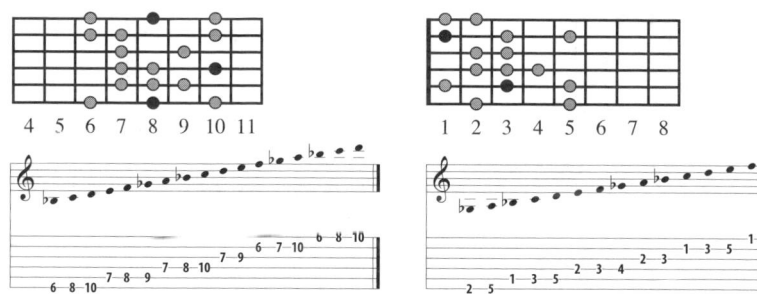

## Dominant ♭5 ♭9 ♯9 (1 ♭2 ♭3 ♭4 ♭5 6 ♭7 8)

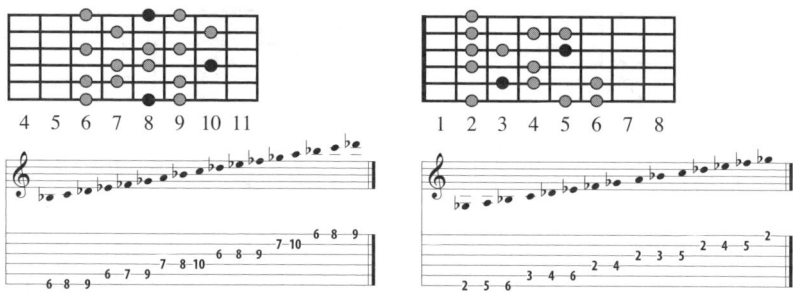

## Dominant ♭9 ♯9 (1 ♭2 ♭3 ♭4 5 6 ♭7 8)

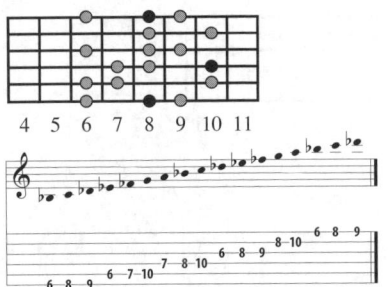
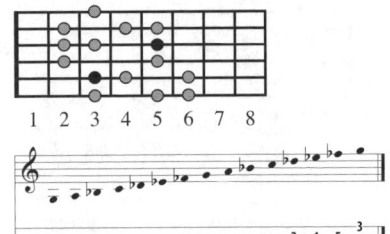

## Dominant ♭9 ♯9 ♭13 (1 ♭2 ♭3 ♭4 5 ♭6 ♭7 8)

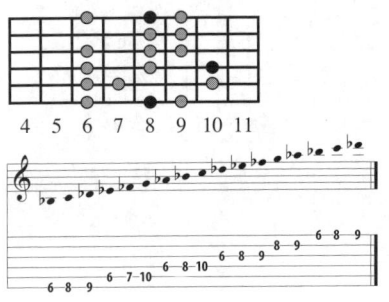

## Dominant ♯9 (1 ♯2 3 4 5 6 ♭7 8)

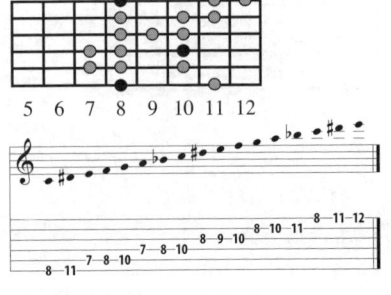

## Dominant ♭9 #11 (1 ♭2 3 #4 5 6 ♭7 8)

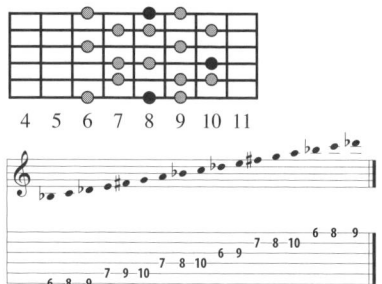
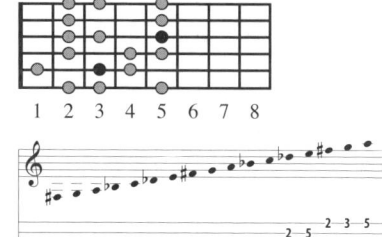

## Dominant ♭9 #11 ♭13 (1 ♭2 3 #4 5 ♭6 ♭7 8)

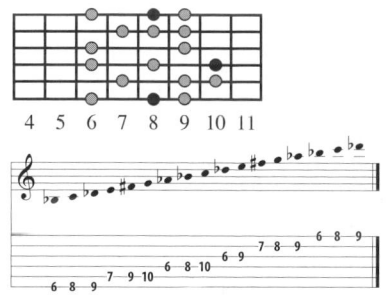
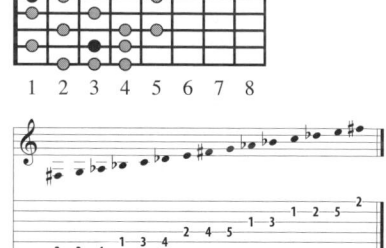

## Dominant 13 (1 2 3 5 6 ♭7 8)

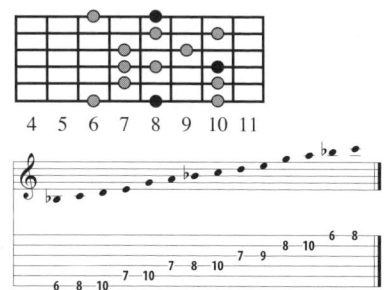
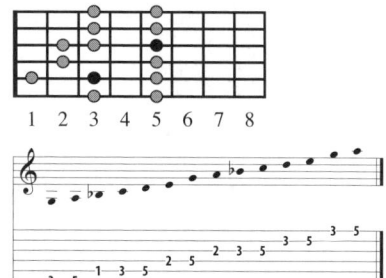

# Major and Dominant Scales

## Major/Ionian (1 2 3 4 5 6 7 8)

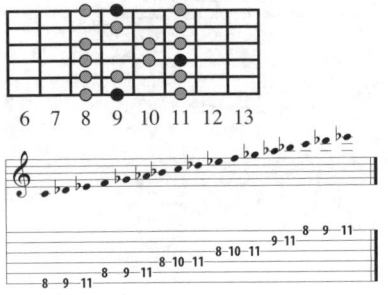
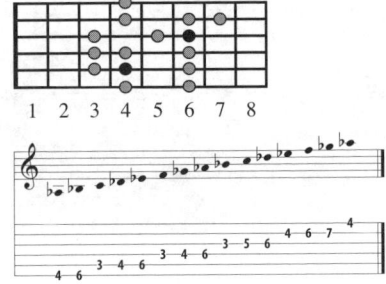

## Mixolydian (1 2 3 4 5 6 ♭7 8)
5th mode of the major scale

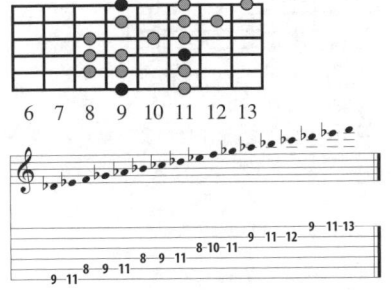
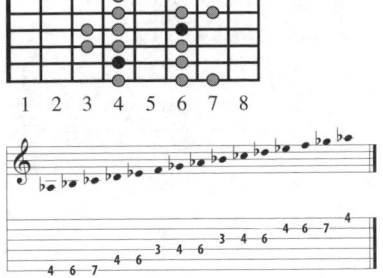

## Lydian (1 2 3 ♯4 5 6 7 8)
4th mode of the major scale

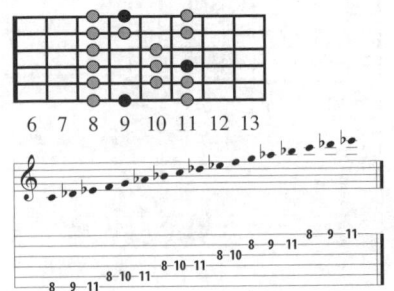
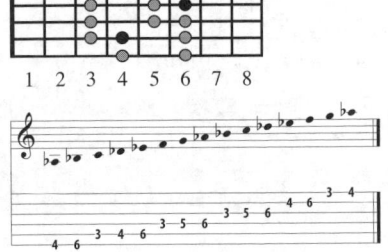

## Major Pentatonic (1 2 3 5 6 8)

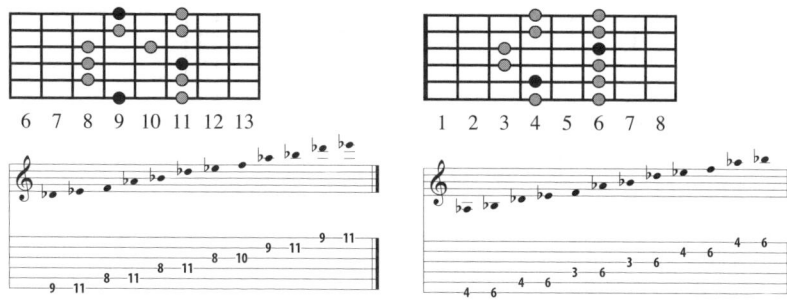

## Major 13 Pentatonic* (1 2 3 5 6 7 8)

## Major Pentatonic Blues* (1 2 ♭3 3 5 6 8)

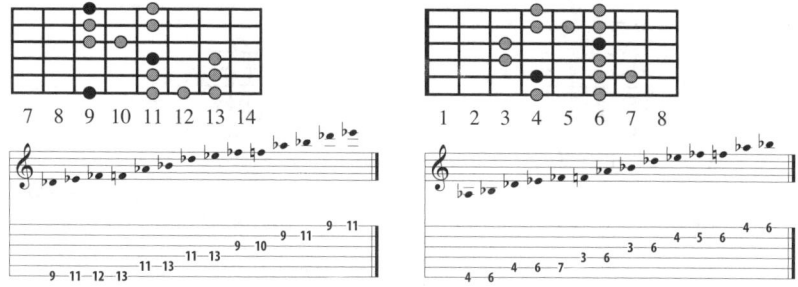

* While this scale has more than five notes, it is based on a five-note, pentatonic scale and it is best to think of it as a pentatonic scale.

# Lydian Pentatonic (1 3 #4 5 7 8)

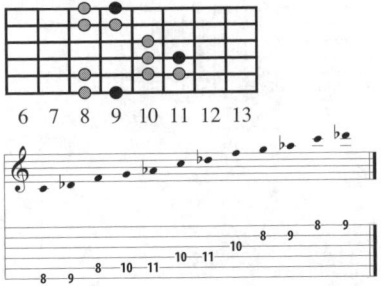
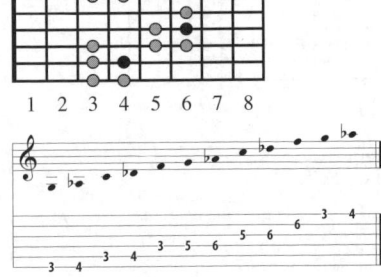

# Lydian ♭7 (1 2 3 #4 5 6 ♭7 8)
4th mode of the melodic minor scale

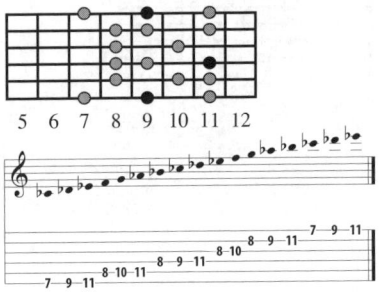
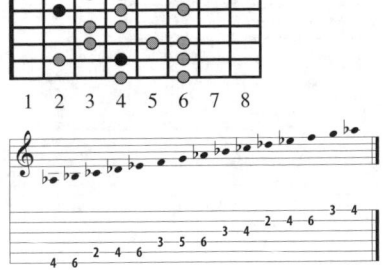

# Lydian #9 (1 #2 3 #4 5 6 7 8)
6th mode of the harmonic minor scale

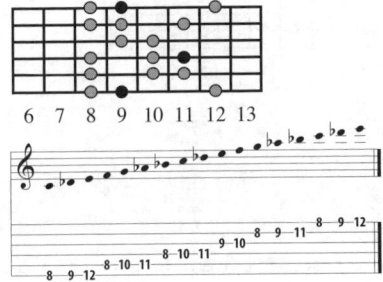
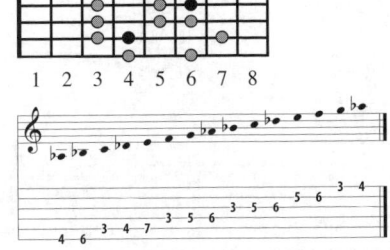

## Aeolian Major (1 2 3 4 5 ♭6 ♭7 8)
5th mode of the melodic minor scale

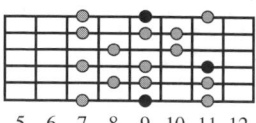
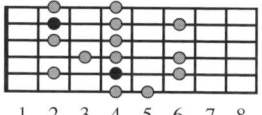

## Phrygian Major (1 ♭2 3 4 5 ♭6 ♭7 8)
5th mode of the harmonic minor scale

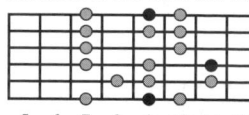
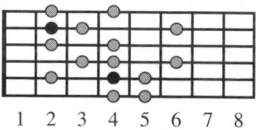

D♭

## Ionian Augmented (1 2 3 4 ♯5 6 7 8)
3rd mode of the harmonic minor scale

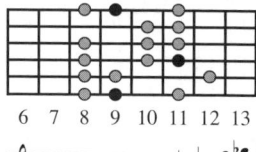
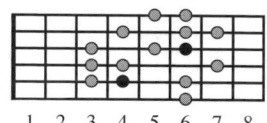

## Lydian Augmented (1 2 3 #4 #5 6 7 8)
3rd mode of the melodic minor scale

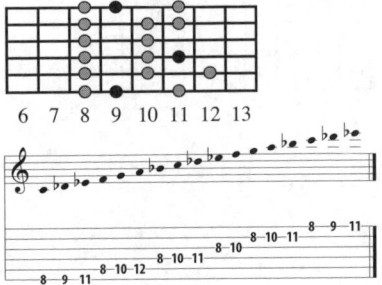
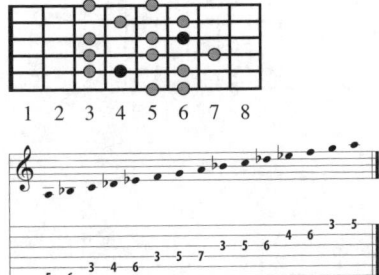

# Minor Scales

## Natural Minor/ Aeolian (1 2 ♭3 4 5 ♭6 ♭7 8)
6th mode of the major scale

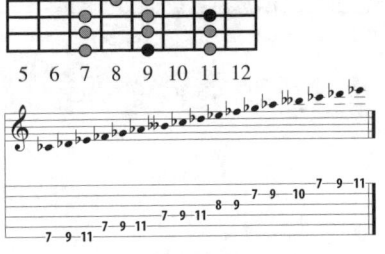
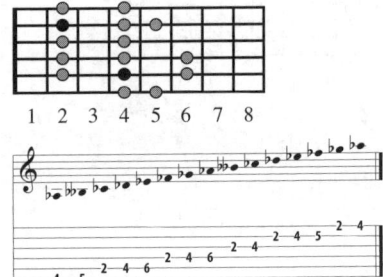

## Harmonic Minor (1 2 ♭3 4 5 ♭6 7 8)

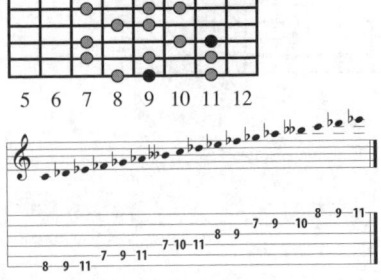
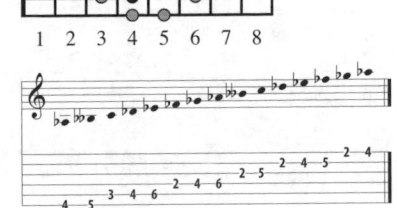

# Jazz Minor/Melodic Minor (1 2 ♭3 4 5 6 7 8)
Melodic Minor descends in Aeolian/Natural Minor

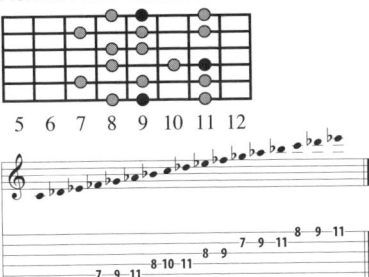
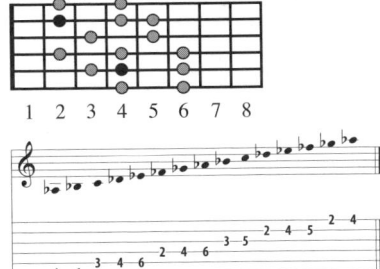

# Dorian (1 2 ♭3 4 5 6 ♭7 8)
2nd mode of the major scale

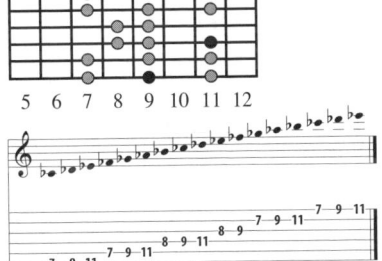
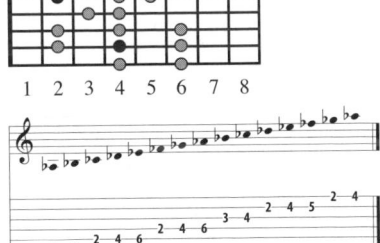

# Phrygian (1 ♭2 ♭3 4 5 ♭6 ♭7 8)
3rd mode of the major scale

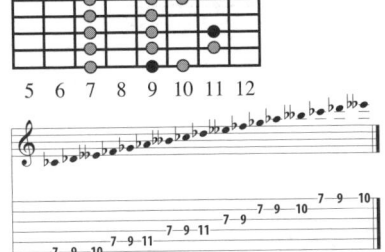
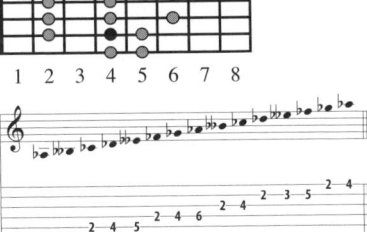

## Locrian (1 ♭2 ♭3 4 ♭5 ♭6 ♭7 8)
7th mode of the major scale

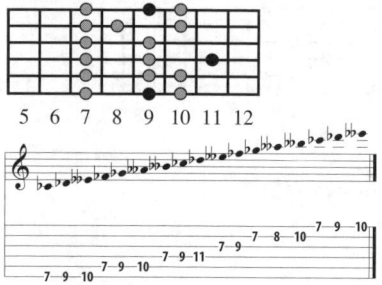
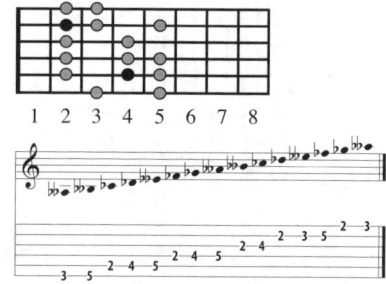

## Minor Pentatonic (1 ♭3 4 5 ♭7 8)

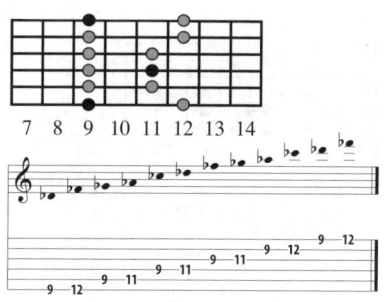
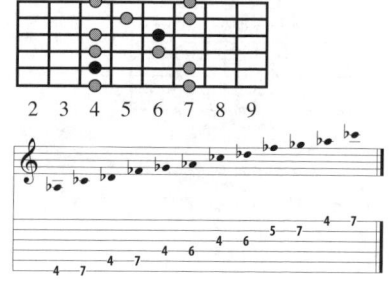

## Minor 13 Pentatonic* (1 ♭3 5 ♭6 ♭7 8)

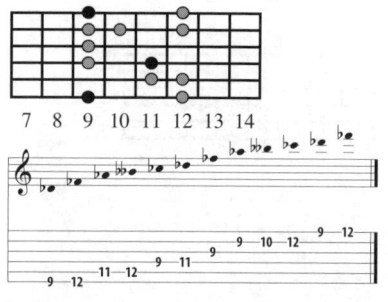
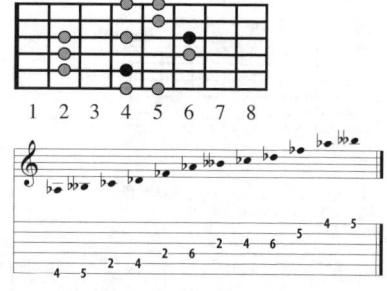

* While this scale has more than five notes, it is based on a five-note, pentatonic scale and it is best to think of it as a pentatonic scale.

# Minor Pentatonic Blues* (1 ♭3 4 ♯4 ♭5 ♭7 8)

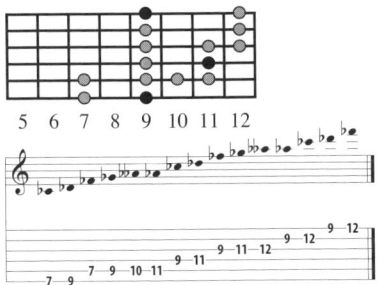
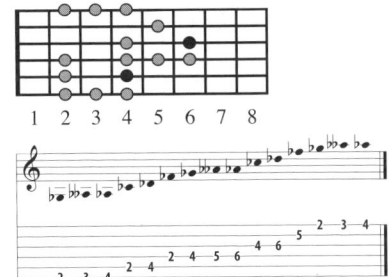

# Dorian Pentatonic (1 2 ♭3 5 ♭7 8)

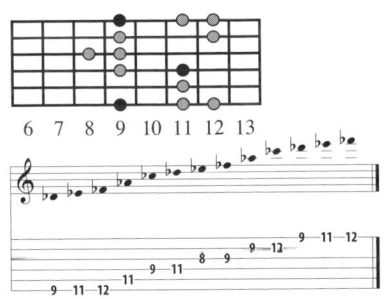
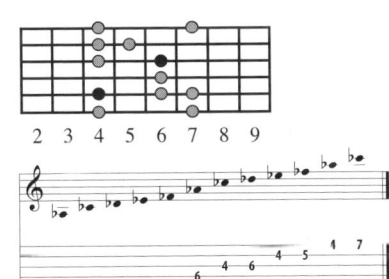

# Phrygian Pentatonic (1 ♭2 4 5 ♭7 8)

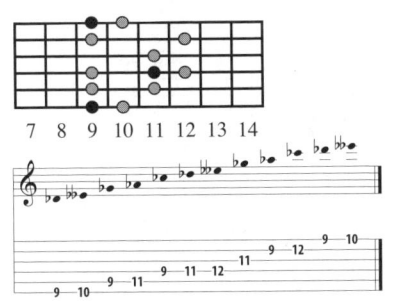
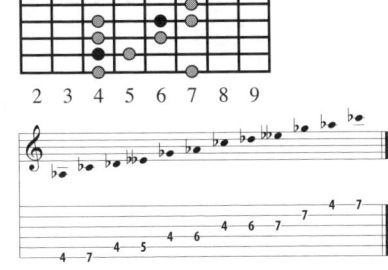

* While this scale has more than five notes, it is based on a five-note, pentatonic scale and it is best to think of it as a pentatonic scale.

## Phrygian ♮6 (1 ♭2 ♭3 4 5 6 ♭7 8)
2nd mode of the melodic minor scale

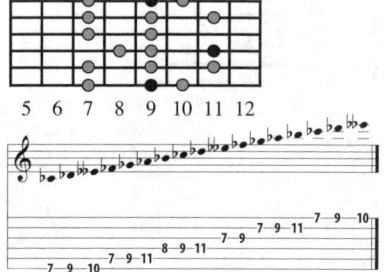
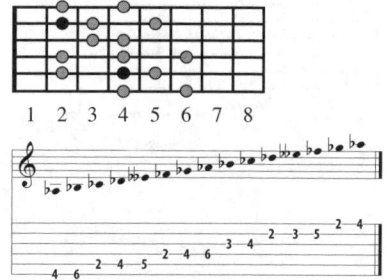

## Locrian ♮2 (1 2 ♭3 4 ♭5 ♭6 ♭7 8)
6th mode of the melodic minor scale

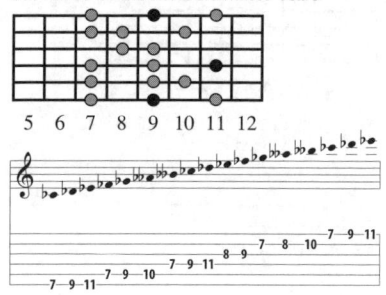
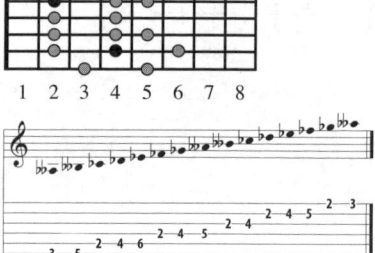

## Locrian ♮6 (1 ♭2 ♭3 4 ♭5 6 ♭7 8)
2nd mode of the harmonic minor scale

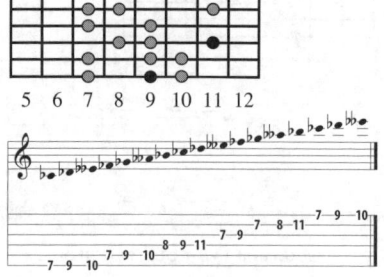

# Symmetrical Scales

## Chromatic (1 b2 2 b3 3 4 b5 5 b6 6 b7 7 8)

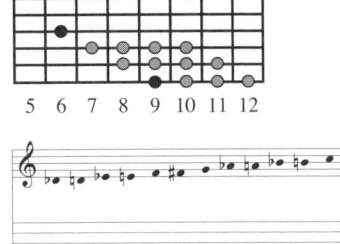
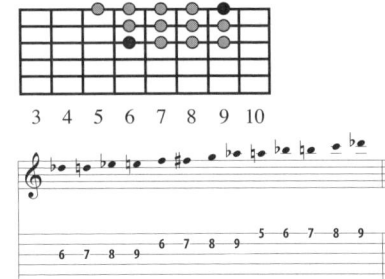

## Whole Tone (1 2 3 #4 #5 #6 8)

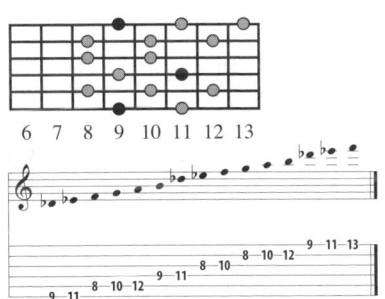
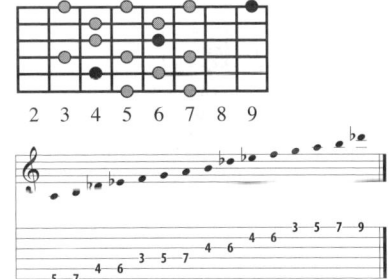

## Auxiliary, Whole/Half Diminished (1 2 b3 4 b5 b6 6 7 8)

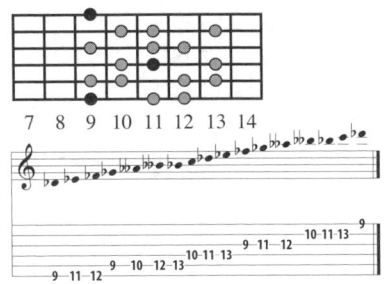
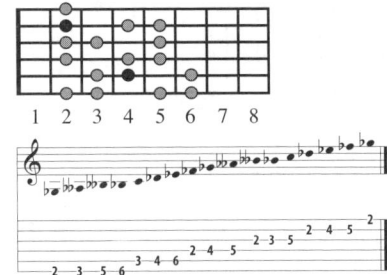

## Symmetrical, Half/Whole Diminished (1 ♭2 ♭3 ♭4 ♭5 5 6 ♭7 8)

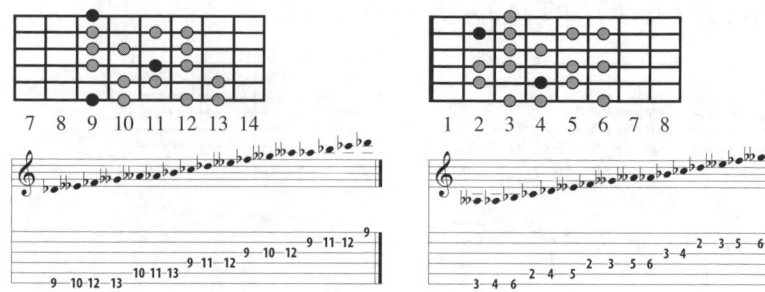

## Augmented (1 ♯2 3 5 ♯5 7 8)

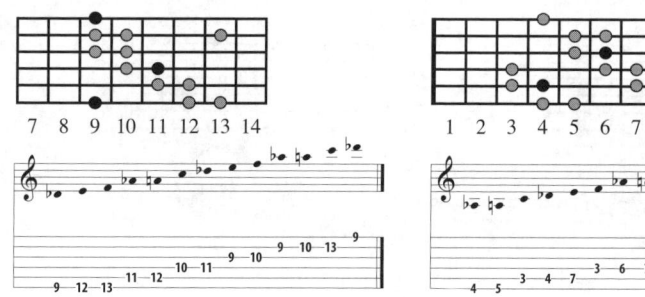

## Chromatic Augmented (1 ♭2 2 ♭3 3 4 ♯4 ♯5 6 ♭7 8)

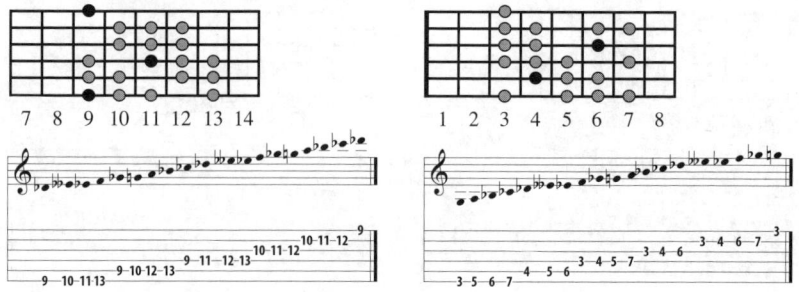

## Augmented ♭9 (1 ♭2 ♭3 3 4 5 ♭6 6 7 8)

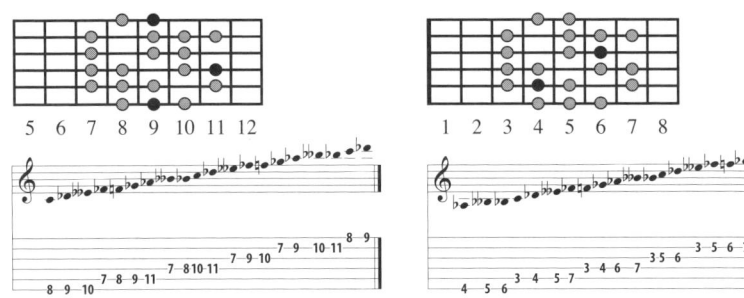

## Augmented 9 (1 2 ♭3 3 ♯4 5 ♭6 ♭7 7 8)

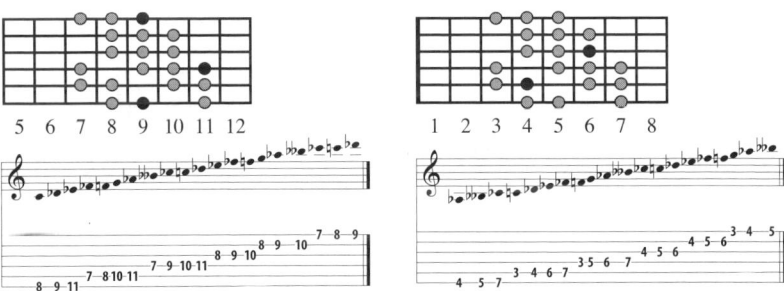

## Diminished Blues (1 ♭2 ♭3 3 ♯5 6 ♭7 8)

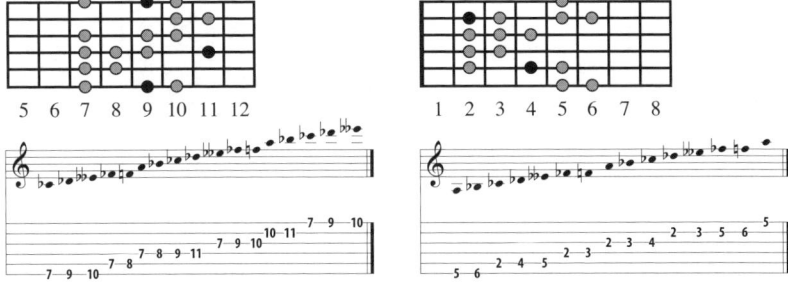

# Four Semitone Tritone (1 b2 2 b3 3 #4 5 b6 6 b7 8)

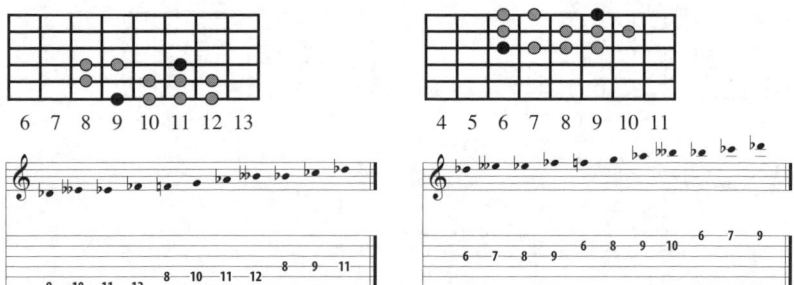

# Tetratonic (1 4 b5 7 8)

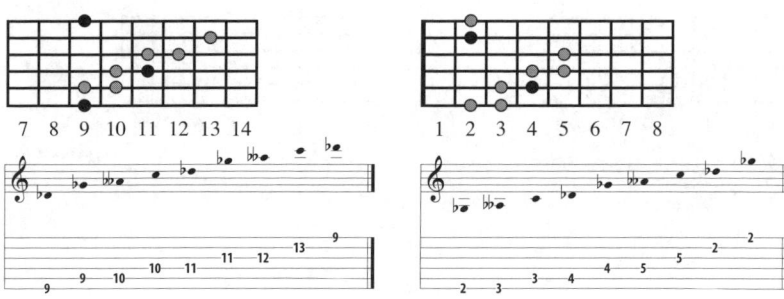

# Three Semitone Tritone (1 b2 2 b3 b5 5 b6 6 8)

## Tritone (1 ♭2 3 ♯4 5 ♭7 8)

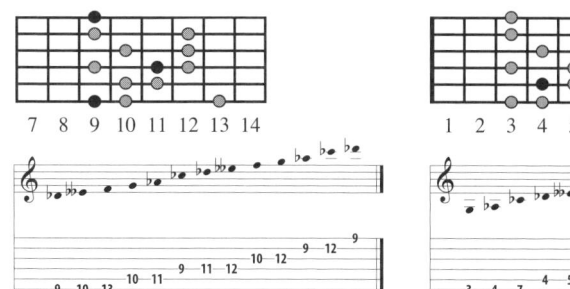
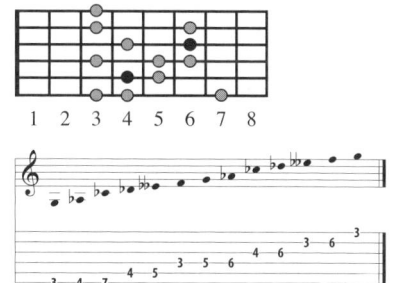

## Two-Semitone Tritone (1 ♭2 2 ♯4 5 ♭6 8)

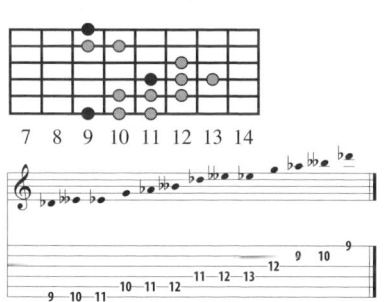
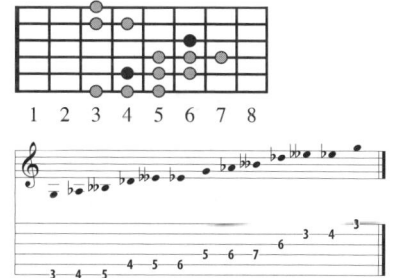

# Hybrid Scales

## Aeolian ♯11 (1 2 ♭3 ♯4 5 ♭6 ♭7 8)

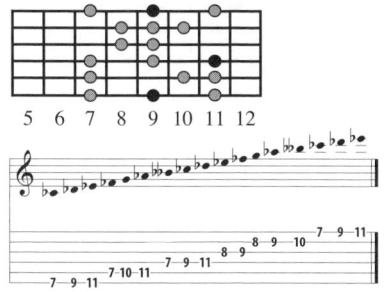
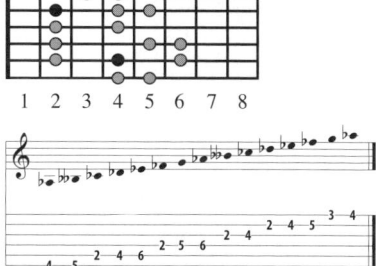

# Augmented Dominant (1 2 3 4 ♯5 6 ♭7 8)

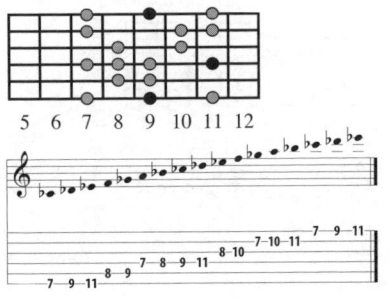

# Augmented Dominant ♭9 (1 ♭2 3 4 ♯5 6 ♭7 8)

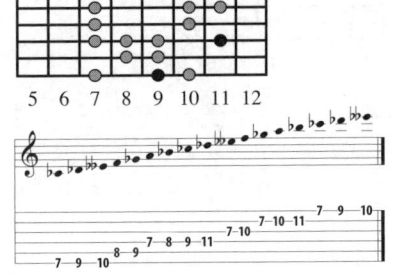
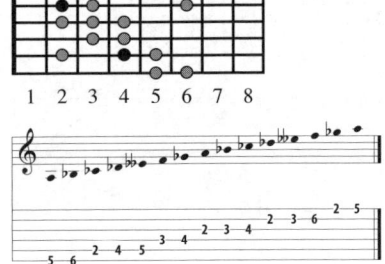

# Augmented Dominant ♯9 (1 ♯2 3 4 ♯5 6 ♭7 8)

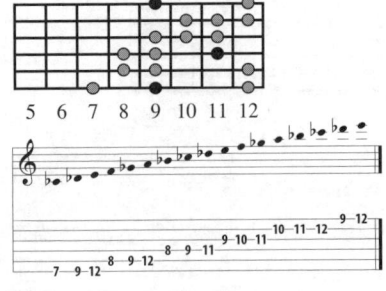
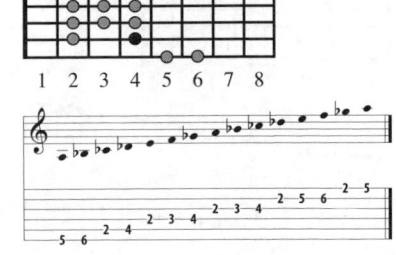

## Augmented #9 (1 #2 3 4 #5 6 7 8)

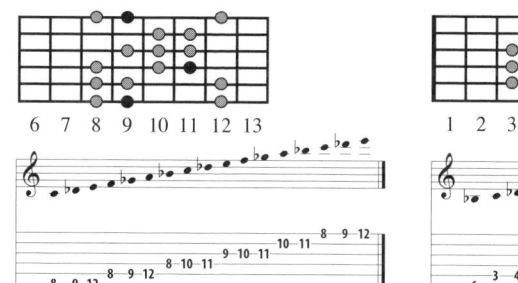
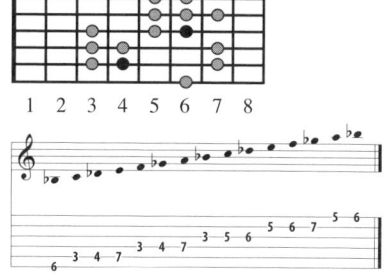

## Augmented Minor/Major 7 (1 2 ♭3 4 #5 6 7 8)

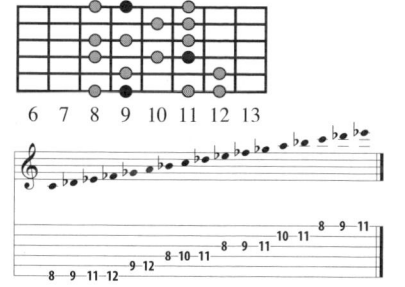
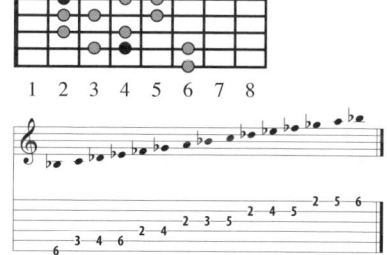

## Bebop Dominant (1 2 3 4 5 6 ♭7 7 8)

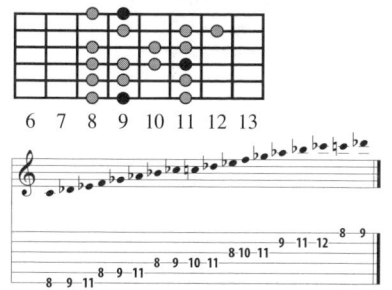
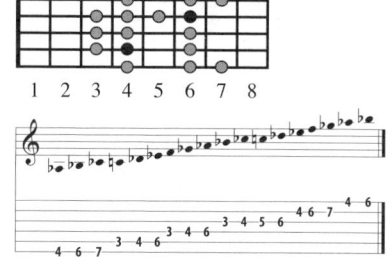

# Bebop Dorian (1 2 ♭3 3 4 5 6 ♭7 8)

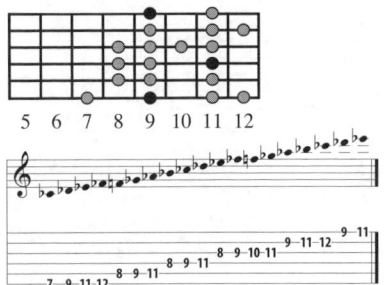
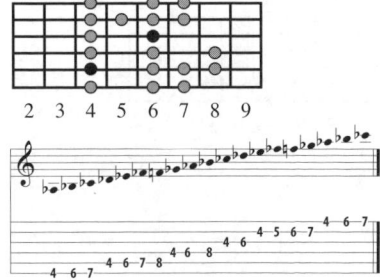

# Bebop Major* (1 2 3 4 ♯4 5 6 7 8)

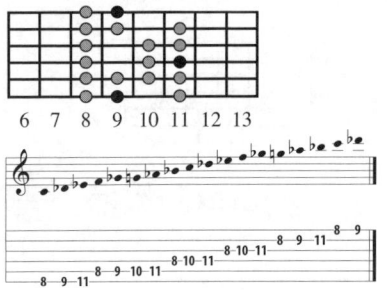
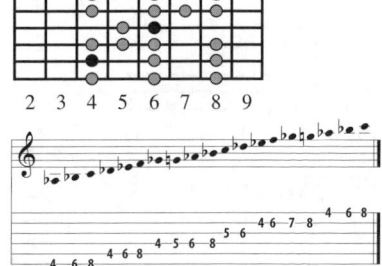

# Bebop Melodic Minor* (1 2 ♭3 4 ♯4 5 6 7 8)

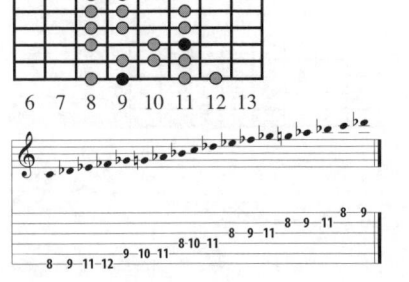
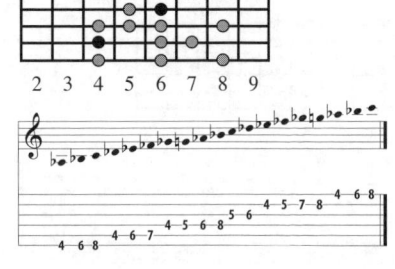

* Many musicians spell this scale with a ♯5 instead of a ♯4.

# Diminished Tritonic (1 ♭3 4 ♭5 8)

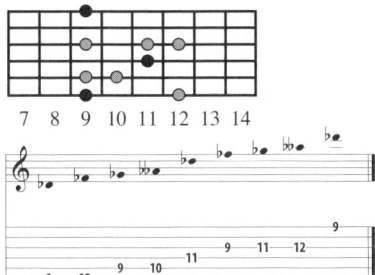

# Dominant ♭5 (1 2 3 4 ♭5 6 ♭7 8)

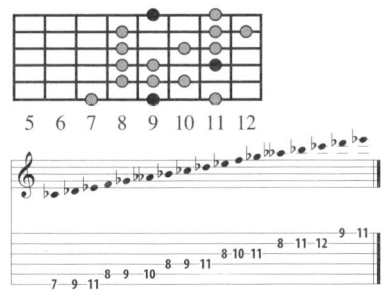
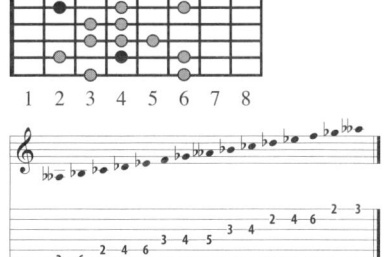

# Dominant ♭5 ♭9 ♯9 (1 ♭2 ♭3 ♭4 ♭5 6 ♭7 8)

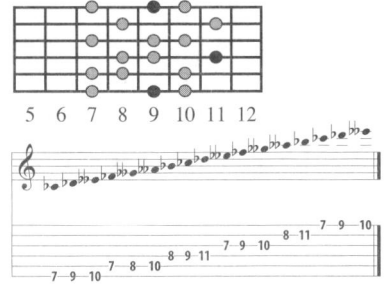
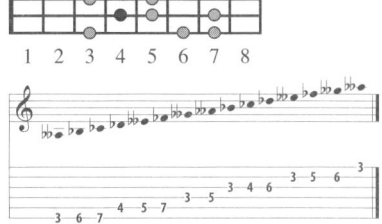

## Dominant ♭9 #9 (1 ♭2 #3 ♭4 5 6 ♭7 8)

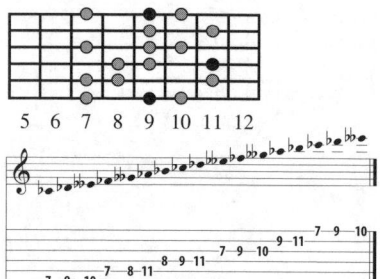
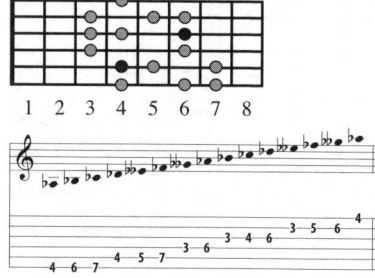

## Dominant ♭9 #9 ♭13 (1 ♭2 #3 ♭4 5 ♭6 ♭7 8)

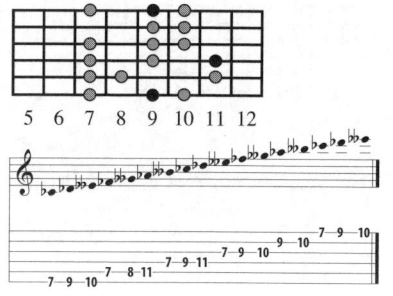
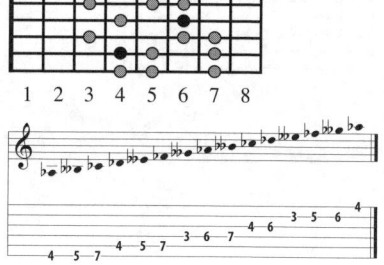

## Dominant #9 (1 #2 3 4 5 6 ♭7 8)

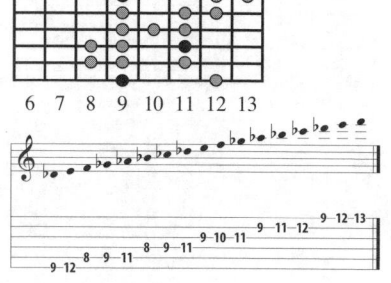
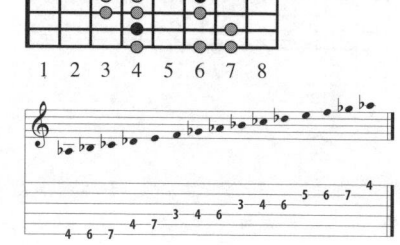

## Dominant ♭9 #11 (1 ♭2 3 #4 5 6 ♭7 8)

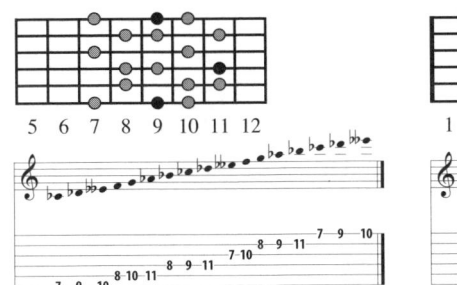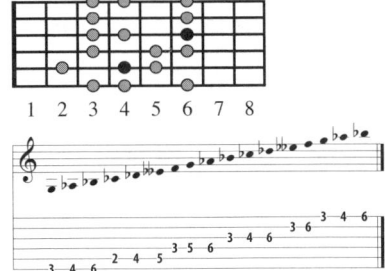

## Dominant ♭9 #11 ♭13 (1 ♭2 3 #4 5 ♭6 ♭7 8)

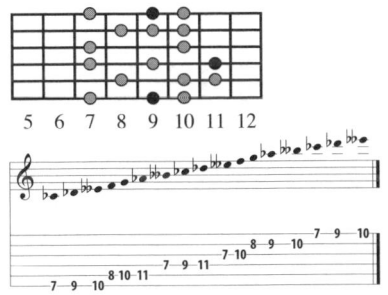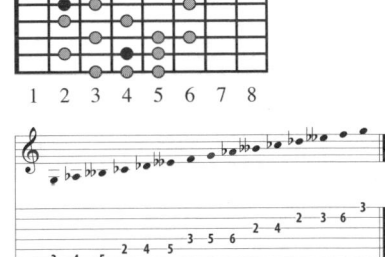

## Dominant 13 (1 2 3 5 6 ♭7 8)

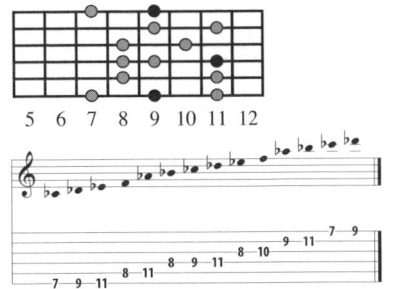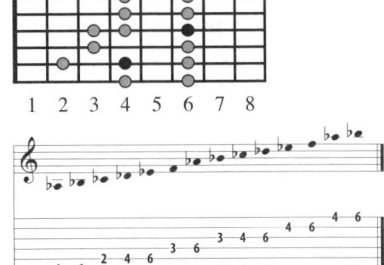

# Major and Dominant Scales

## Major/Ionian (1 2 3 4 5 6 7 8)

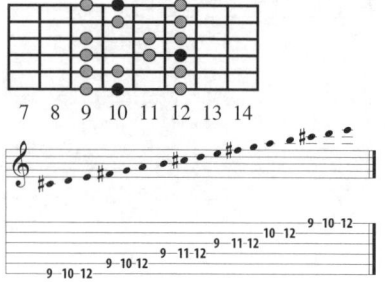
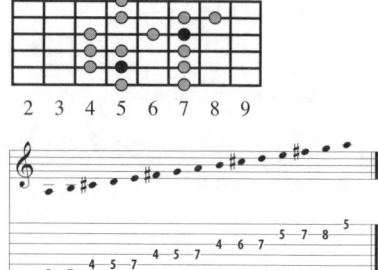

## Mixolydian (1 2 3 4 5 6 ♭7 8)
5th mode of the major scale

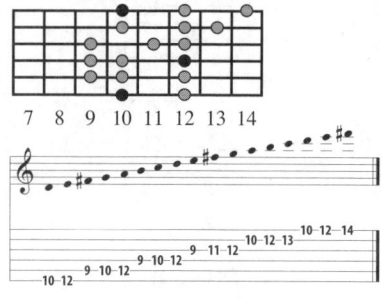
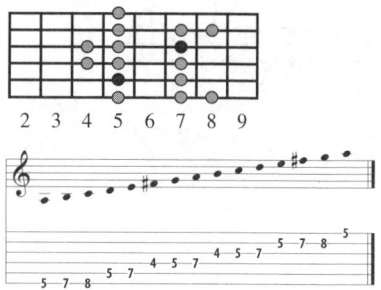

## Lydian (1 2 3 ♯4 5 6 7 8)
4th mode of the major scale

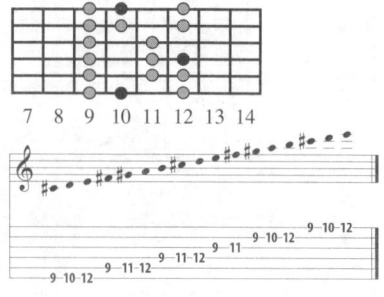
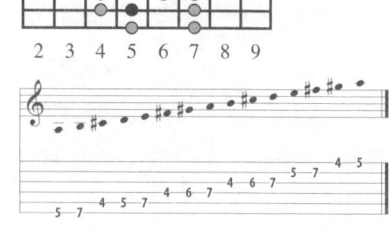

## Major Pentatonic (1 2 3 5 6 8)

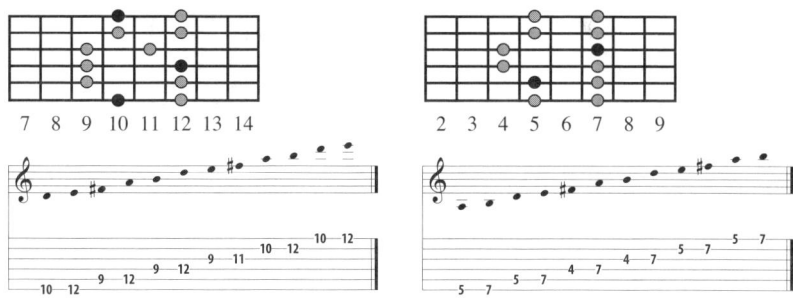

## Major 13 Pentatonic* (1 2 3 5 6 7 8)

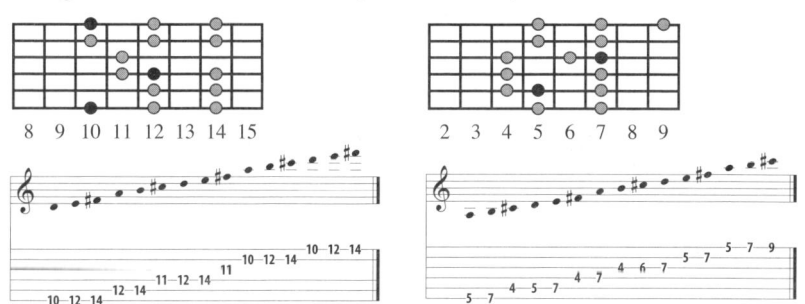

## Major Pentatonic Blues* (1 2 ♭3 3 5 6 8)

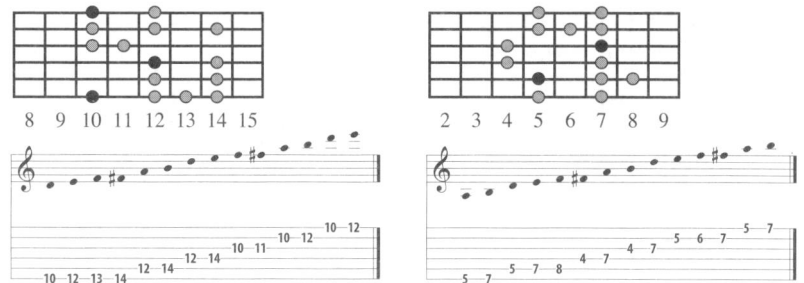

\* While this scale has more than five notes, it is based on a five-note, pentatonic scale and it is best to think of it as a pentatonic scale.

# Lydian Pentatonic (1 3 #4 5 7 8)

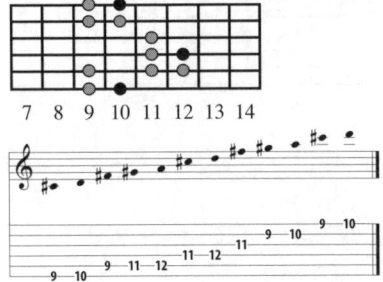

# Lydian ♭7 (1 2 3 #4 5 6 ♭7 8)
4th mode of the melodic minor scale

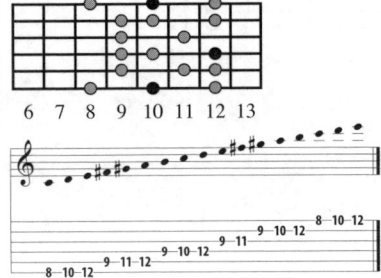
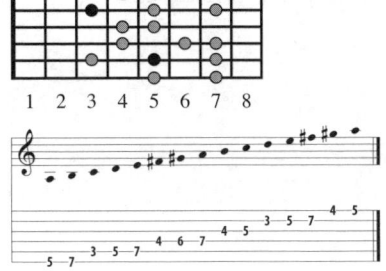

# Lydian #9 (1 #2 3 #4 5 6 7 8)
6th mode of the harmonic minor scale

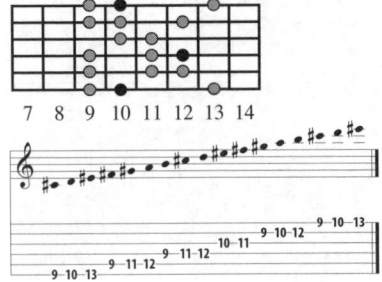
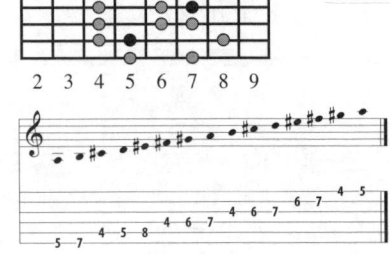

# Aeolian Major (1 2 3 4 5 ♭6 ♭7 8)
5th mode of the melodic minor scale

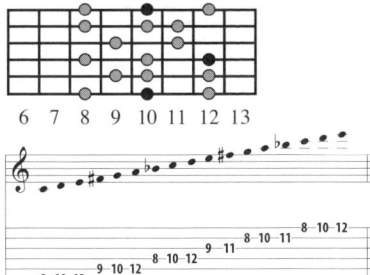
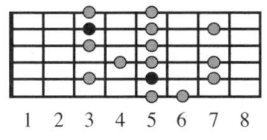

# Phrygian Major (1 ♭2 3 4 5 ♭6 ♭7 8)
5th mode of the harmonic minor scale

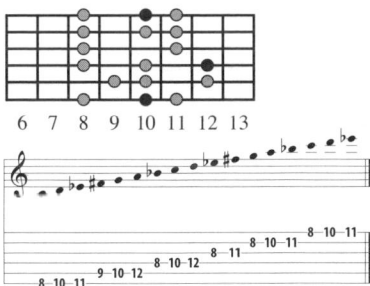
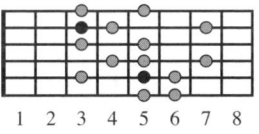

# Ionian Augmented (1 2 3 4 ♯5 6 7 8)
3rd mode of the harmonic minor scale

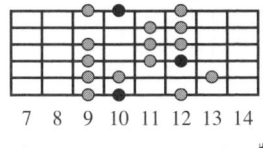

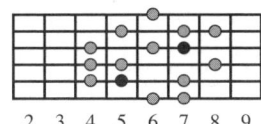

## Lydian Augmented (1 2 3 #4 #5 6 7 8)
3rd mode of the melodic minor scale

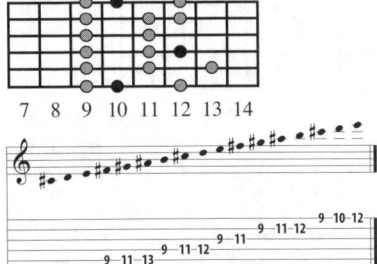
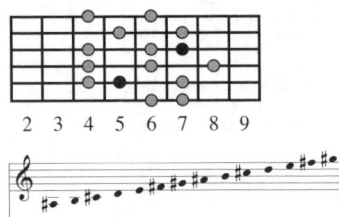

# Minor Scales

## Natural Minor/Aeolian (1 2 ♭3 4 5 ♭6 ♭7 8)
6th mode of the major scale

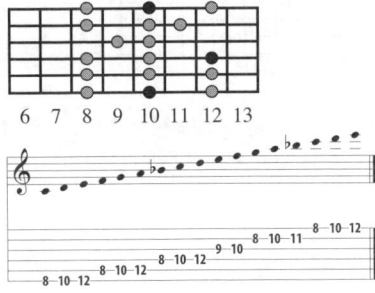
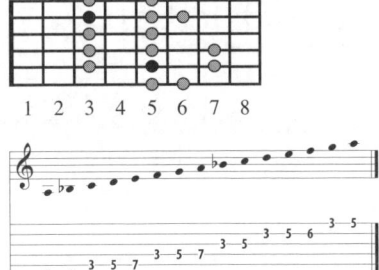

## Harmonic Minor (1 2 ♭3 4 5 ♭6 7 8)

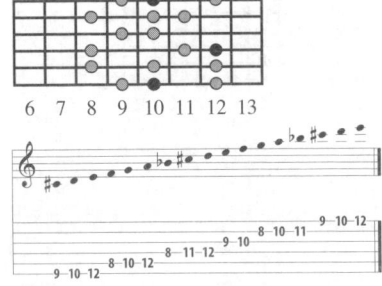
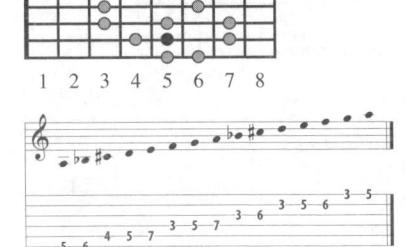

# Jazz Minor/Melodic Minor (1 2 ♭3 4 5 6 7 8)
Melodic Minor descends in Aeolian/Natural Minor

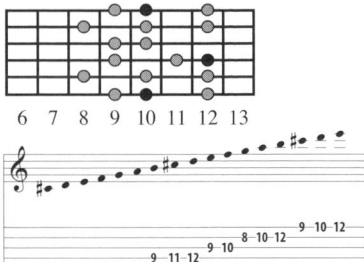 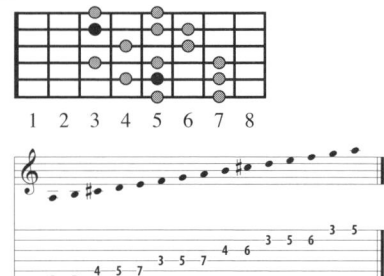

# Dorian (1 2 ♭3 4 5 6 ♭7 8)
2nd mode of the major scale

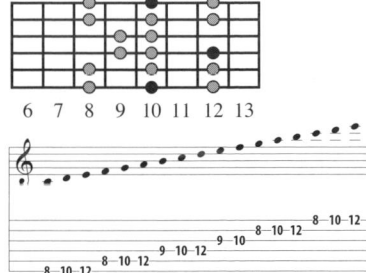 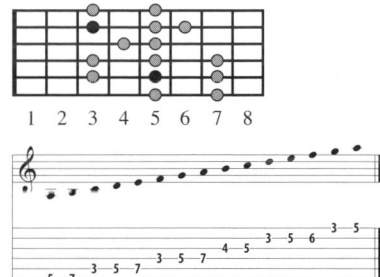

# Phrygian (1 ♭2 ♭3 4 5 ♭6 ♭7 8)
3rd mode of the major scale

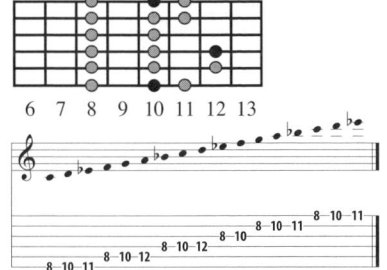 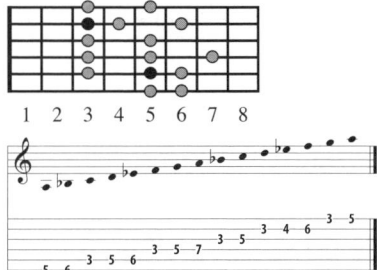

## Locrian (1 ♭2 ♭3 4 ♭5 ♭6 ♭7 8)
7th mode of the major scale

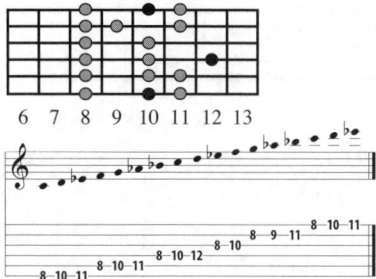
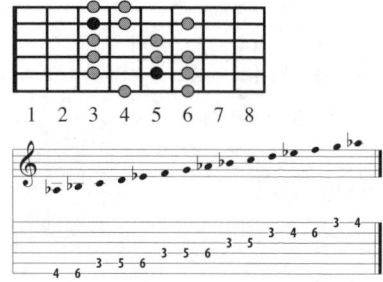

## Minor Pentatonic (1 ♭3 4 5 ♭7 8)

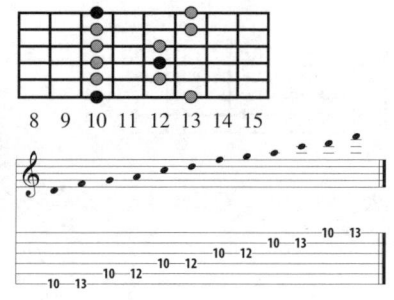
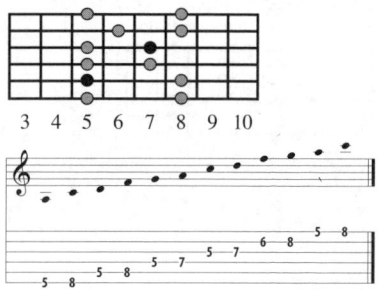

## Minor 13 Pentatonic* (1 ♭3 5 ♭6 ♭7 8)

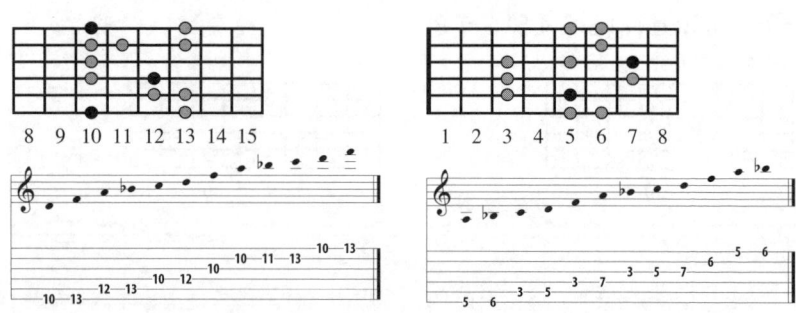

* While this scale has more than five notes, it is based on a five-note, pentatonic scale and it is best to think of it as a pentatonic scale.

## Minor Pentatonic Blues* (1 ♭3 4 ♭5 5 ♭7 8)

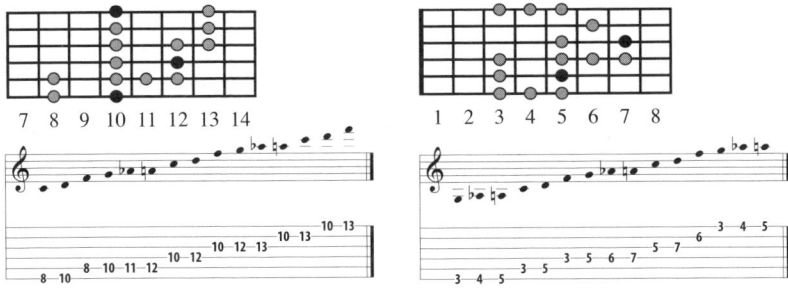

## Dorian Pentatonic (1 2 ♭3 5 ♭7 8)

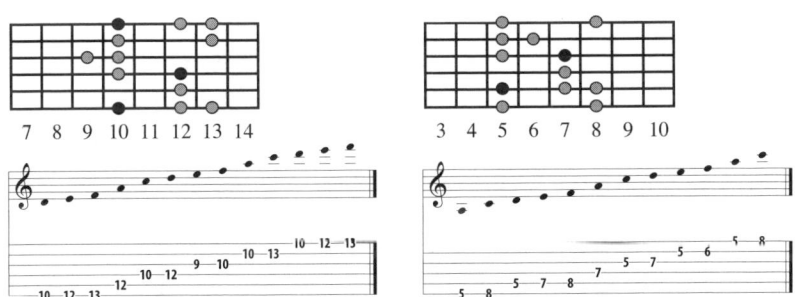

## Phrygian Pentatonic (1 ♭2 4 5 ♭7 8)

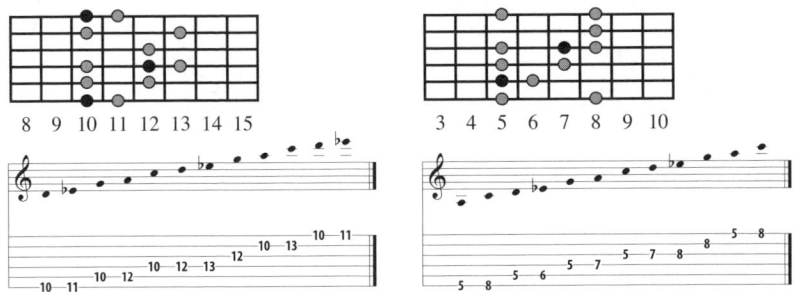

\* While this scale has more than five notes, it is based on a five-note, pentatonic scale and it is best to think of it as a pentatonic scale.

# Phrygian ♮6 (1 ♭2 ♭3 4 5 6 ♭7 8)
2nd mode of the melodic minor scale

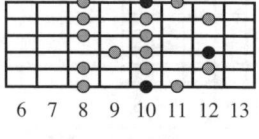
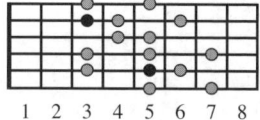
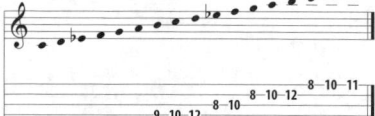
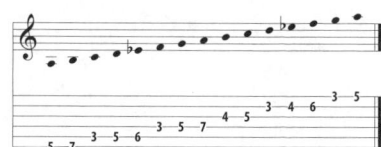

# Locrian ♮2 (1 2 ♭3 4 ♭5 ♭6 ♭7 8)
6th mode of the melodic minor scale

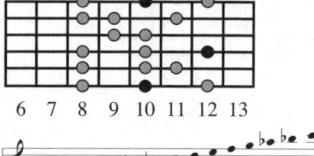
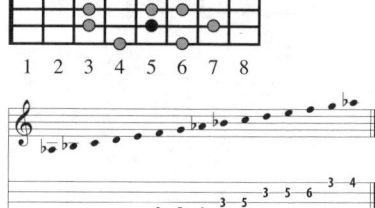
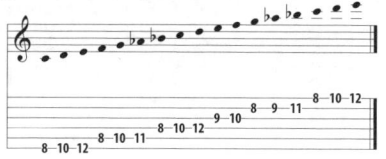

# Locrian ♮6 (1 ♭2 ♭3 4 ♭5 6 ♭7 8)
2nd mode of the harmonic minor scale

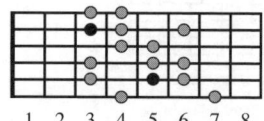
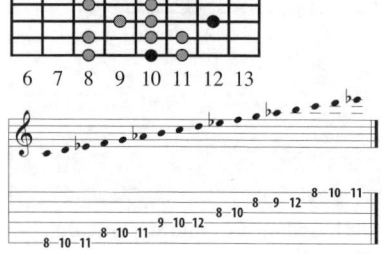

# Symmetrical Scales

## Chromatic (1 ♭2 2 ♭3 3 4 ♭5 5 ♭6 6 ♭7 7 8)

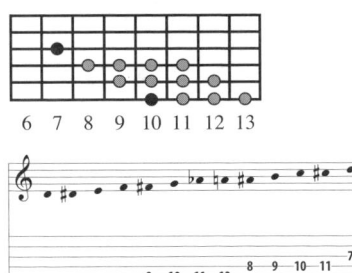
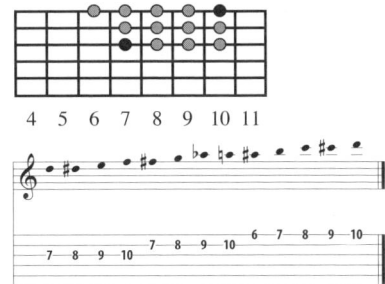

## Whole Tone (1 2 3 ♯4 ♯5 ♯6 8)

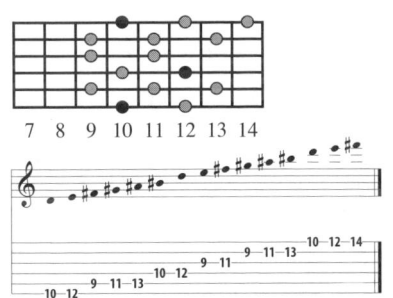
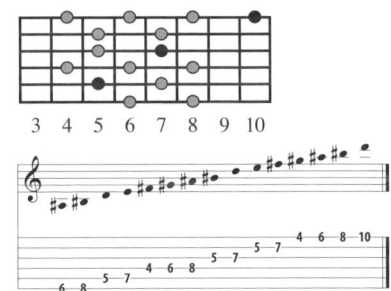

## Auxiliary, Whole/Half Diminished (1 2 ♭3 4 ♭5 ♭6 6 7 8)

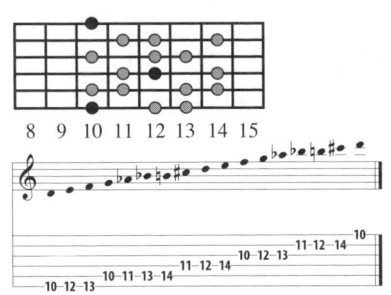
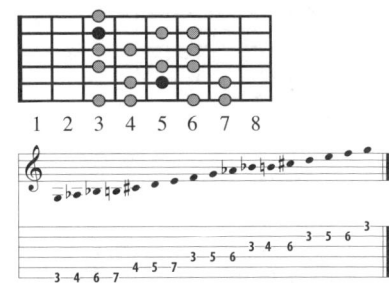

## Symmetrical, Half/Whole Diminished (1 ♭2 ♭3 ♭4 ♭5 5 6 ♭7 8)

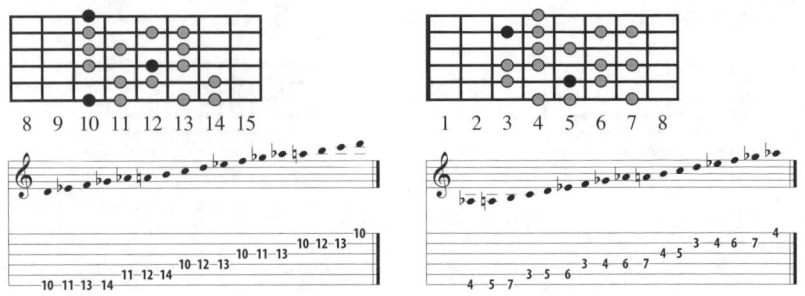

## Augmented (1 ♯2 3 5 ♯5 7 8)

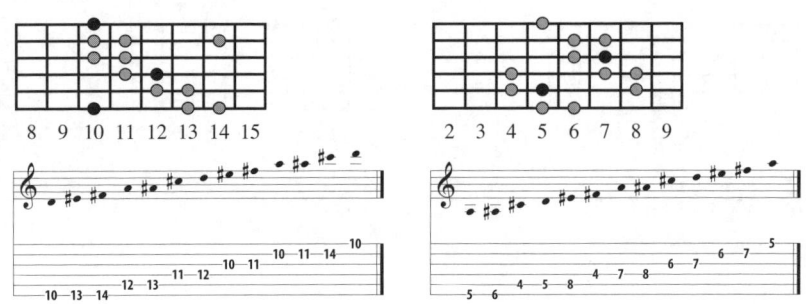

## Chromatic Augmented (1 ♭2 2 3 4 ♯4 ♯5 6 ♭7 8)

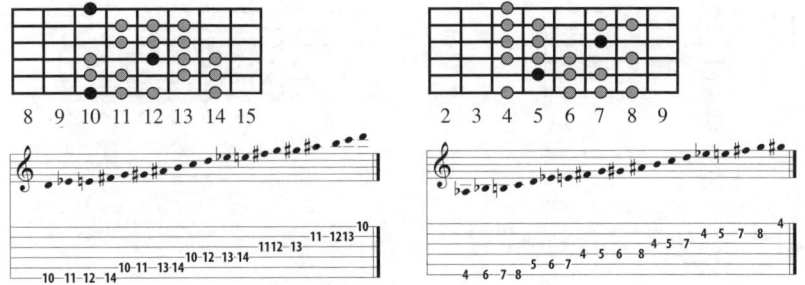

## Augmented ♭9 (1 ♭2 ♭3 3 4 5 ♭6 6 7 8)

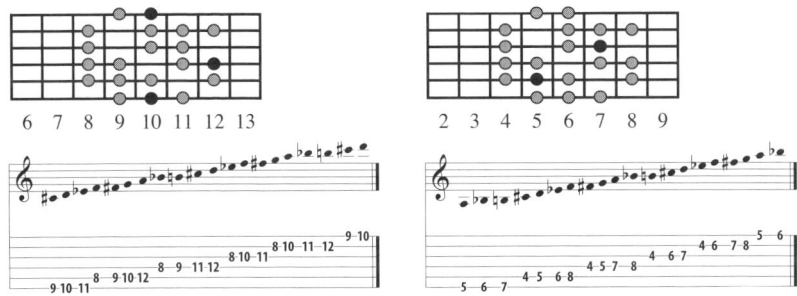

## Augmented 9 (1 2 ♭3 3 ♯4 5 ♭6 ♭7 7 8)

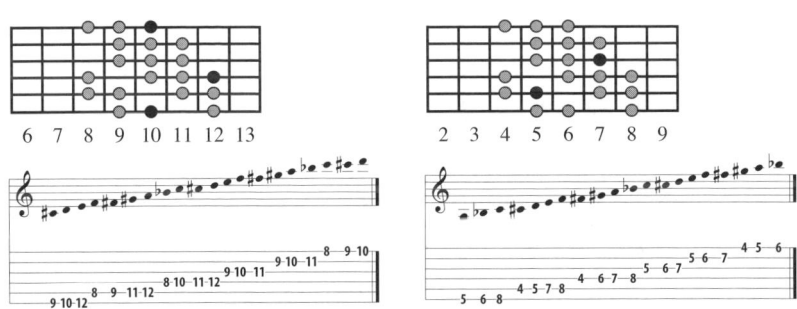

## Diminished Blues (1 ♭2 ♭3 3 ♯5 6 ♭7 8)

# Four Semitone Tritone (1 ♭2 2 ♭3 3 #4 5 ♭6 6 ♭7 8)

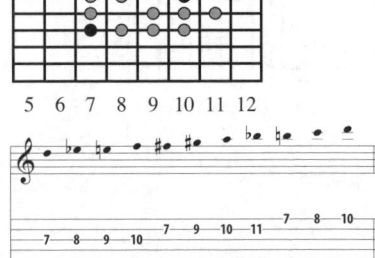

# Tetratonic (1 4 ♭5 7 8)

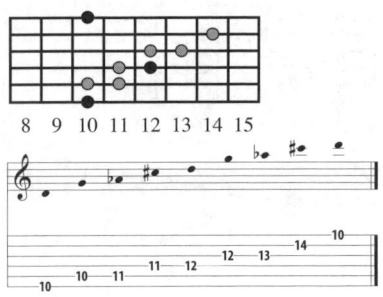

# Three Semitone Tritone (1 ♭2 2 ♭3 ♭5 5 ♭6 6 8)

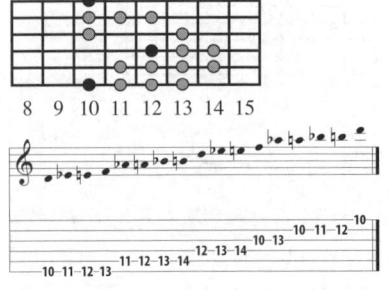

## Tritone (1 ♭2 3 ♯4 5 ♭7 8)

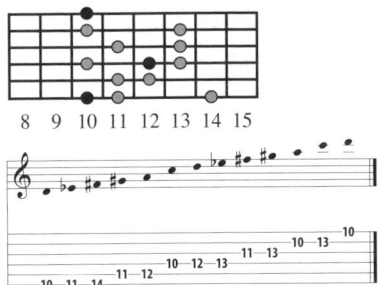
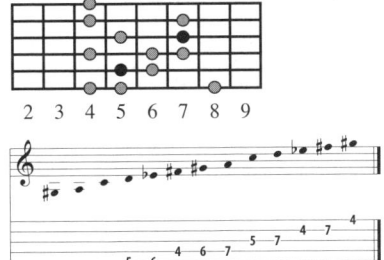

## Two-Semitone Tritone (1 ♭2 2 ♯4 5 ♭6 8)

# Hybrid Scales
## Aeolian ♯11 (1 2 ♭3 ♯4 5 ♭6 ♭7 8)

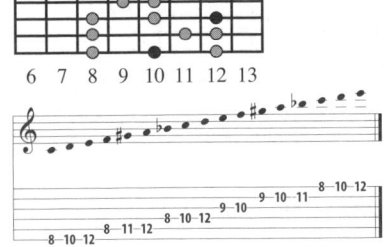
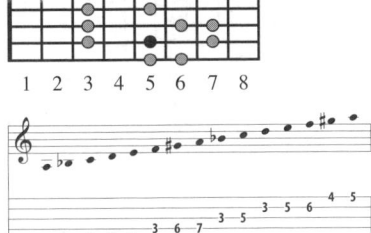

## Augmented Dominant (1 2 3 4 ♯5 6 ♭7 8)

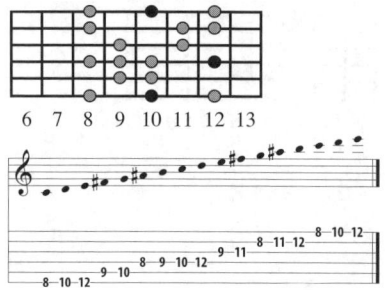
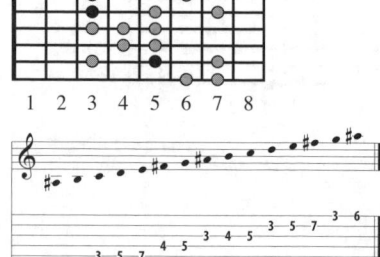

## Augmented Dominant ♭9 (1 ♭2 3 4 ♯5 6 ♭7 8)

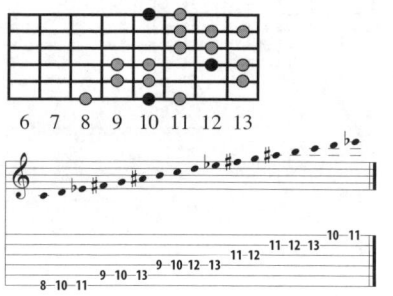
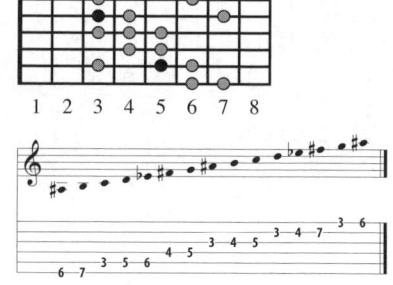

## Augmented Dominant ♯9 (1 ♯2 3 4 ♯5 6 ♭7 8)

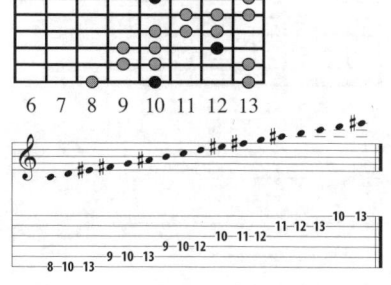

## Augmented #9 (1 #2 3 4 #5 6 7 8)

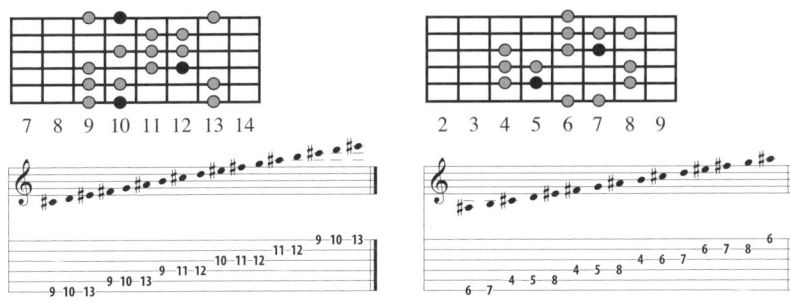

## Augmented Minor/Major 7 (1 2 b3 4 #5 6 7 8)

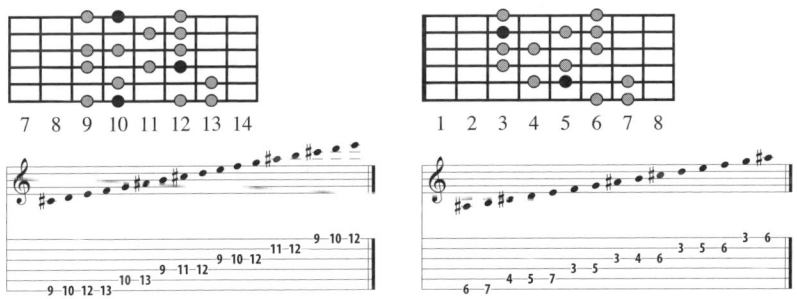

## Bebop Dominant (1 2 3 4 5 6 b7 7 8)

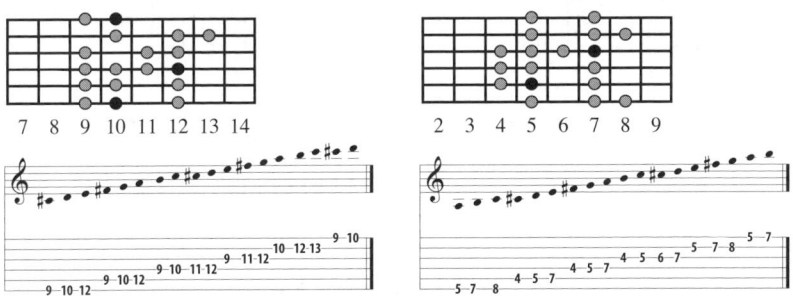

## Bebop Dorian (1 2 ♭3 3 4 5 6 ♭7 8)

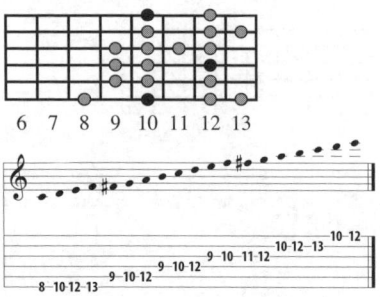
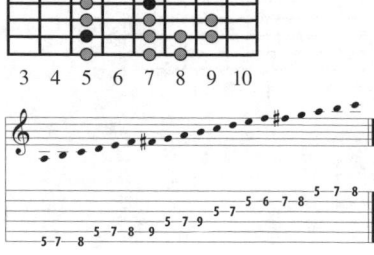

## Bebop Major* (1 2 3 4 ♯4 5 6 7 8)

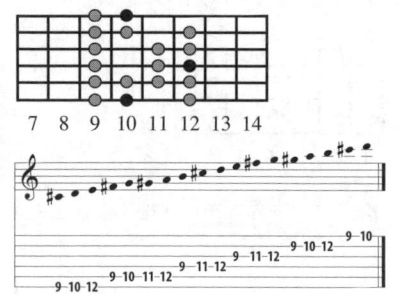
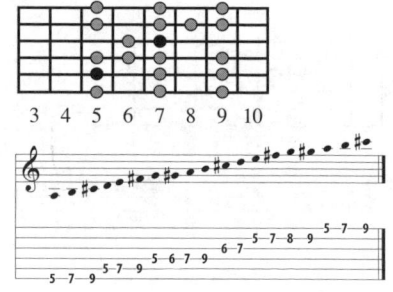

## Bebop Melodic Minor* (1 2 ♭3 4 ♯4 5 6 7 8)

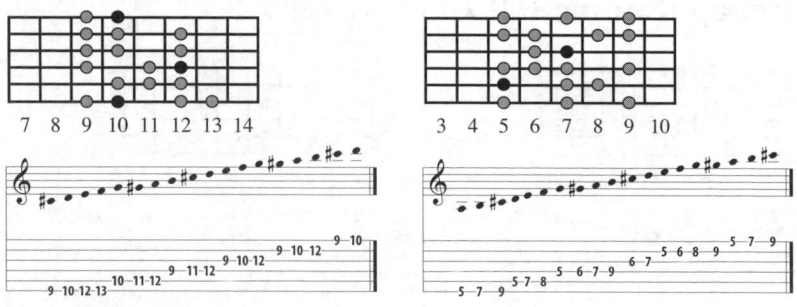

* Many musicians spell this scale with a ♯5 instead of a ♯4.

## Diminished Tritonic (1 b3 4 b5 8)

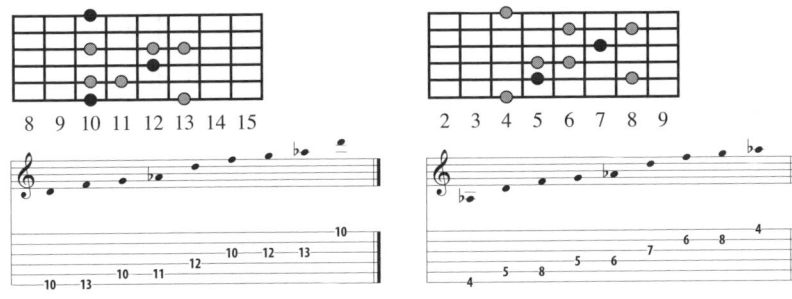

## Dominant b5 (1 2 3 4 b5 6 b7 8)

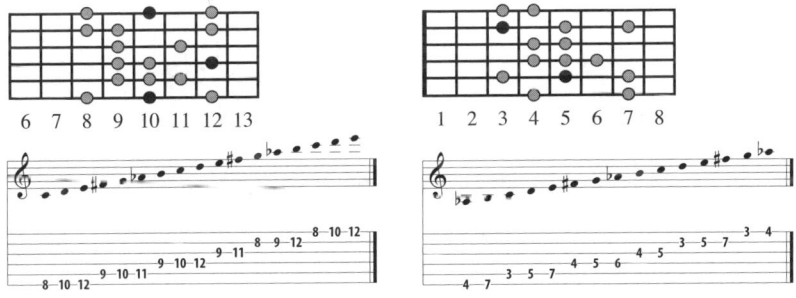

## Dominant b5 b9 #9 (1 b2 b3 b4 b5 6 b7 8)

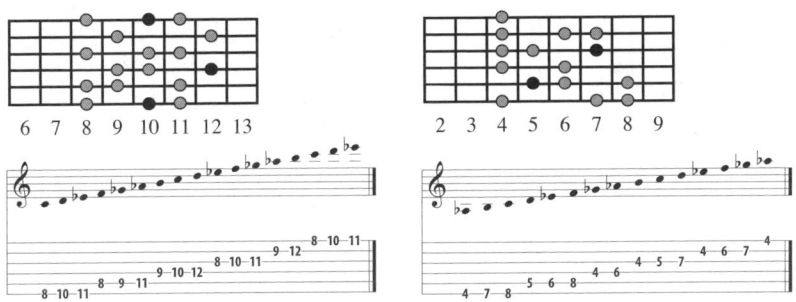

## Dominant ♭9 ♯9 (1 ♭2 ♭3 ♭4 5 6 ♭7 8)

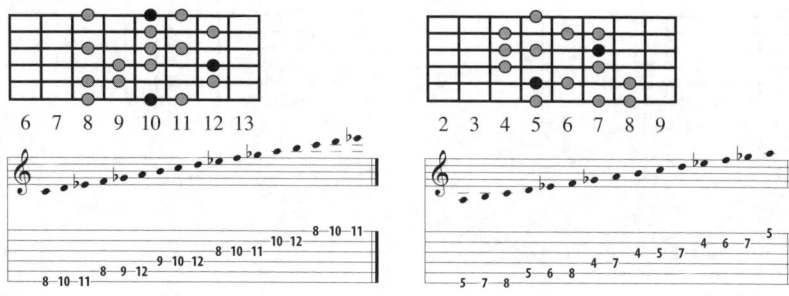

## Dominant ♭9 ♯9 ♭13 (1 ♭2 ♭3 ♭4 5 ♭6 ♭7 8)

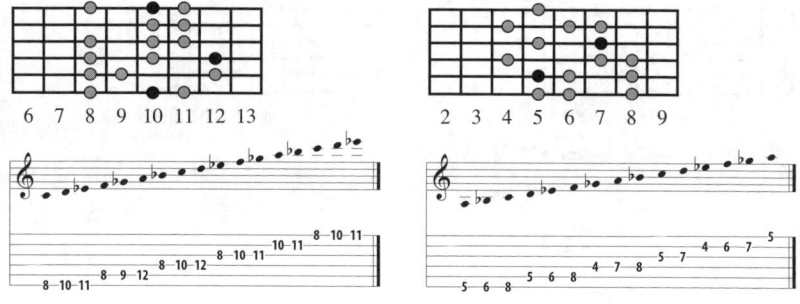

## Dominant ♯9 (1 ♯2 3 4 5 6 ♭7 8)

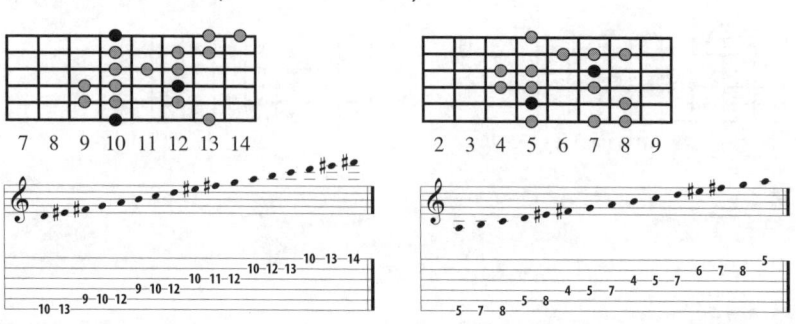

## Dominant ♭9 ♯11 (1 ♭2 3 ♯4 5 6 ♭7 8)

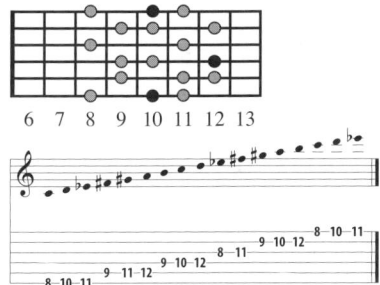
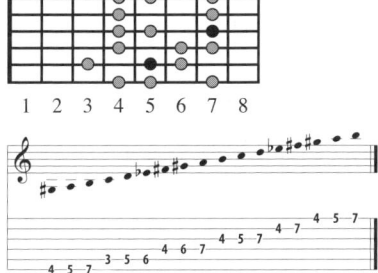

## Dominant ♭9 ♯11 ♭13 (1 ♭2 3 ♯4 5 ♭6 ♭7 8)

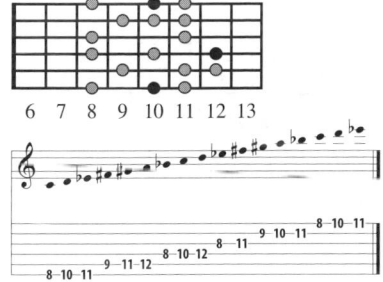
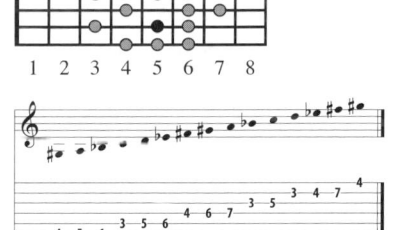

## Dominant 13 (1 2 3 5 6 ♭7 8)

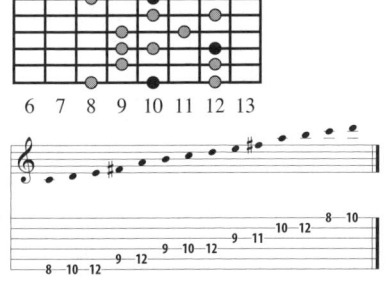
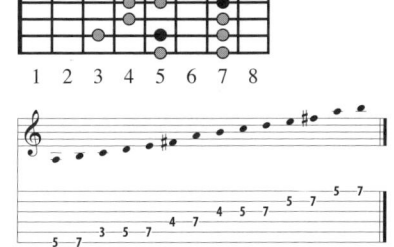

# Major and Dominant Scales

## Major/Ionian (1 2 3 4 5 6 7 8)

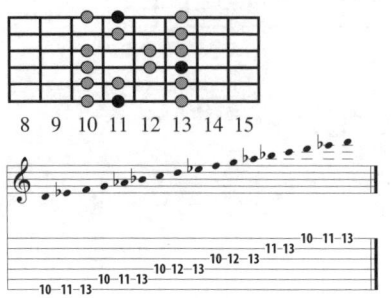
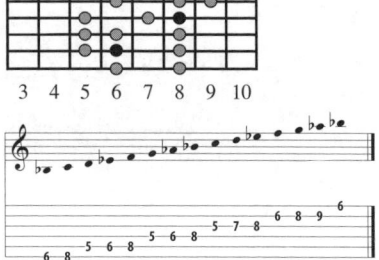

## Mixolydian (1 2 3 4 5 6 ♭7 8)
5th mode of the major scale

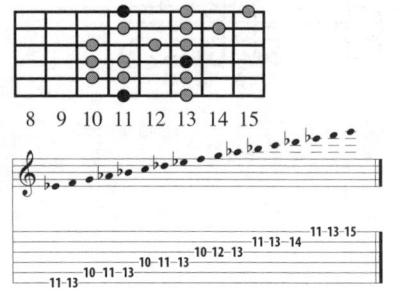
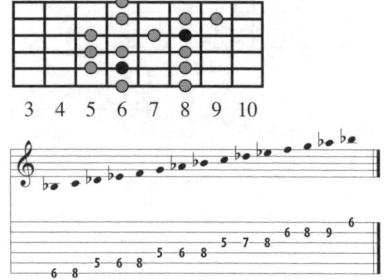

## Lydian (1 2 3 ♯4 5 6 7 8)
4th mode of the major scale

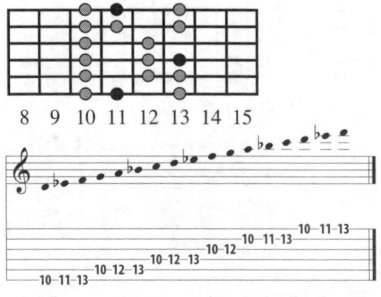
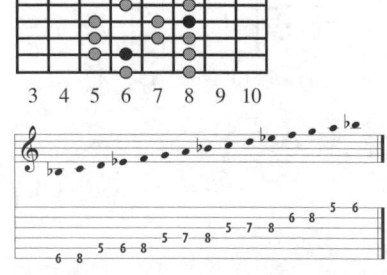

## Major Pentatonic (1 2 3 5 6 8)

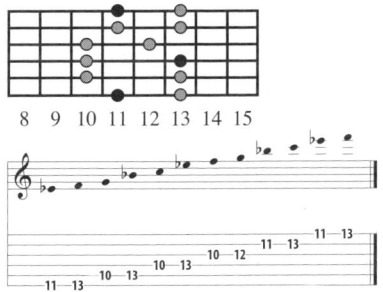
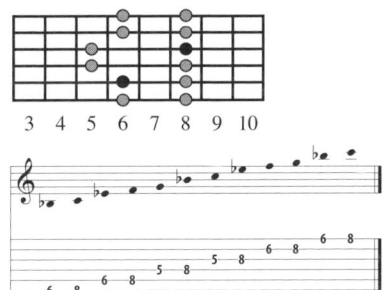

## Major 13 Pentatonic* (1 2 3 5 6 7 8)

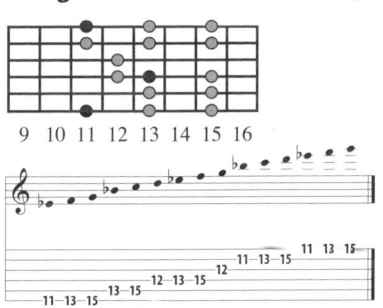
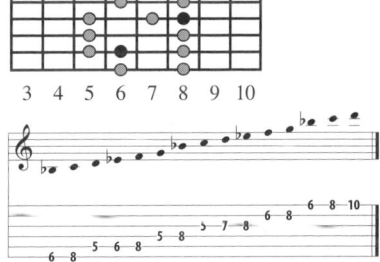

## Major Pentatonic Blues* (1 2 b3 3 5 6 8)

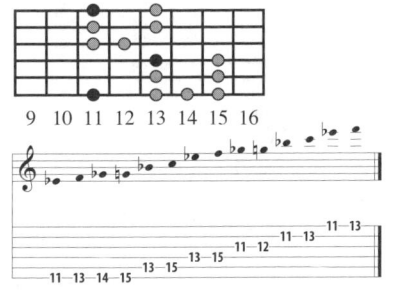
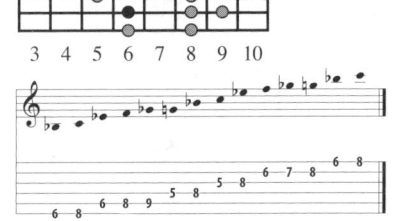

* While this scale has more than five notes, it is based on a five-note, pentatonic scale and it is best to think of it as a pentatonic scale.

# Lydian Pentatonic (1 3 #4 5 7 8)

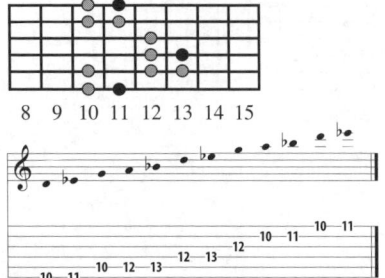
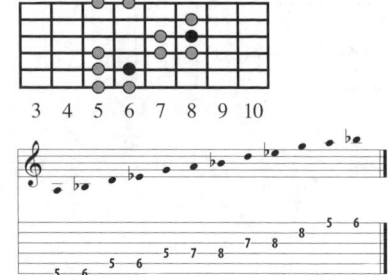

# Lydian ♭7 (1 2 3 #4 5 6 ♭7 8)
4th mode of the melodic minor scale

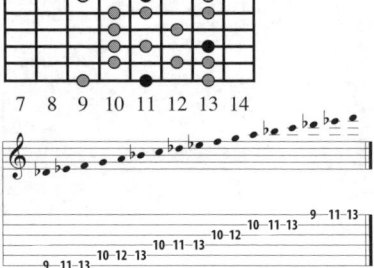
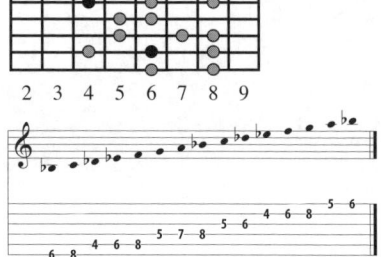

# Lydian #9 (1 #2 3 #4 5 6 7 8)
6th mode of the harmonic minor scale

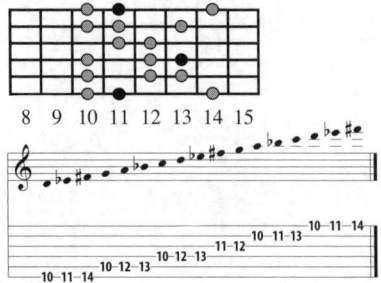
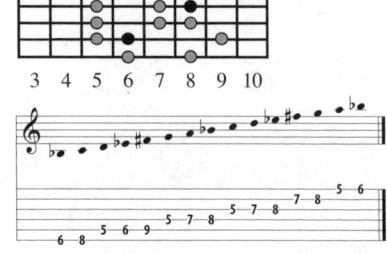

# Aeolian Major (1 2 3 4 5 ♭6 ♭7 8)
5th mode of the melodic minor scale

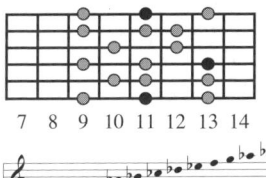
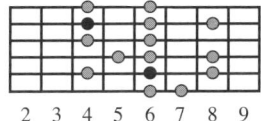
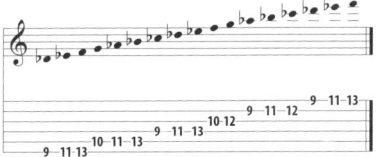

# Phrygian Major (1 ♭2 3 4 5 ♭6 ♭7 8)
5th mode of the harmonic minor scale

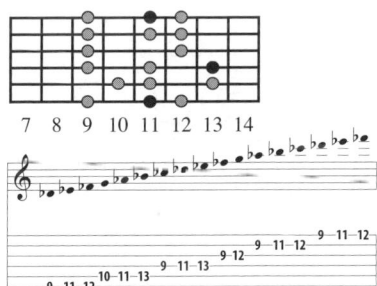
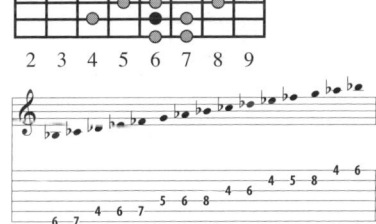

# Ionian Augmented (1 2 3 4 ♯5 6 7 8)
3rd mode of the harmonic minor scale

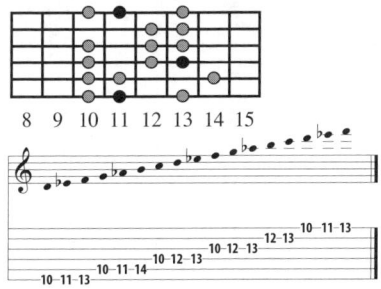
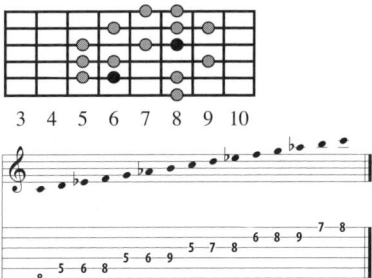

## Lydian Augmented (1 2 3 #4 #5 6 7 8)
3rd mode of the melodic minor scale

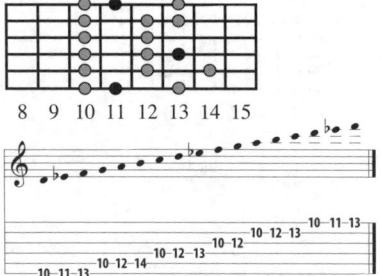
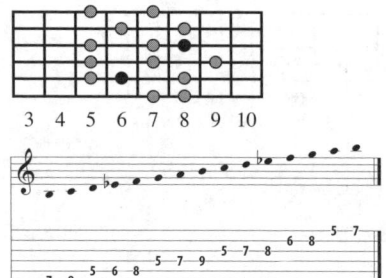

# Minor Scales

## Natural Minor/Aeolian (1 2 b3 4 5 b6 b7 8)
6th mode of the major scale

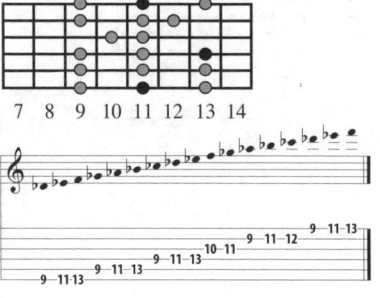
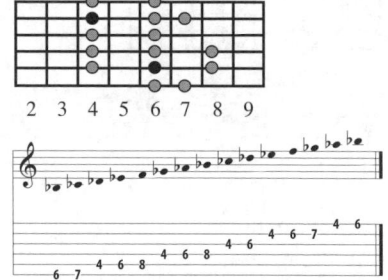

## Harmonic Minor (1 2 b3 4 5 b6 7 8)

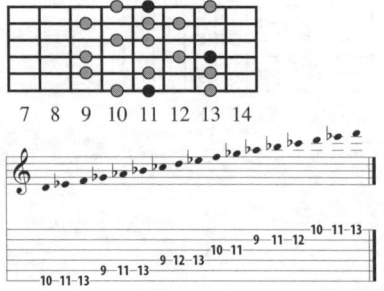
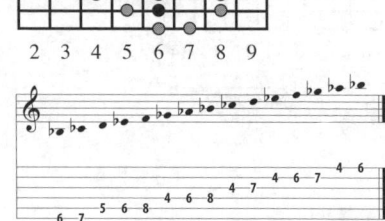

# Jazz Minor/Melodic Minor (1 2 b3 4 5 6 7 8)
Melodic Minor descends in Aeolian/Natural Minor

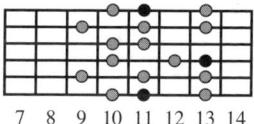
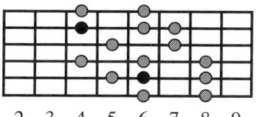
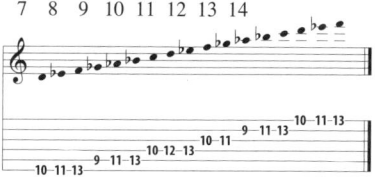

# Dorian (1 2 b3 4 5 6 b7 8)
2nd mode of the major scale

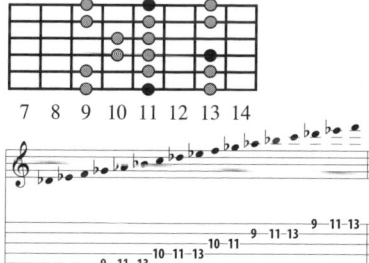
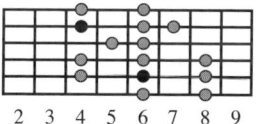

# Phrygian (1 b2 b3 4 5 b6 b7 8)
3rd mode of the major scale

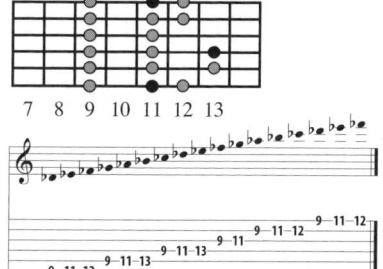
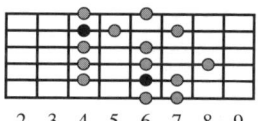

Eb

# Locrian (1 ♭2 ♭3 4 ♭5 ♭6 ♭7 8)
7th mode of the major scale

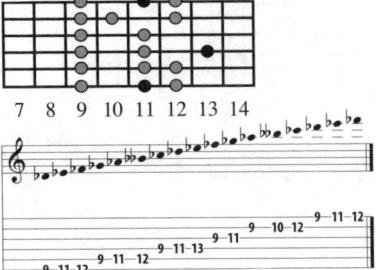
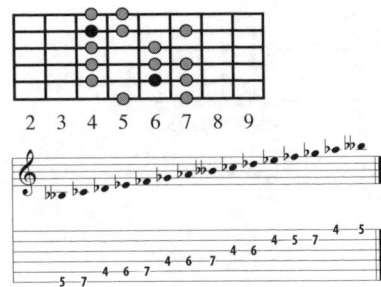

# Minor Pentatonic (1 ♭3 4 5 ♭7 8)

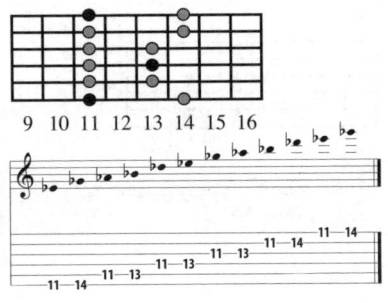
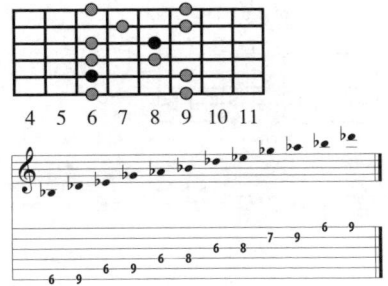

# Minor 13 Pentatonic* (1 ♭3 5 ♭6 ♭7 8)

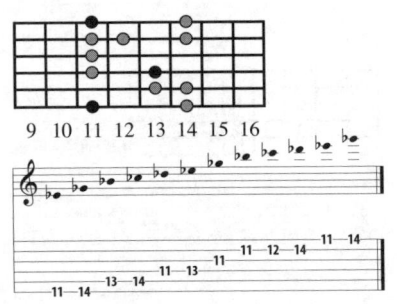
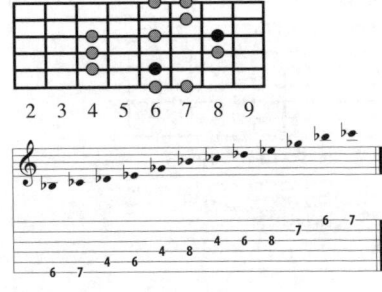

* While this scale has more than five notes, it is based on a five-note, pentatonic scale and it is best to think of it as a pentatonic scale.

## Minor Pentatonic Blues* (1 ♭3 4 ♭5 5 ♭7 8)

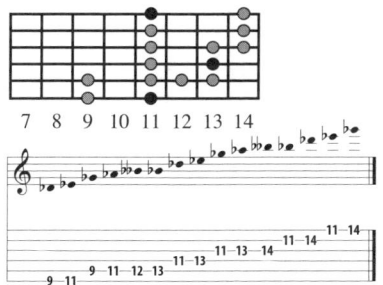
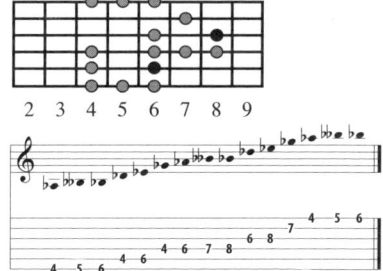

## Dorian Pentatonic (1 2 ♭3 5 ♭7 8)

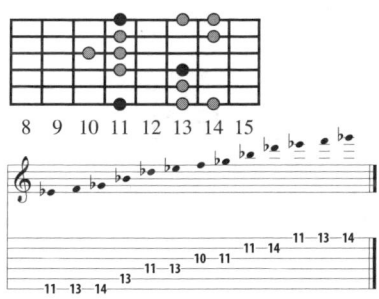

E♭

## Phrygian Pentatonic (1 ♭2 4 5 ♭7 8)

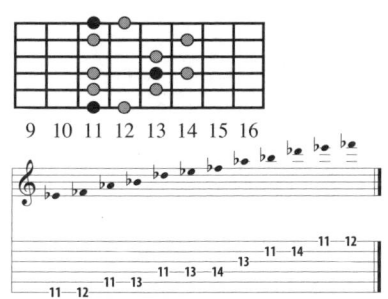
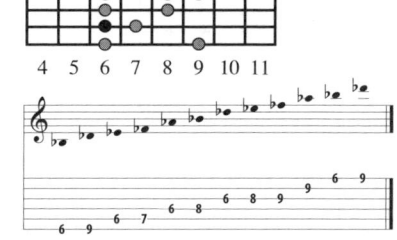

* While this scale has more than five notes, it is based on a five-note, pentatonic scale and it is best to think of it as a pentatonic scale.

## Phrygian ♮6 (1 ♭2 ♭3 4 5 6 ♭7 8)
2nd mode of the melodic minor scale

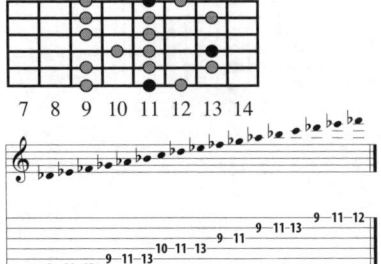
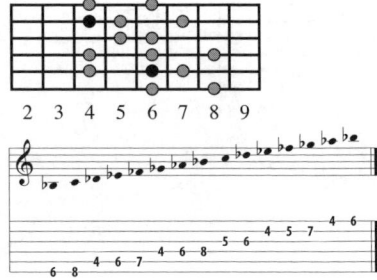

## Locrian ♮2 (1 2 ♭3 4 ♭5 ♭6 ♭7 8)
6th mode of the melodic minor scale

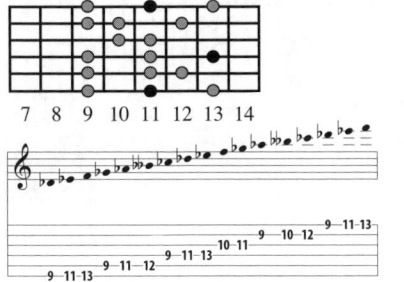
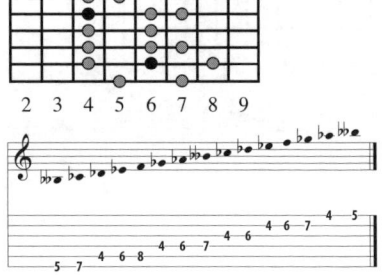

## Locrian ♮6 (1 ♭2 ♭3 4 ♭5 6 ♭7 8)
2nd mode of the harmonic minor scale

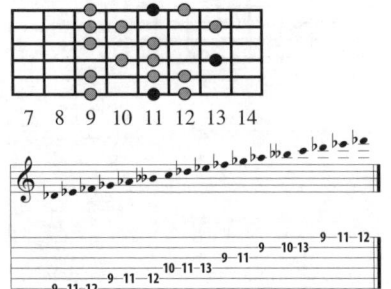

# Symmetrical Scales

## Chromatic (1 b2 2 b3 3 4 b5 5 b6 6 b7 7 8)

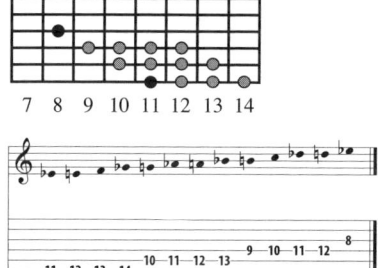
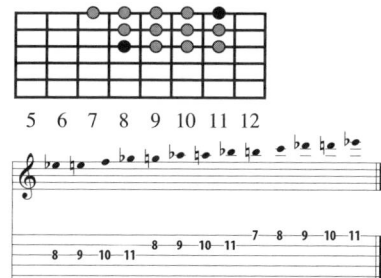

## Whole Tone (1 2 3 #4 #5 #6 8)

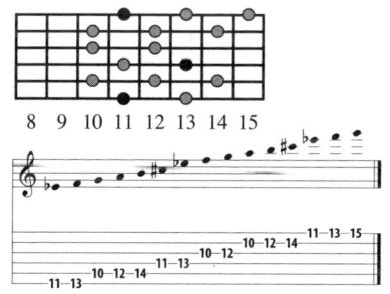
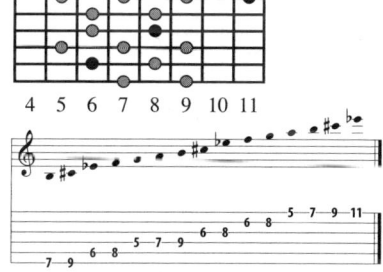

## Auxiliary, Whole/Half Diminished (1 2 b3 4 b5 b6 6 7 8)

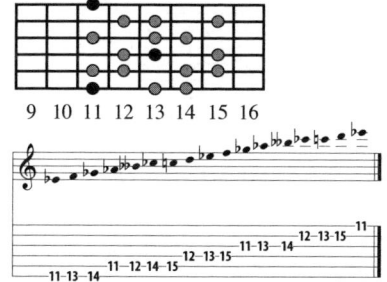

# Symmetrical, Half/Whole Diminished (1 ♭2 ♭3 ♭4 ♭5 5 6 ♭7 8)

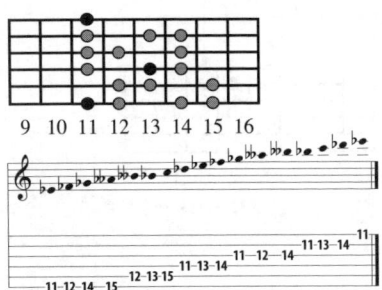
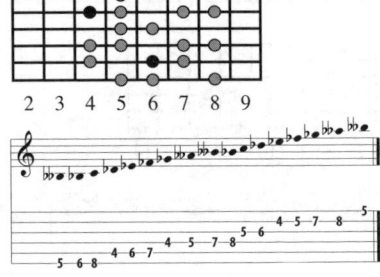

# Augmented (1 ♯2 3 5 ♯5 7 8)

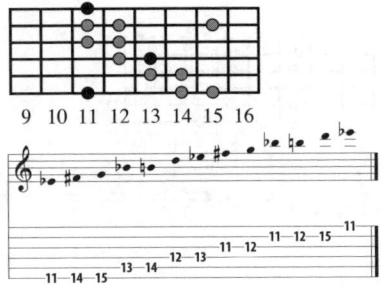
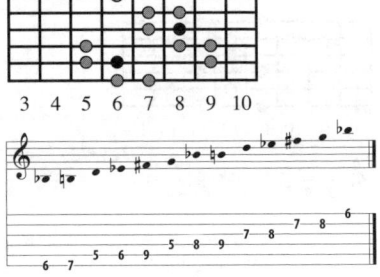

# Chromatic Augmented (1 ♭2 2 3 4 ♯4 ♯5 6 ♭7 8)

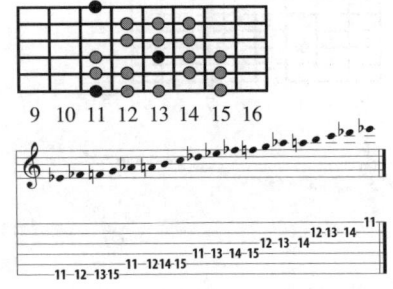

# Augmented ♭9 (1 ♭2 ♭3 3 4 5 ♭6 6 7 8)

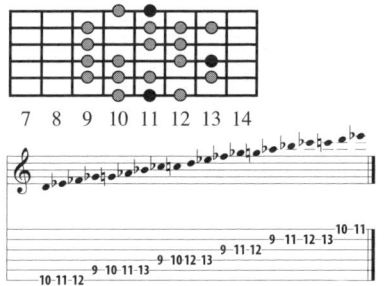
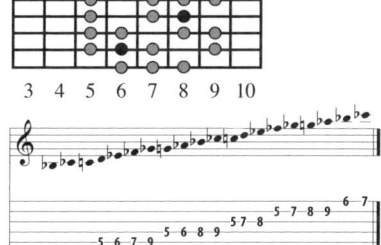

# Augmented 9 (1 2 ♭3 3 ♯4 5 ♭6 ♭7 7 8)

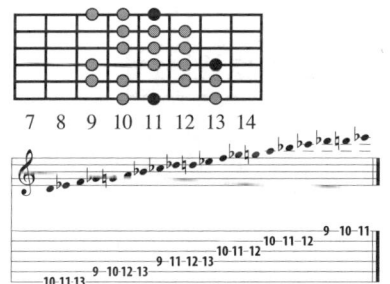
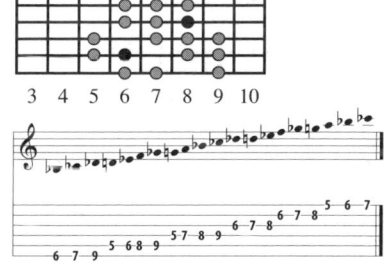

# Diminished Blues (1 ♭2 ♭3 3 ♯5 6 ♭7 8)

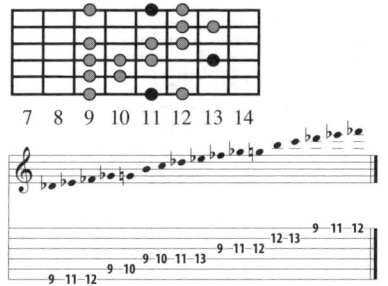
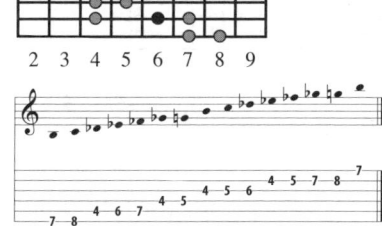

# Four Semitone Tritone (1 b2 2 b3 3 #4 5 b6 6 b7 8)

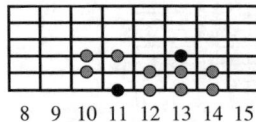
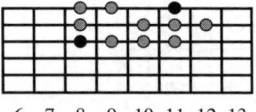

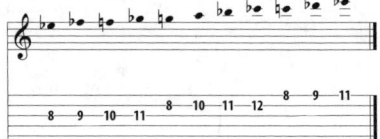

# Tetratonic (1 4 b5 7 8)

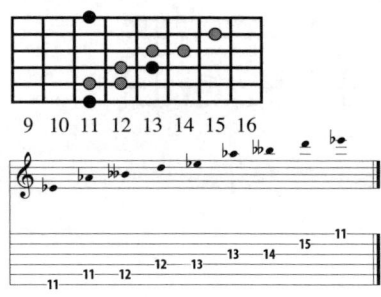
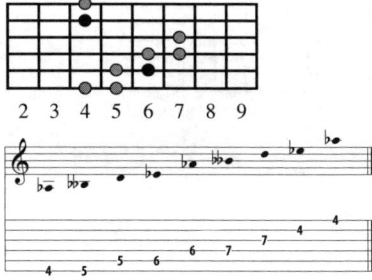

# Three Semitone Tritone (1 b2 2 b3 b5 5 b6 6 8)

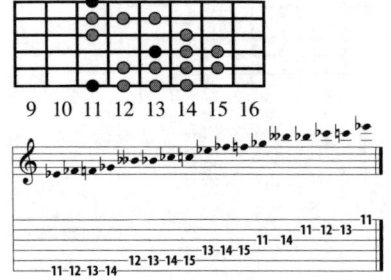

# Tritone (1 ♭2 3 ♯4 5 ♭7 8)

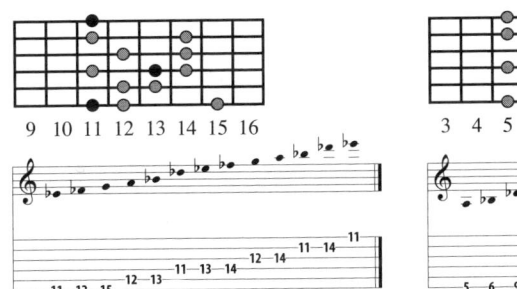
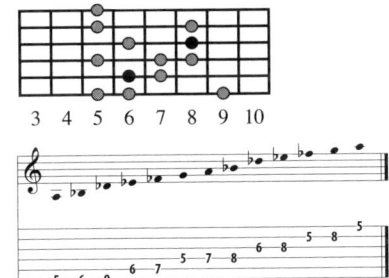

# Two-Semitone Tritone (1 ♭2 2 ♯4 5 ♭6 8)

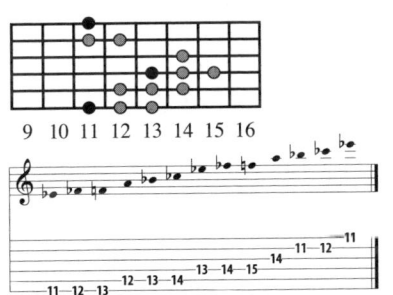
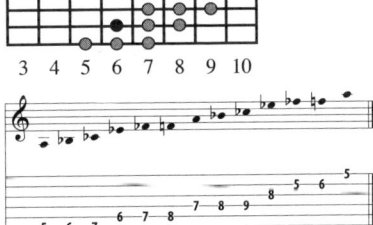

# Hybrid Scales

## Aeolian ♯11 (1 2 ♭3 ♯4 5 ♭6 ♭7 8)

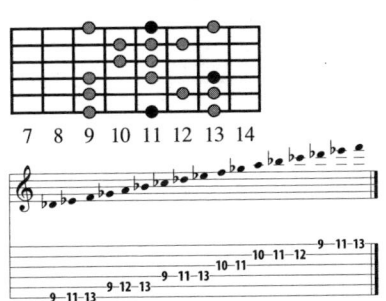
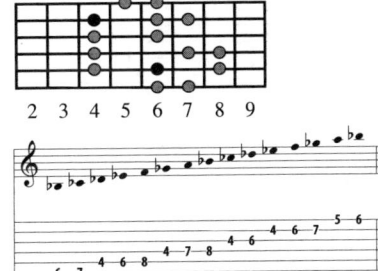

## Augmented Dominant (1 2 3 4 #5 6 b7 8)

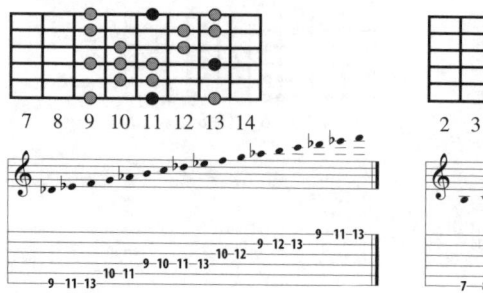
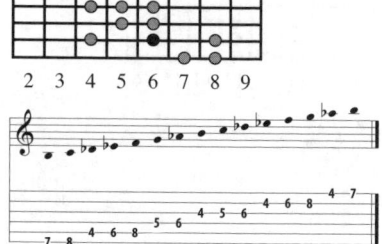

## Augmented Dominant b9 (1 b2 3 4 #5 6 b7 8)

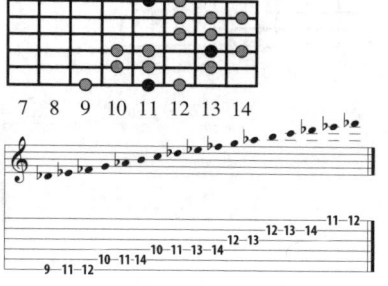

## Augmented Dominant #9 (1 #2 3 4 #5 6 b7 8)

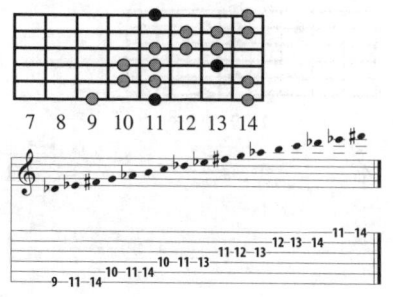
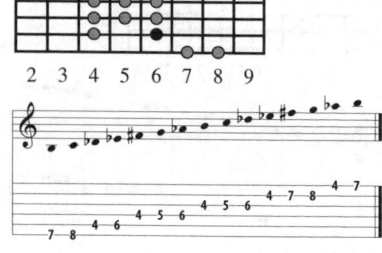

## Augmented ♯9 (1 ♯2 3 4 ♯5 6 7 8)

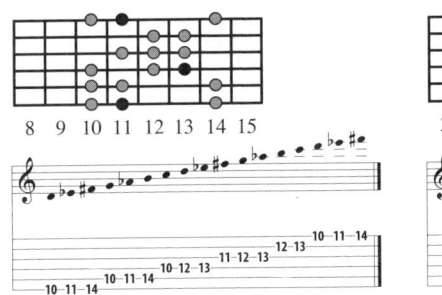
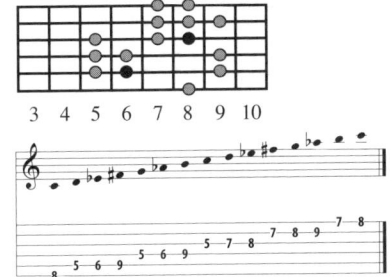

## Augmented Minor/Major 7 (1 2 ♭3 4 ♯5 6 7 8)

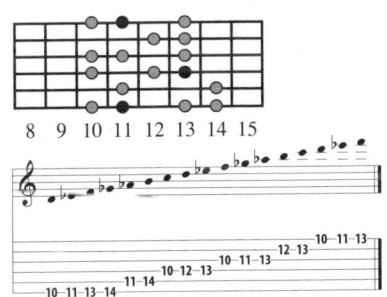
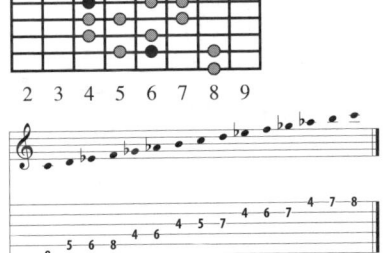

## Bebop Dominant (1 2 3 4 5 6 ♭7 7 8)

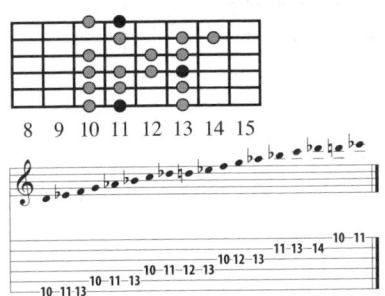
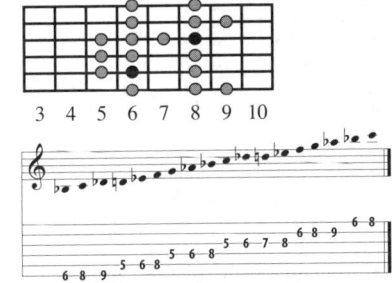

## Bebop Dorian (1 2 ♭3 3 4 5 6 ♭7 8)

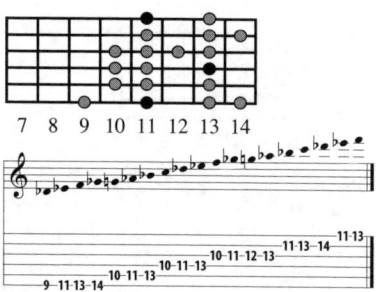
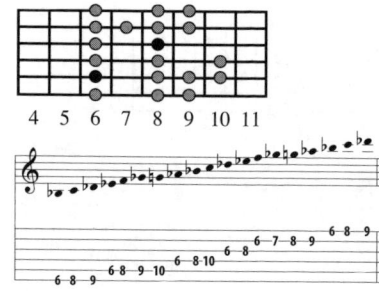

## Bebop Major* (1 2 3 4 ♯4 5 6 7 8)

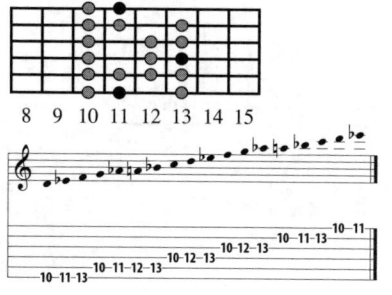
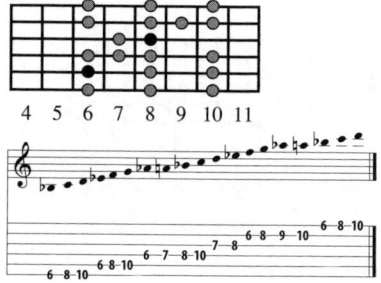

## Bebop Melodic Minor* (1 2 ♭3 4 ♯4 5 6 7 8)

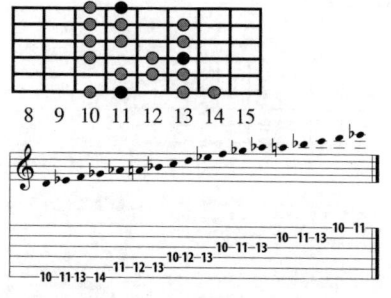
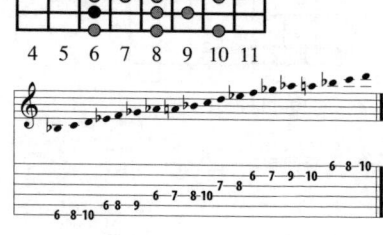

* Many musicians spell this scale with a ♯5 instead of a ♯4.

# Diminished Tritonic (1 ♭3 4 ♭5 8)

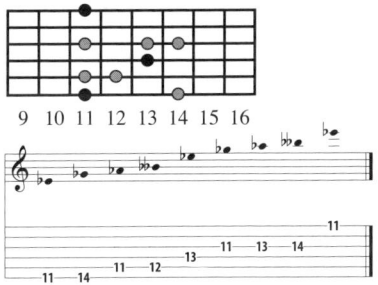
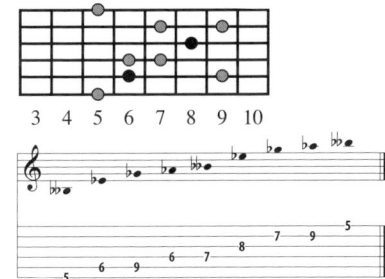

# Dominant ♭5 (1 2 3 4 ♭5 6 ♭7 8)

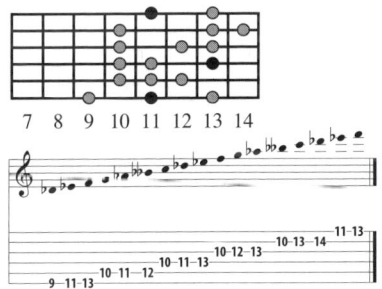
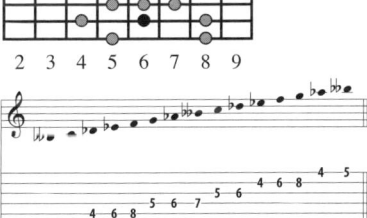

# Dominant ♭5 ♭9 ♯9 (1 ♭2 ♭3 ♭4 ♭5 6 ♭7 8)

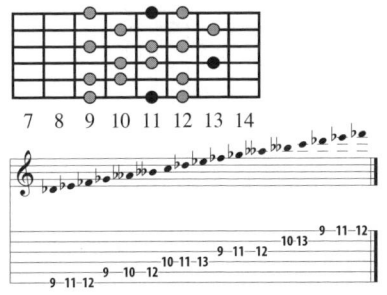
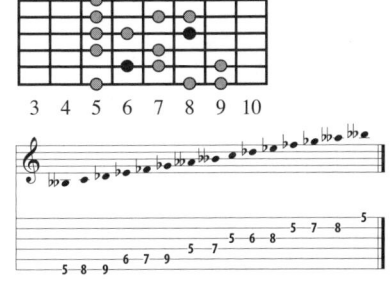

## Dominant ♭9 ♯9 (1 ♭2 ♯3 ♭4 5 6 ♭7 8)

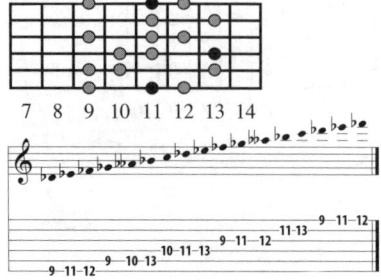
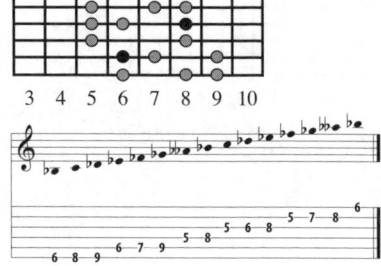

## Dominant ♭9 ♯9 ♭13 (1 ♭2 ♯3 ♭4 5 ♭6 ♭7 8)

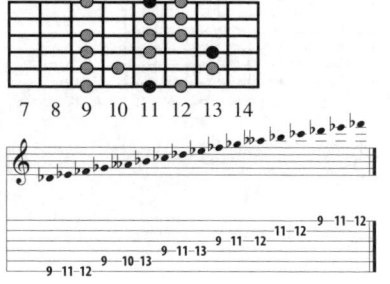
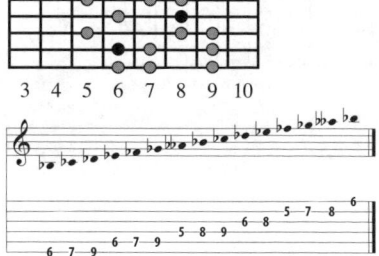

## Dominant ♯9 (1 ♯2 3 4 5 6 ♭7 8)

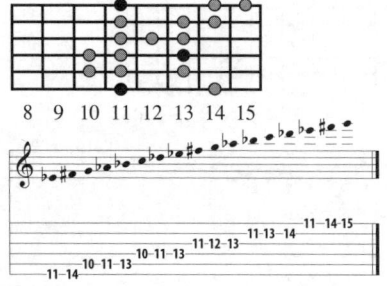

## Dominant ♭9 #11 (1 ♭2 3 #4 5 6 ♭7 8)

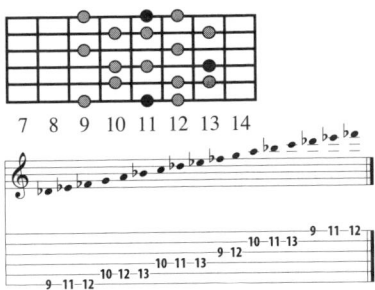
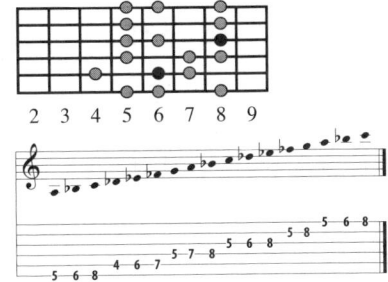

## Dominant ♭9 #11 ♭13 (1 ♭2 3 #4 5 ♭6 ♭7 8)

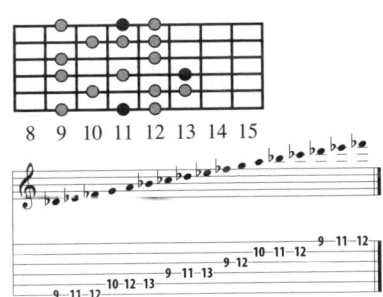
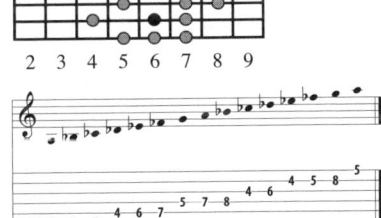

## Dominant 13 (1 2 3 5 6 ♭7 8)

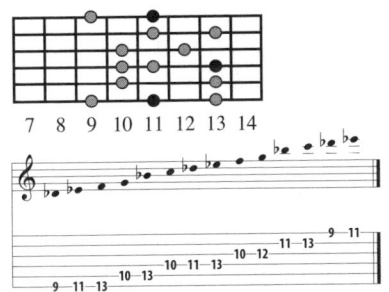
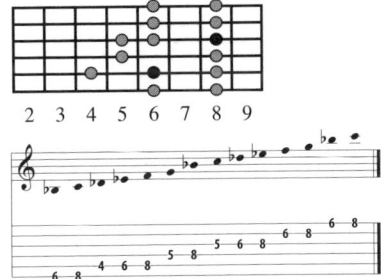

# Major and Dominant Scales

## Major/Ionian (1 2 3 4 5 6 7 8)

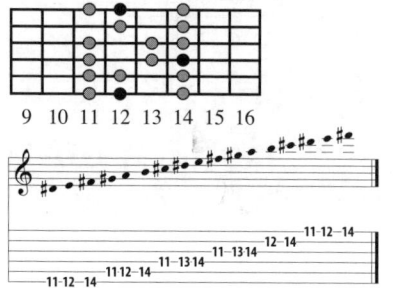
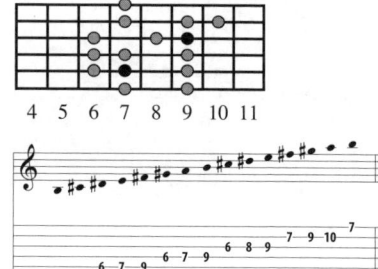

## Mixolydian (1 2 3 4 5 6 ♭7 8)
5th mode of the major scale

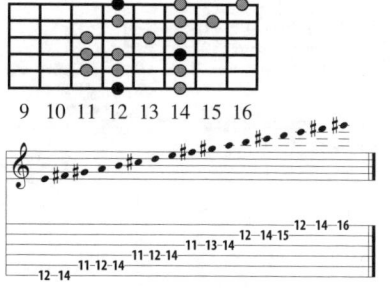

## Lydian (1 2 3 ♯4 5 6 7 8)
4th mode of the major scale

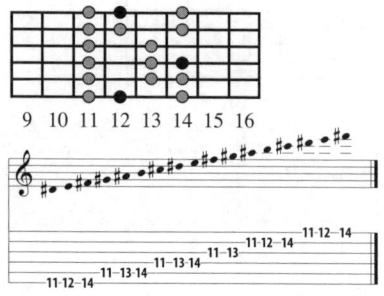
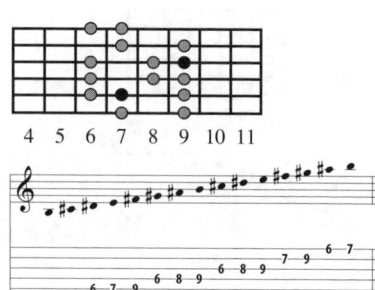

## Major Pentatonic (1 2 3 5 6 8)

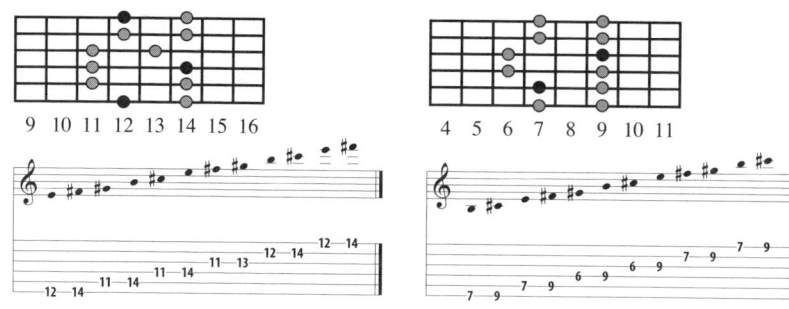

## Major 13 Pentatonic* (1 2 3 5 6 7 8)

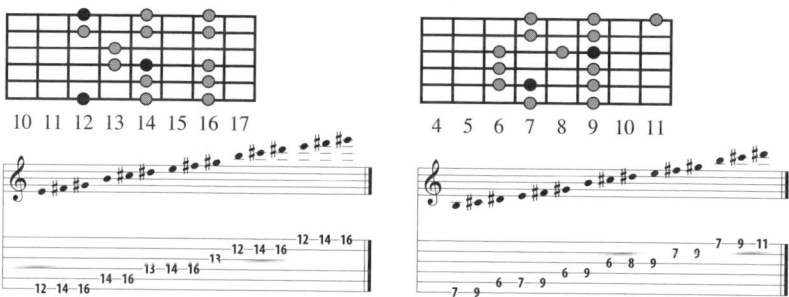

## Major Pentatonic Blues* (1 2 ♭3 3 5 6 8)

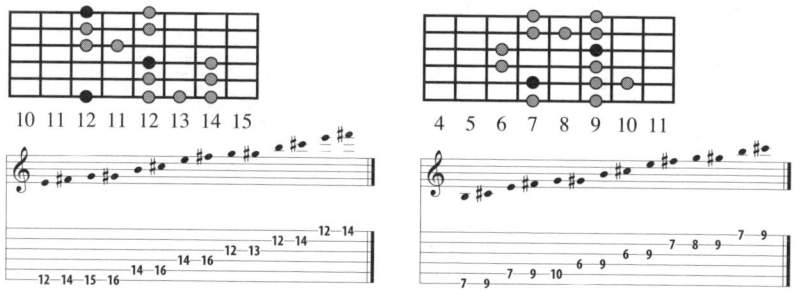

\* While this scale has more than five notes, it is based on a five-note, pentatonic scale and it is best to think of it as a pentatonic scale.

## Lydian Pentatonic (1 3 #4 5 7 8)

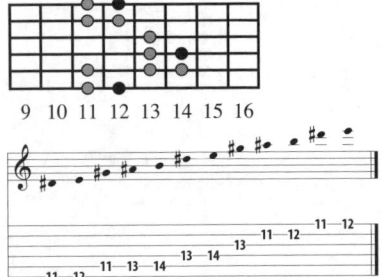
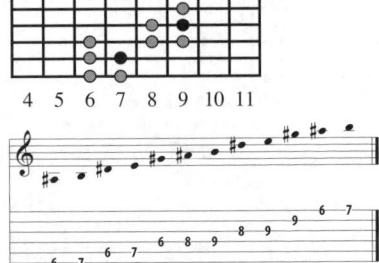

## Lydian ♭7 (1 2 3 #4 5 6 ♭7 8)
4th mode of the melodic minor scale

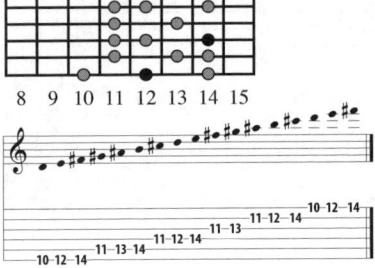
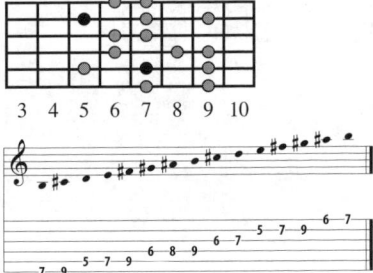

## Lydian #9 (1 #2 3 #4 5 6 7 8)
6th mode of the harmonic minor scale

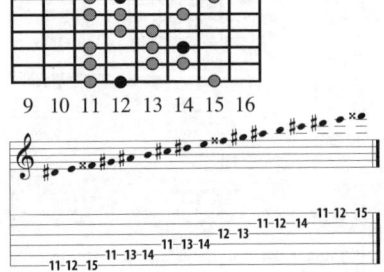
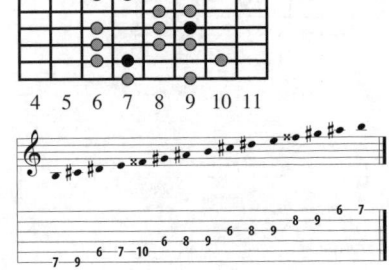

## Aeolian Major (1 2 3 4 5 ♭6 ♭7 8)
5th mode of the melodic minor scale

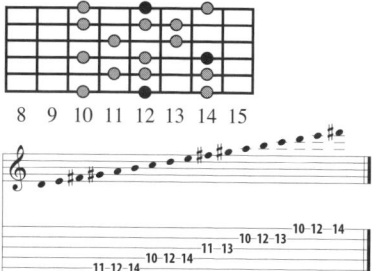
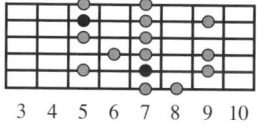

## Phrygian Major (1 ♭2 3 4 5 ♭6 ♭7 8)
5th mode of the harmonic minor scale

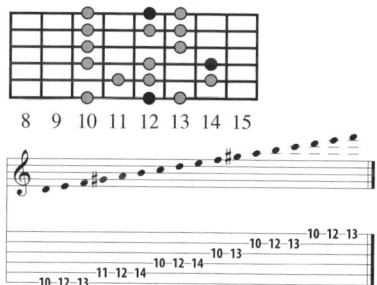
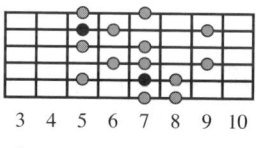

## Ionian Augmented (1 2 3 4 ♯5 6 7 8)
3rd mode of the harmonic minor scale

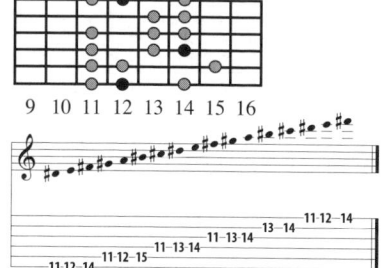
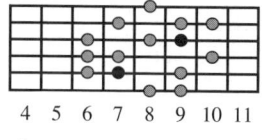

## Lydian Augmented (1 2 3 #4 #5 6 7 8)
3rd mode of the melodic minor scale

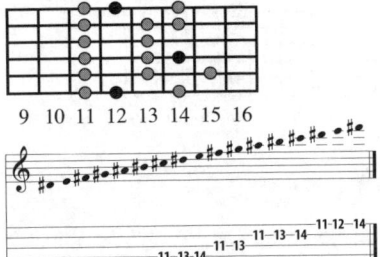
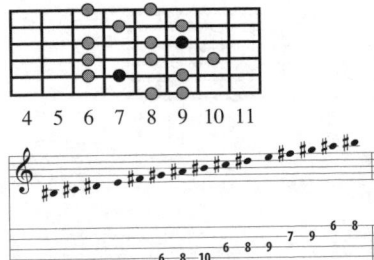

# Minor Scales

## Natural Minor/ Aeolian (1 2 b3 4 5 b6 b7 8)
6th mode of the major scale

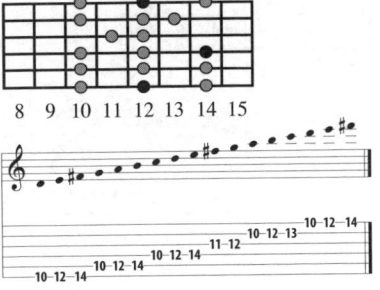
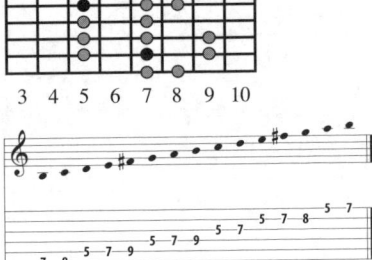

## Harmonic Minor (1 2 b3 4 5 b6 7 8)

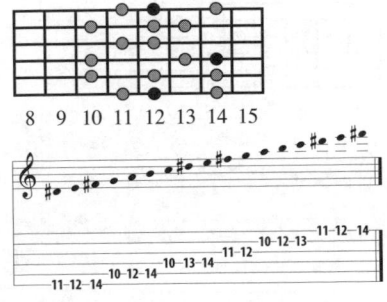

## Jazz Minor/Melodic Minor (1 2 ♭3 4 5 6 7 8)
Melodic Minor descends in Aeolian/Natural Minor

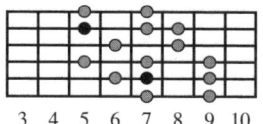
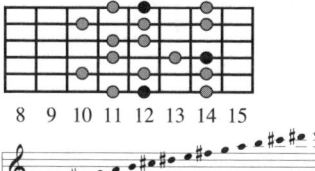

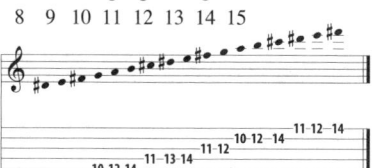

## Dorian (1 2 ♭3 4 5 6 ♭7 8)
2nd mode of the major scale

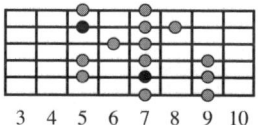
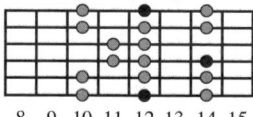
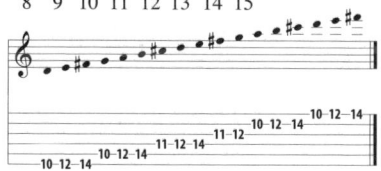

## Phrygian (1 ♭2 ♭3 4 5 ♭6 ♭7 8)
3rd mode of the major scale

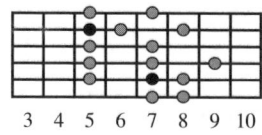
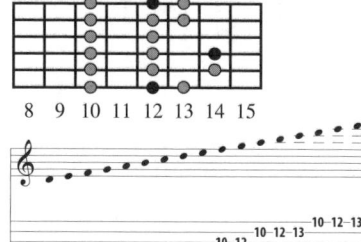
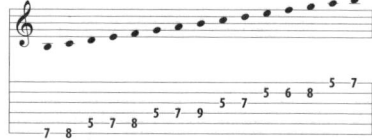

## Locrian (1 ♭2 ♭3 4 ♭5 ♭6 ♭7 8)
7th mode of the major scale

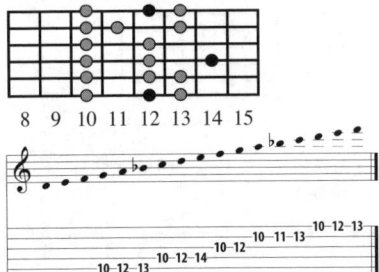
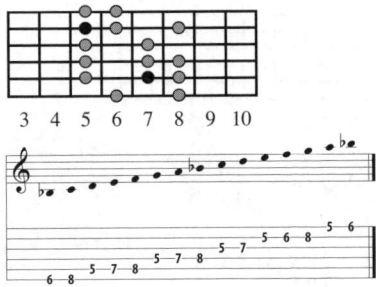

## Minor Pentatonic (1 ♭3 4 5 ♭7 8)

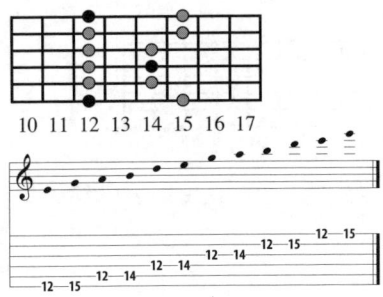
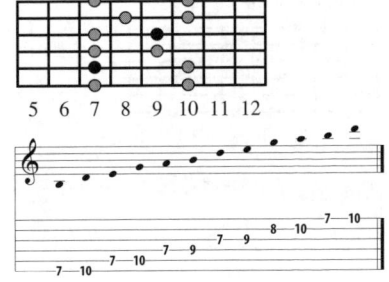

## Minor 13 Pentatonic* (1 ♭3 5 ♭6 ♭7 8)

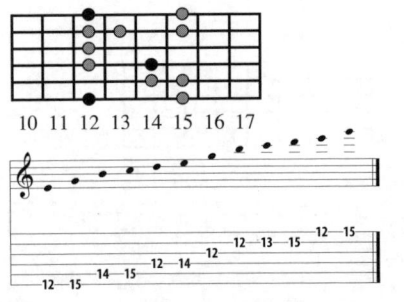
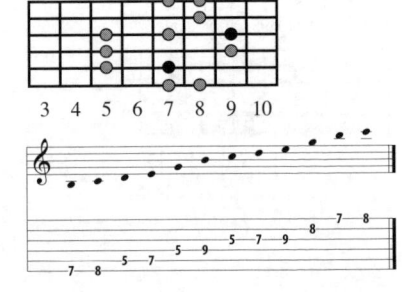

\* While this scale has more than five notes, it is based on a five-note, pentatonic scale and it is best to think of it as a pentatonic scale.

## Minor Pentatonic Blues* (1 ♭3 4 ♭5 5 ♭7 8)

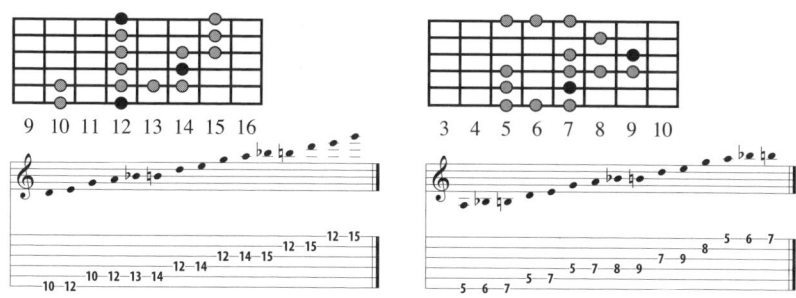

## Dorian Pentatonic (1 2 ♭3 5 ♭7 8)

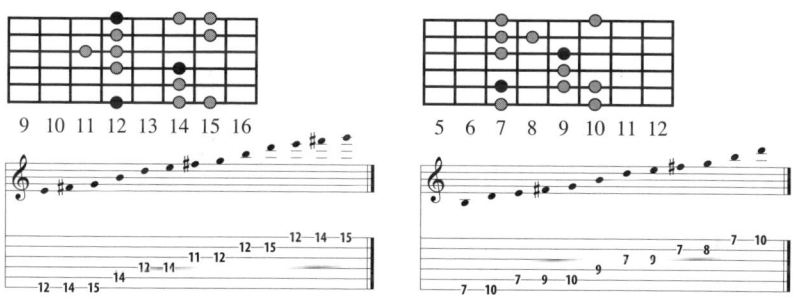

## Phrygian Pentatonic (1 ♭2 4 5 ♭7 8)

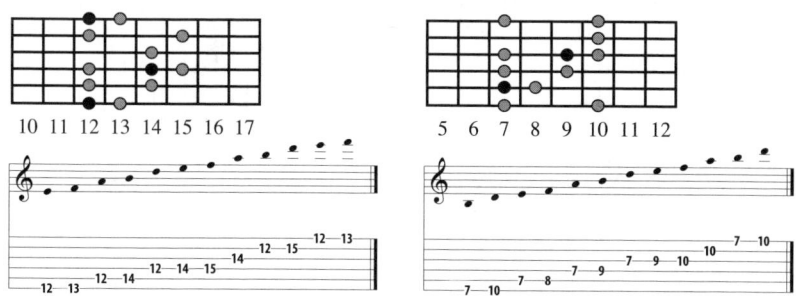

* While this scale has more than five notes, it is based on a five-note, pentatonic scale and it is best to think of it as a pentatonic scale.

# Phrygian ♮6 (1 ♭2 ♭3 4 5 6 ♭7 8)
2nd mode of the melodic minor scale

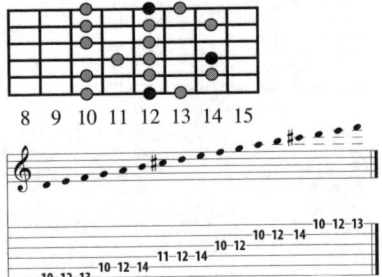
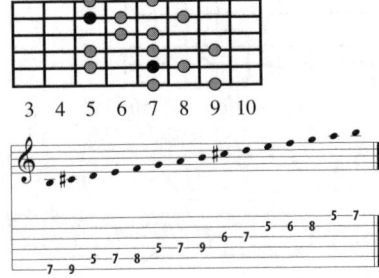

# Locrian ♮2 (1 2 ♭3 4 ♭5 ♭6 ♭7 8)
6th mode of the melodic minor scale

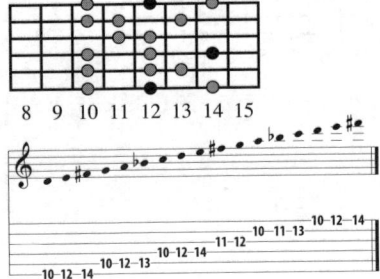
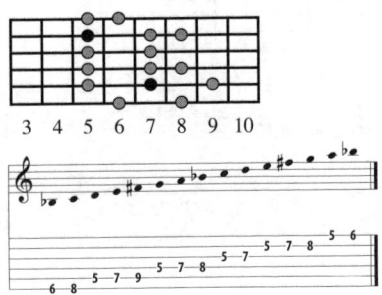

# Locrian ♮6 (1 ♭2 ♭3 4 ♭5 6 ♭7 8)
2nd mode of the harmonic minor scale

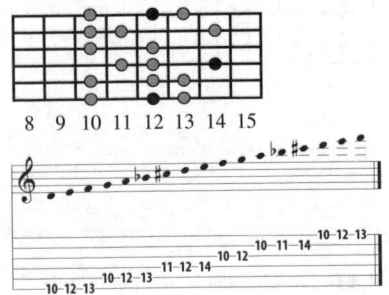
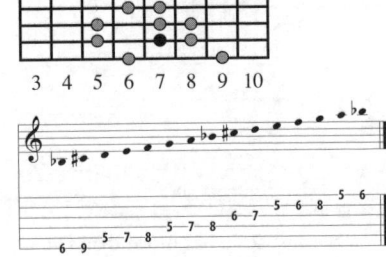

# Symmetrical Scales

## Chromatic (1 ♭2 2 ♭3 3 4 ♭5 5 ♭6 6 ♭7 7 8)

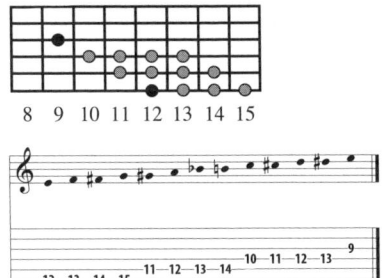
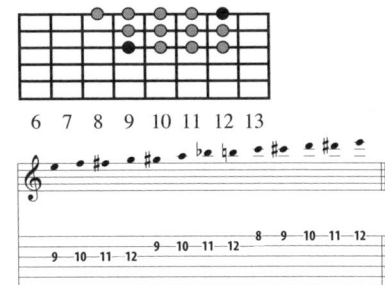

## Whole Tone (1 2 3 ♯4 ♯5 ♯6 8)

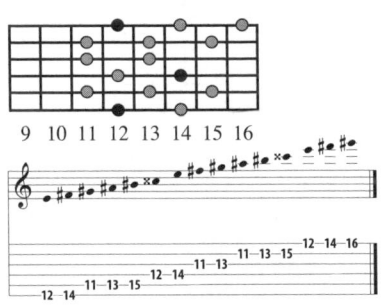
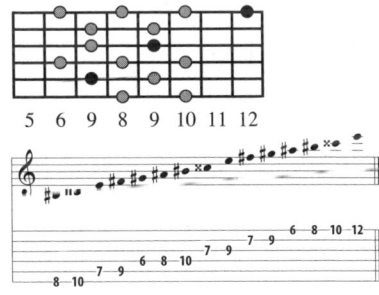

## Auxiliary, Whole/Half Diminished (1 2 ♭3 4 ♭5 ♭6 6 7 8)

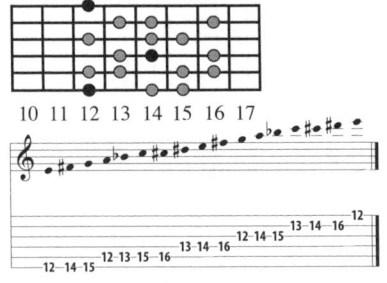
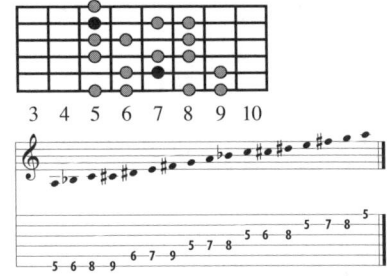

## Symmetrical, Half/Whole Diminished (1 ♭2 ♭3 ♭4 ♭5 5 6 ♭7 8)

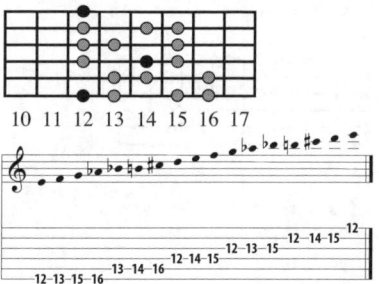
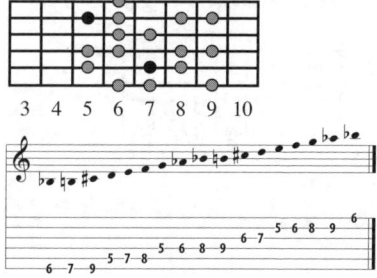

## Augmented (1 #2 3 5 #5 7 8)

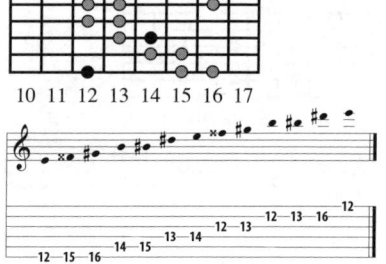
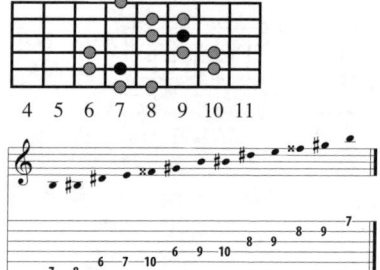

## Chromatic Augmented (1 ♭2 2 3 4 #4 #5 6 ♭7 8)

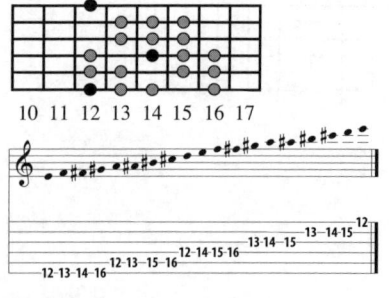
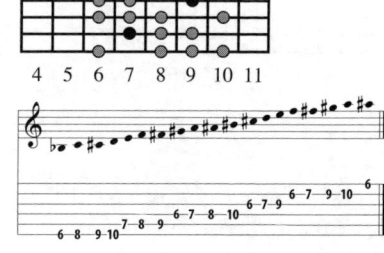

## Augmented ♭9 (1 ♭2 ♭3 3 4 5 ♭6 6 7 8)

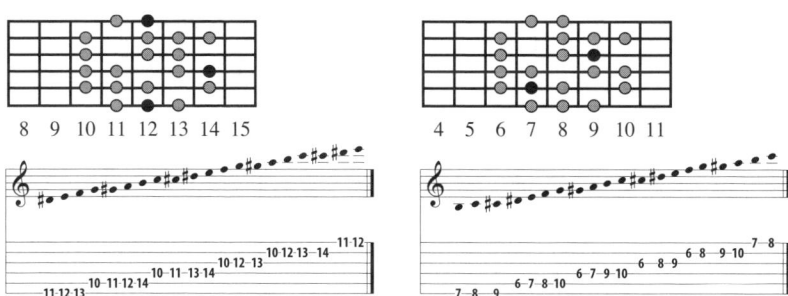

## Augmented 9 (1 2 ♭3 3 ♯4 5 ♭6 ♭7 7 8)

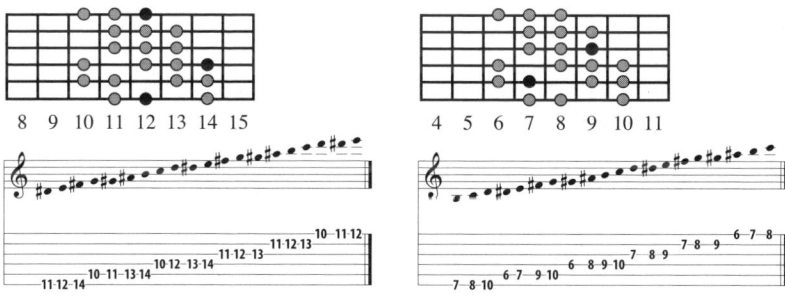

## Diminished Blues (1 ♭2 ♭3 3 ♯5 6 ♭7 8)

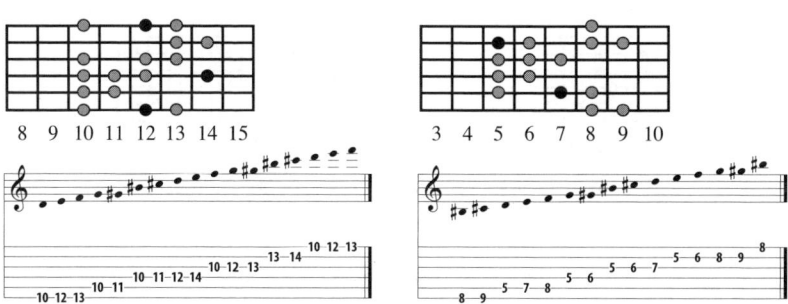

# Four Semitone Tritone (1 b2 2 b3 3 #4 5 b6 6 b7 8)

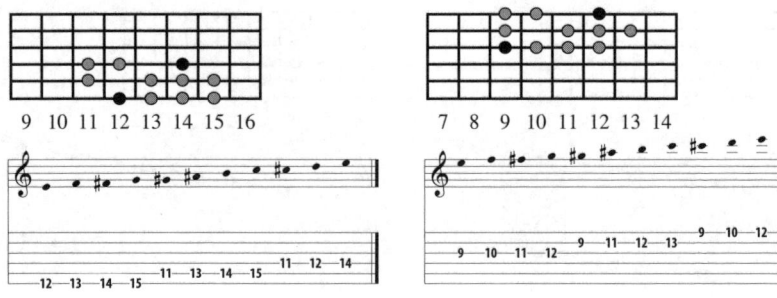

# Tetratonic (1 4 b5 7 8)

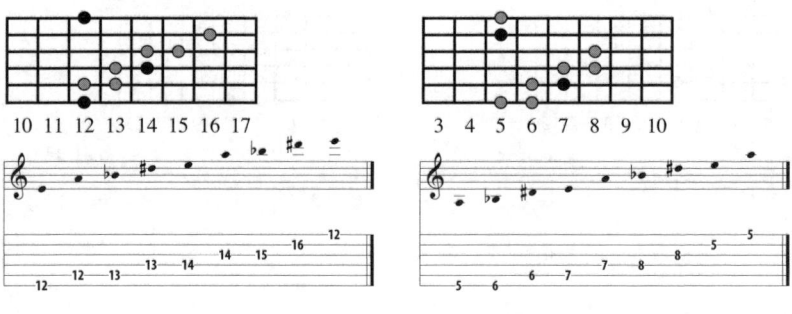

# Three Semitone Tritone (1 b2 2 b3 b5 5 b6 6 8)

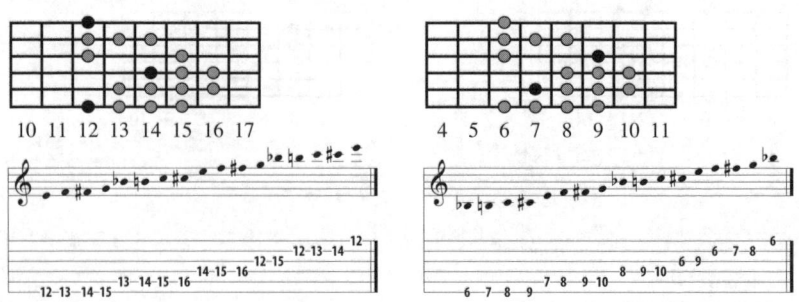

## Tritone (1 ♭2 3 ♯4 5 ♭7 8)

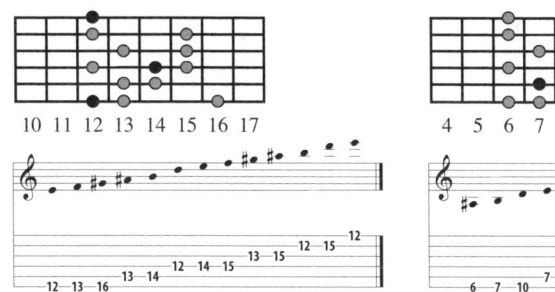
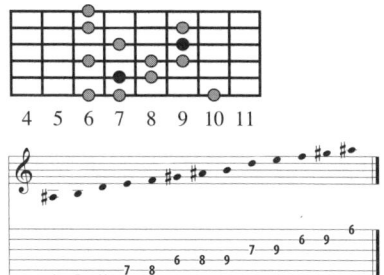

## Two-Semitone Tritone (1 ♭2 2 ♯4 5 ♭6 8)

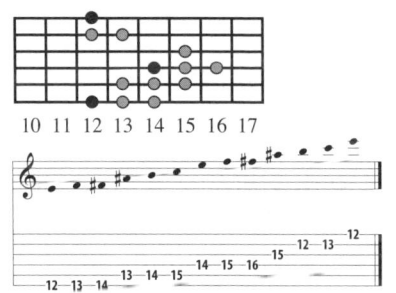
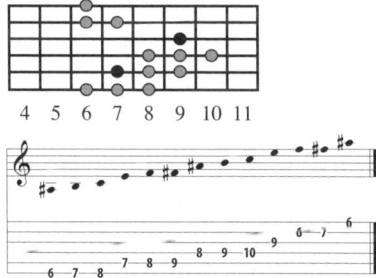

# Hybrid Scales

## Aeolian ♯11 (1 2 ♭3 ♯4 5 ♭6 ♭7 8)

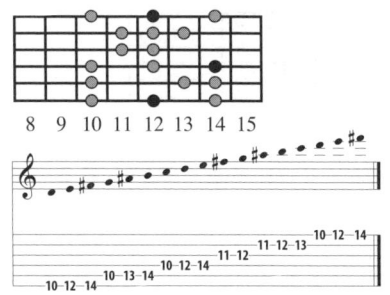
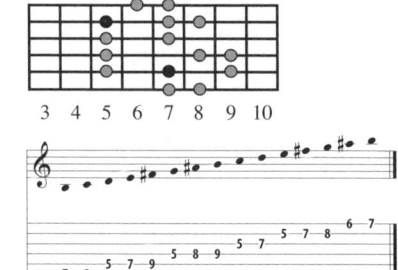

## Augmented Dominant (1 2 3 4 ♯5 6 ♭7 8)

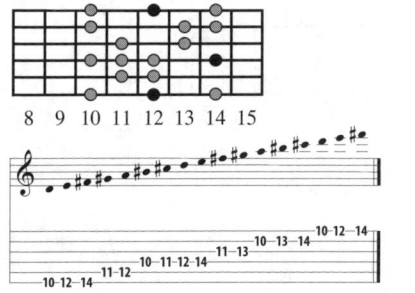
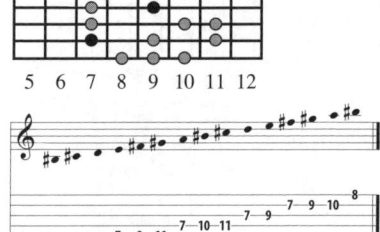

## Augmented Dominant ♭9 (1 ♭2 3 4 ♯5 6 ♭7 8)

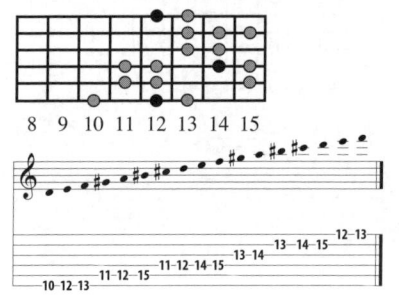
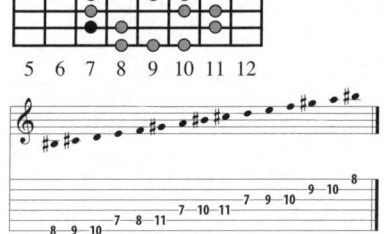

## Augmented Dominant ♯9 (1 ♯2 3 4 ♯5 6 ♭7 8)

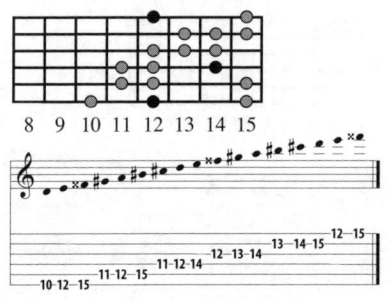
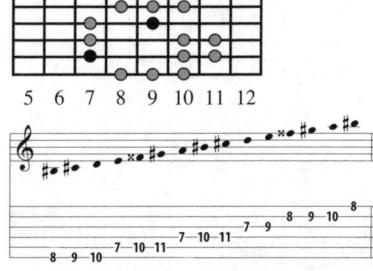

## Augmented #9 (1 #2 3 4 #5 6 7 8)

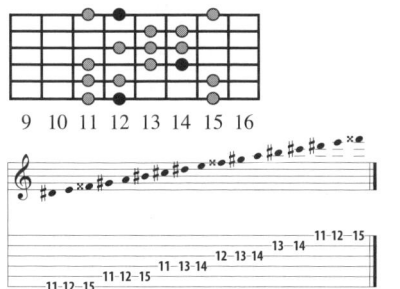
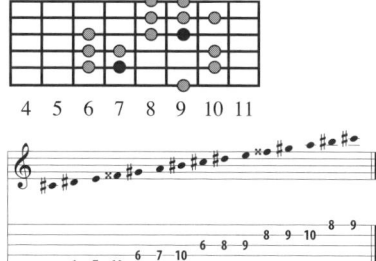

## Augmented Minor/Major 7 (1 2 ♭3 4 #5 6 7 8)

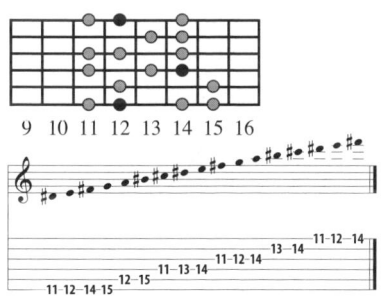
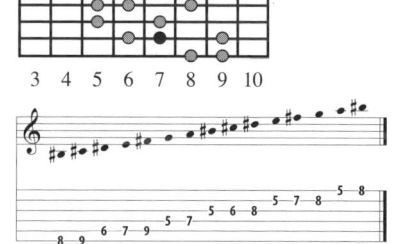

## Bebop Dominant (1 2 3 4 5 6 ♭7 7 8)

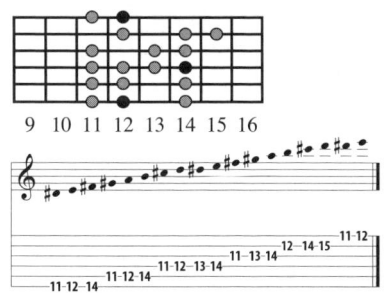
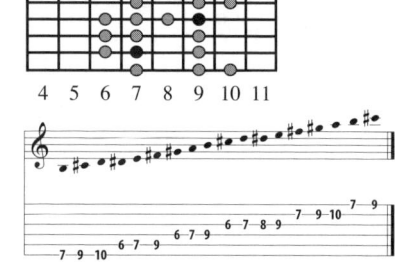

## Bebop Dorian (1 2 ♭3 3 4 5 6 ♭7 8)

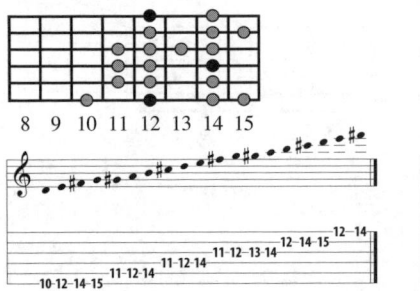
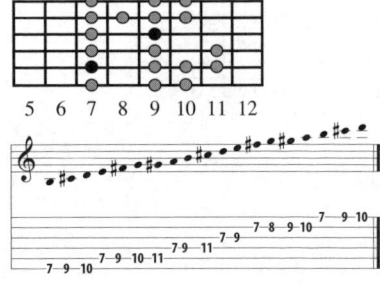

## Bebop Major* (1 2 3 4 ♯4 5 6 7 8)

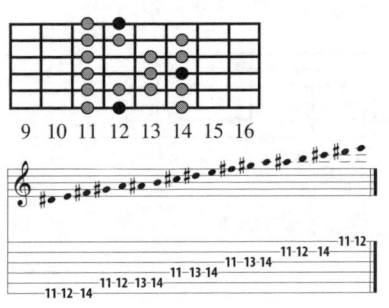
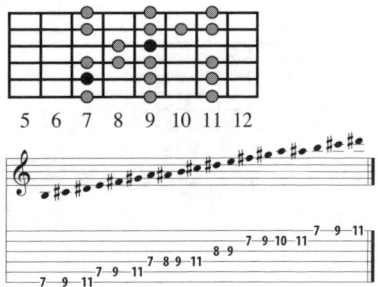

## Bebop Melodic Minor* (1 2 ♭3 4 ♯4 5 6 7 8)

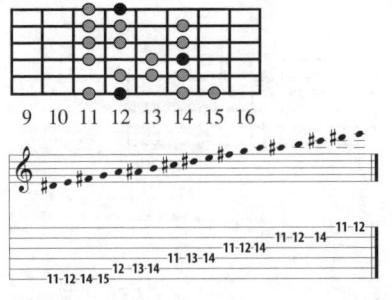
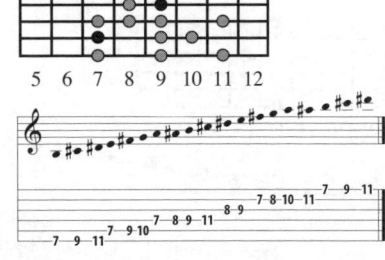

* Many musicians spell this scale with a ♯5 instead of a ♯4.

## Diminished Tritonic (1 ♭3 4 ♭5 8)

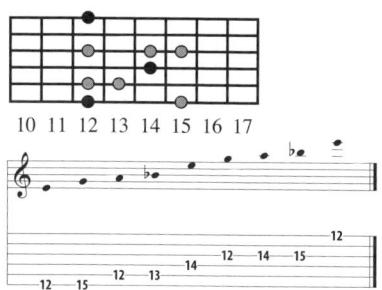
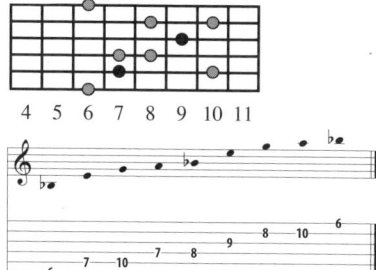

## Dominant ♭5 (1 2 3 4 ♭5 6 ♭7 8)

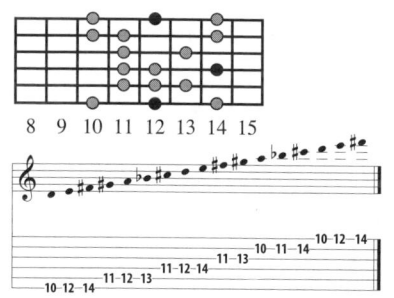
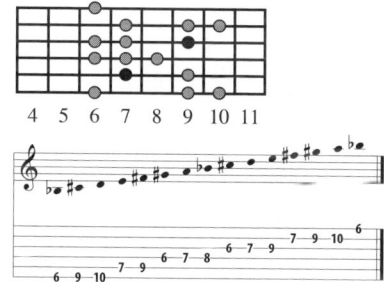

## Dominant ♭5 ♭9 #9 (1 ♭2 ♭3 ♭4 ♭5 6 ♭7 8)

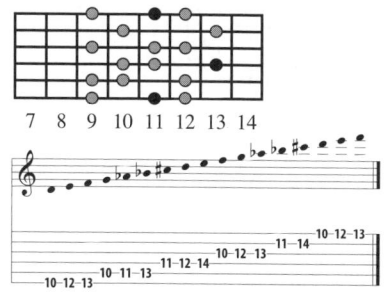

## Dominant ♭9 ♯9 (1 ♭2 ♭3 ♭4 5 6 ♭7 8)

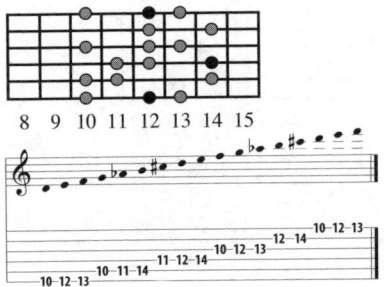
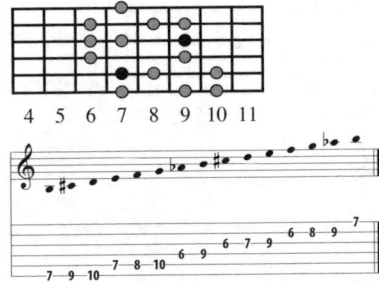

## Dominant ♭9 ♯9 ♭13 (1 ♭2 ♭3 ♭4 5 ♭6 ♭7 8)

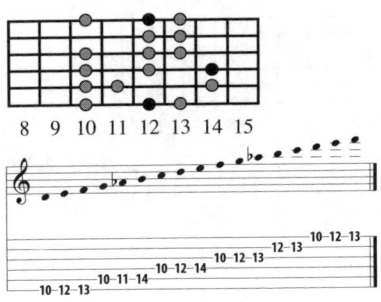
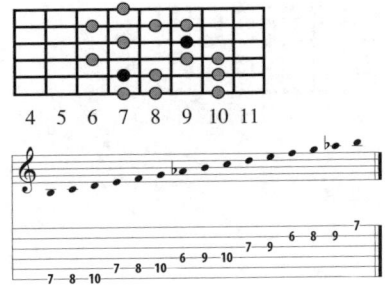

## Dominant ♯9 (1 ♯2 3 4 5 6 ♭7 8)

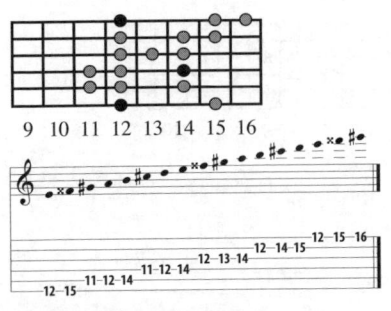
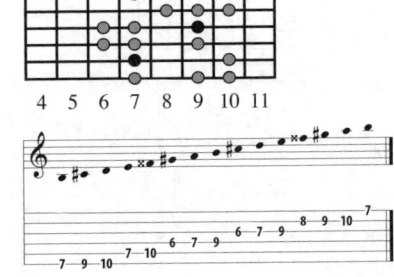

## Dominant ♭9 #11 (1 ♭2 3 #4 5 6 ♭7 8)

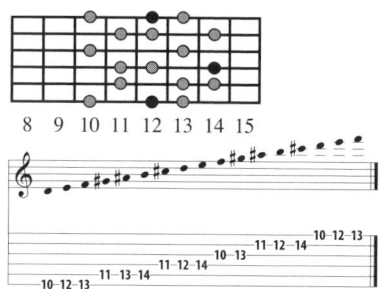
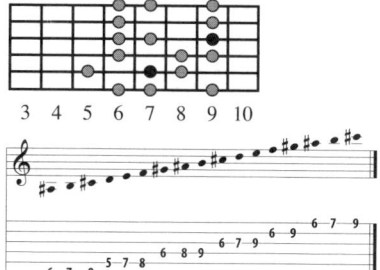

## Dominant ♭9 #11 ♭13 (1 ♭2 3 #4 5 ♭6 ♭7 8)

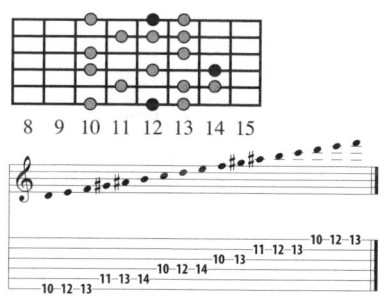
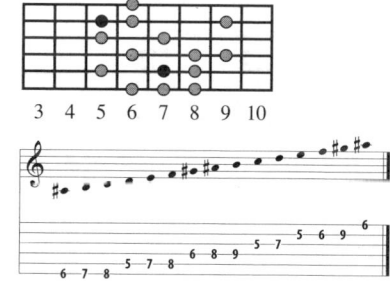

## Dominant 13 (1 2 3 5 6 ♭7 8)

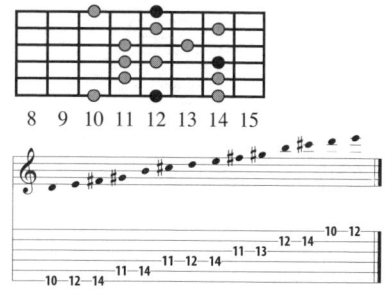
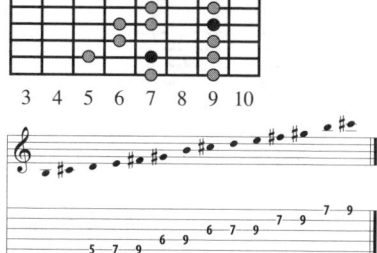

# Major and Dominant Scales

## Major/Ionian (1 2 3 4 5 6 7 8)

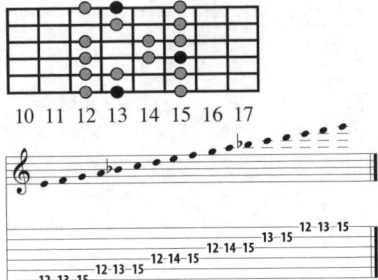
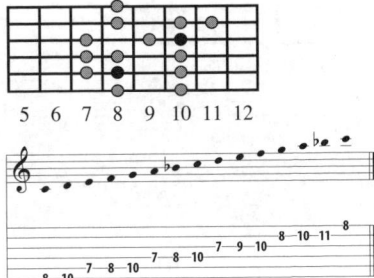

## Mixolydian (1 2 3 4 5 6 ♭7 8)
5th mode of the major scale

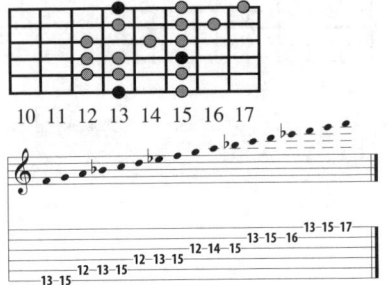
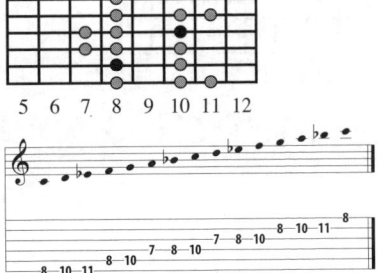

## Lydian (1 2 3 ♯4 5 6 7 8)
4th mode of the major scale

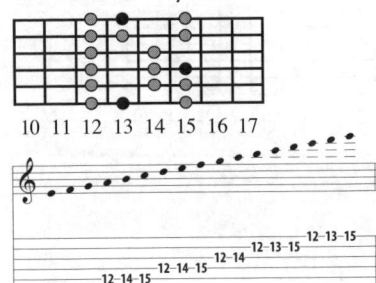
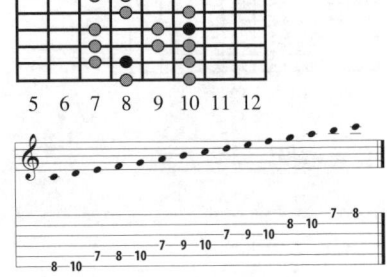

## Major Pentatonic (1 2 3 5 6 8)

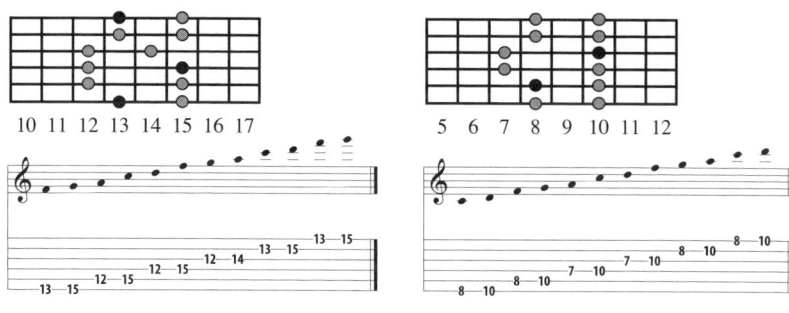

## Major 13 Pentatonic* (1 2 3 5 6 7 8)

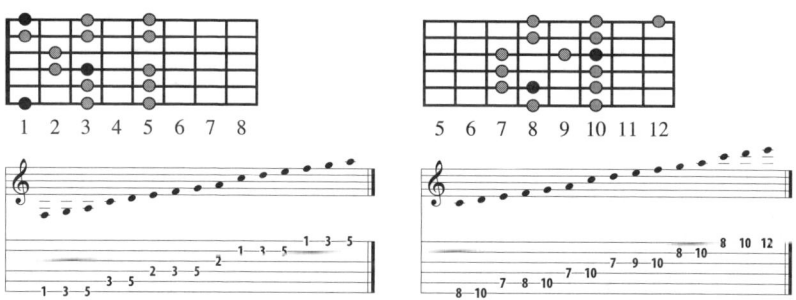

## Major Pentatonic Blues* (1 2 ♭3 3 5 6 8)

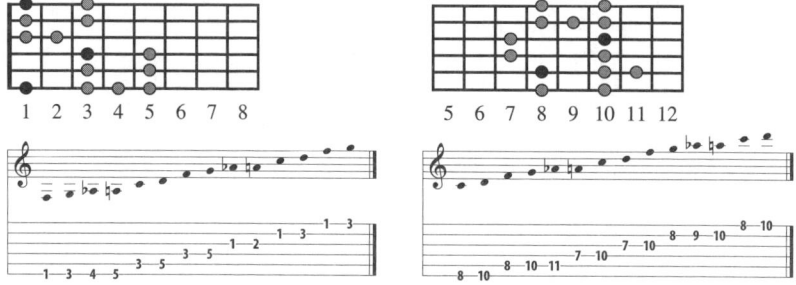

* While this scale has more than five notes, it is based on a five-note, pentatonic scale and it is best to think of it as a pentatonic scale.

## Lydian Pentatonic (1 3 #4 5 7 8)

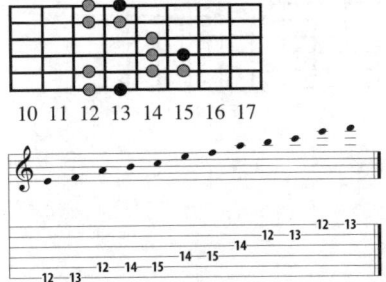
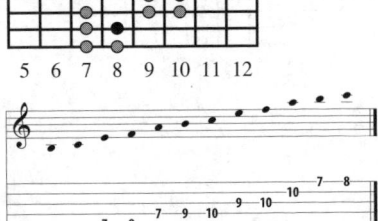

## Lydian ♭7 (1 2 3 #4 5 6 ♭7 8)
4th mode of the melodic minor scale

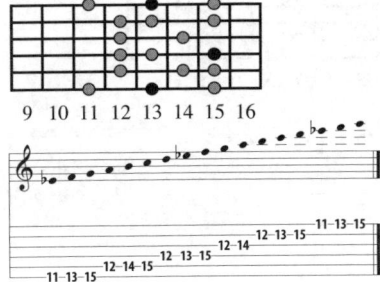
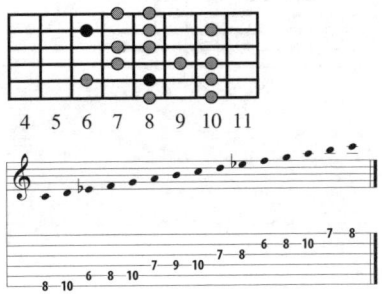

## Lydian #9 (1 #2 3 #4 5 6 7 8)
6th mode of the harmonic minor scale

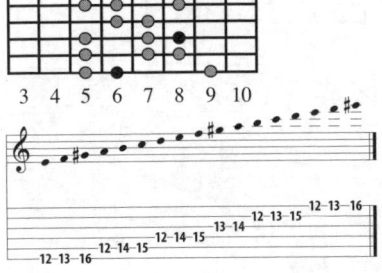
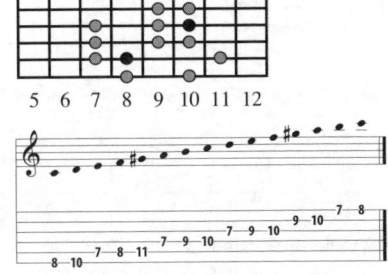

## Aeolian Major (1 2 3 4 5 ♭6 ♭7 8)
5th mode of the melodic minor scale

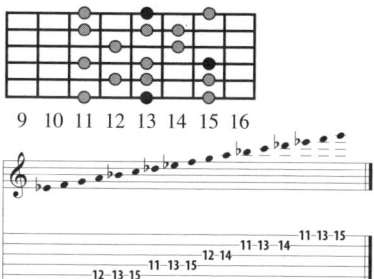
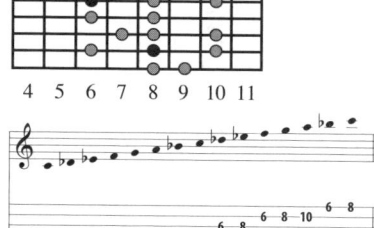

## Phrygian Major (1 ♭2 3 4 5 ♭6 ♭7 8)
5th mode of the harmonic minor scale

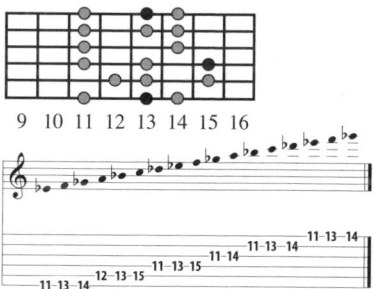
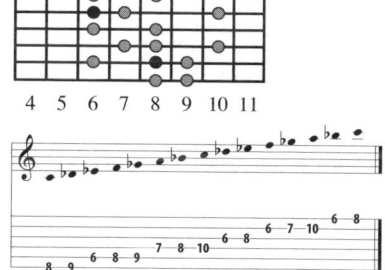

## Ionian Augmented (1 2 3 4 ♯5 6 7 8)
3rd mode of the harmonic minor scale

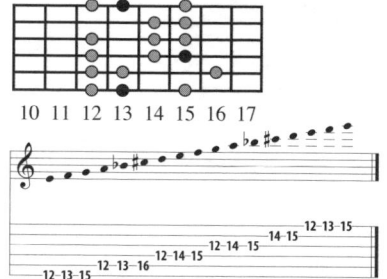
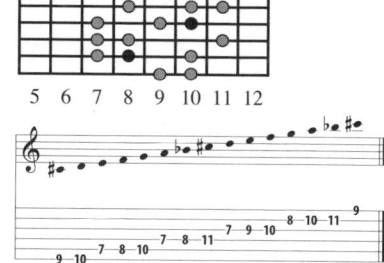

## Lydian Augmented (1 2 3 #4 #5 6 7 8)
3rd mode of the melodic minor scale

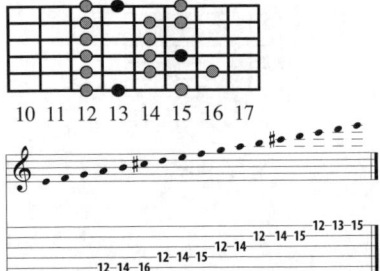
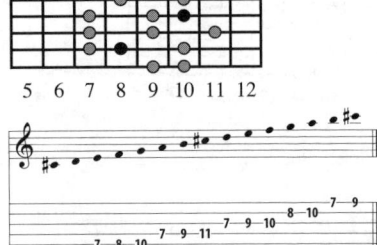

# Minor Scales

## Natural Minor/Aeolian (1 2 ♭3 4 5 ♭6 ♭7 8)
6th mode of the major scale

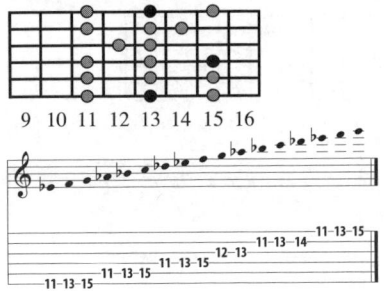
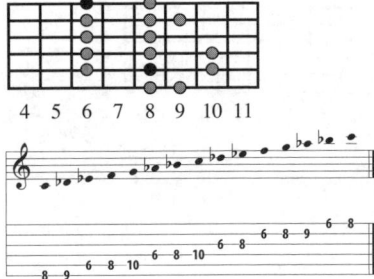

## Harmonic Minor (1 2 ♭3 4 5 ♭6 7 8)

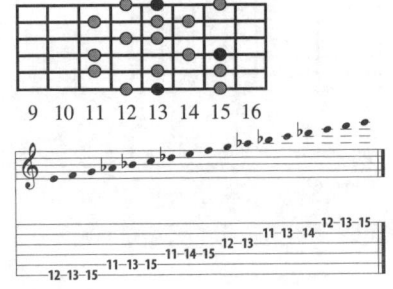
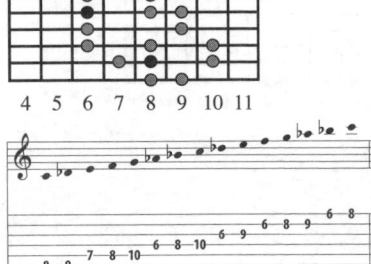

# Jazz Minor/Melodic Minor (1 2 ♭3 4 5 6 7 8)
Melodic Minor descends in Aeolian/Natural Minor

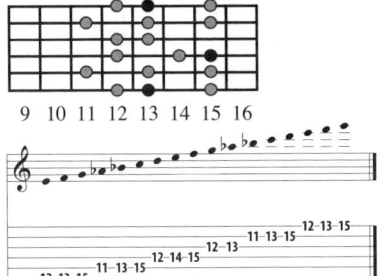
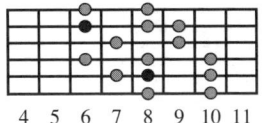
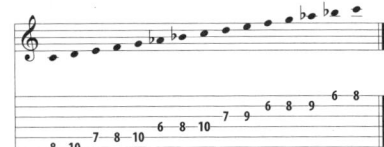

# Dorian (1 2 ♭3 4 5 6 ♭7 8)
2nd mode of the major scale

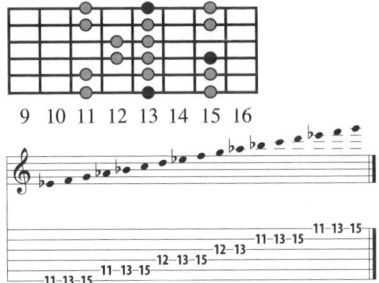
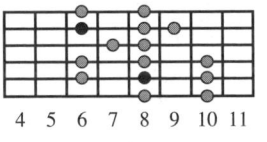

# Phrygian (1 ♭2 ♭3 4 5 ♭6 ♭7 8)
3rd mode of the major scale

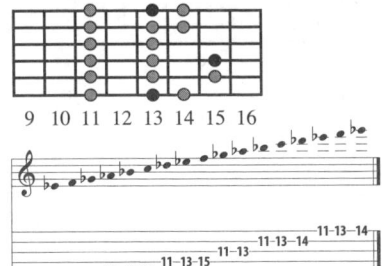
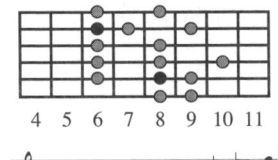

## **Locrian** (1 ♭2 ♭3 4 ♭5 ♭6 ♭7 8)
7th mode of the major scale

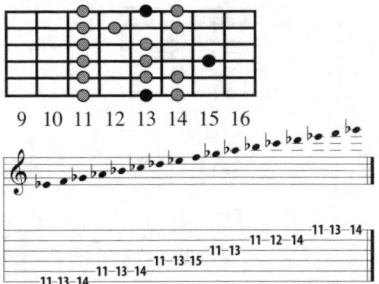
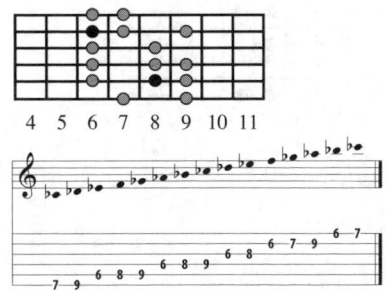

## **Minor Pentatonic** (1 ♭3 4 5 ♭7 8)

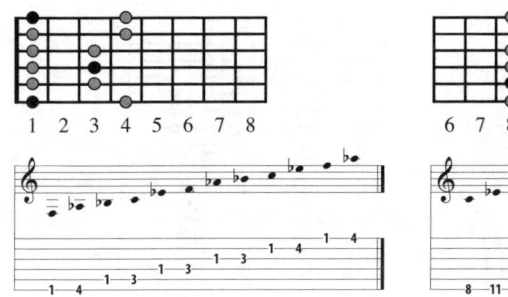
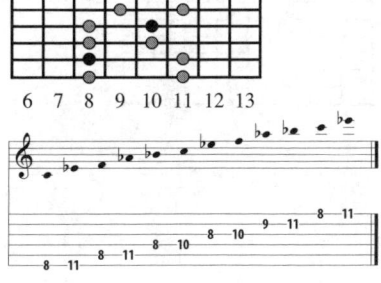

## **Minor 13 Pentatonic**\* (1 ♭3 5 ♭6 ♭7 8)

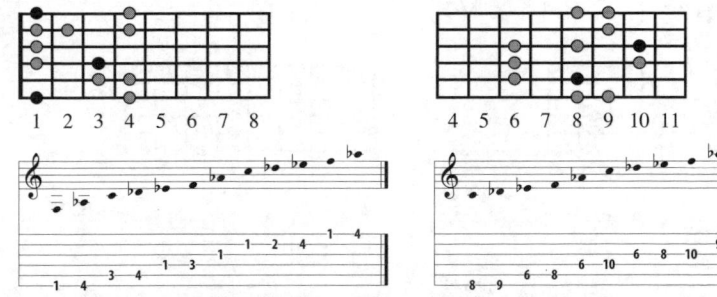

\* While this scale has more than five notes, it is based on a five-note, pentatonic scale and it is best to think of it as a pentatonic scale.

# Minor Pentatonic Blues* (1 ♭3 4 ♭5 5 ♭7 8)

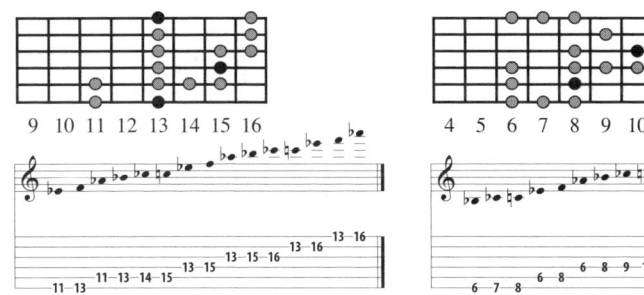

# Dorian Pentatonic (1 2 ♭3 5 ♭7 8)

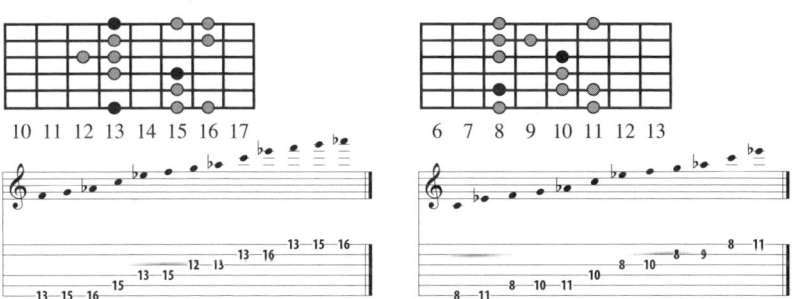

# Phrygian Pentatonic (1 ♭2 4 5 ♭7 8)

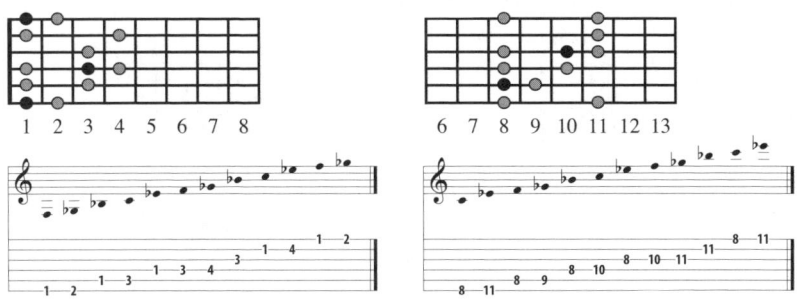

* While this scale has more than five notes, it is based on a five-note, pentatonic scale and it is best to think of it as a pentatonic scale.

## Phrygian ♮6 (1 ♭2 ♭3 4 5 6 ♭7 8)
2nd mode of the melodic minor scale

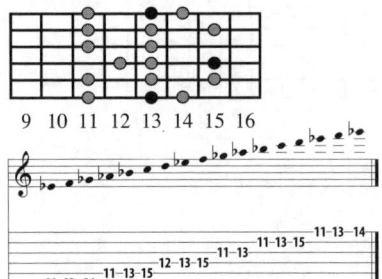
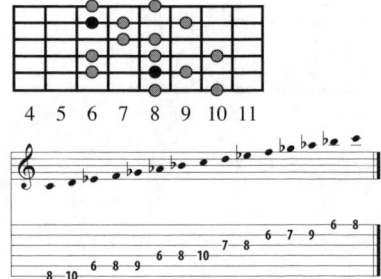

## Locrian ♮2 (1 2 ♭3 4 ♭5 ♭6 ♭7 8)
6th mode of the melodic minor scale

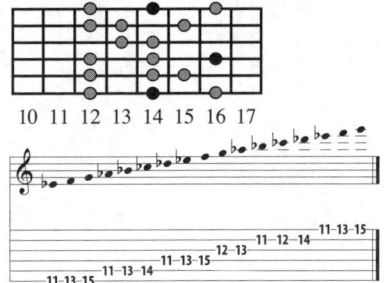
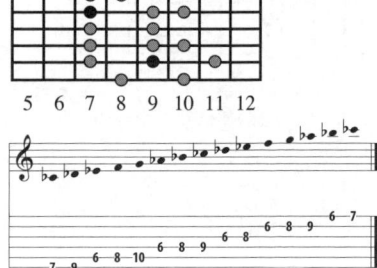

## Locrian ♮6 (1 ♭2 ♭3 4 ♭5 6 ♭7 8)
2nd mode of the harmonic minor scale

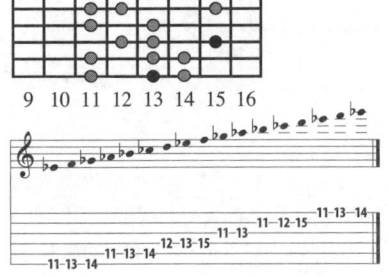
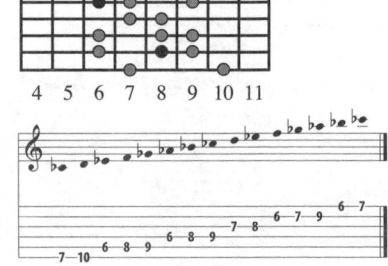

# Symmetrical Scales

## Chromatic (1 b2 2 b3 3 4 b5 5 b6 6 b7 7 8)

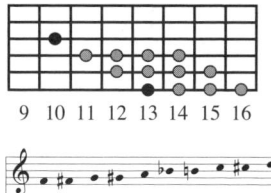
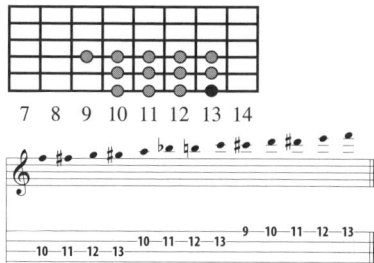

## Whole Tone (1 2 3 #4 #5 #6 8)

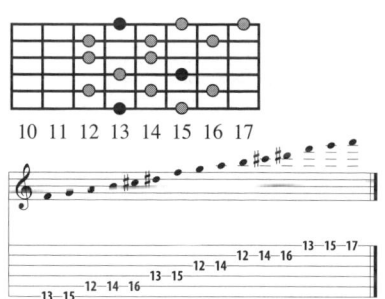
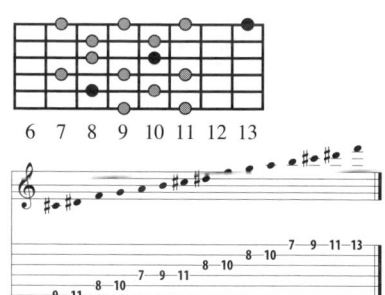

## Auxiliary, Whole/Half Diminished (1 2 b3 4 b5 b6 6 7 8)

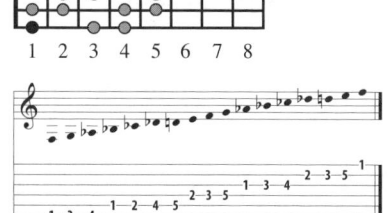
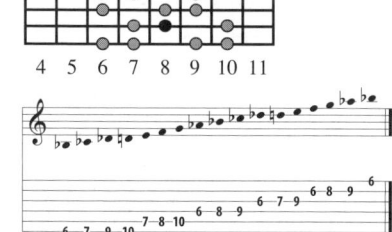

## Symmetrical, Half/Whole Diminished (1 b2 b3 b4 b5 5 6 b7 8)

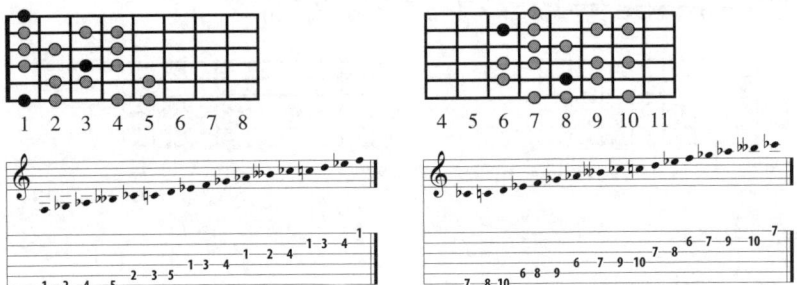

## Augmented (1 #2 3 5 #5 7 8)

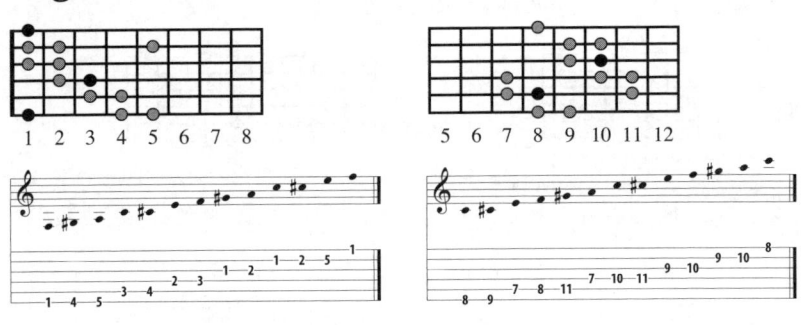

## Chromatic Augmented (1 b2 2 3 4 #4 #5 6 b7 8)

## Augmented ♭9 (1 ♭2 ♭3 3 4 5 ♭6 6 7 8)

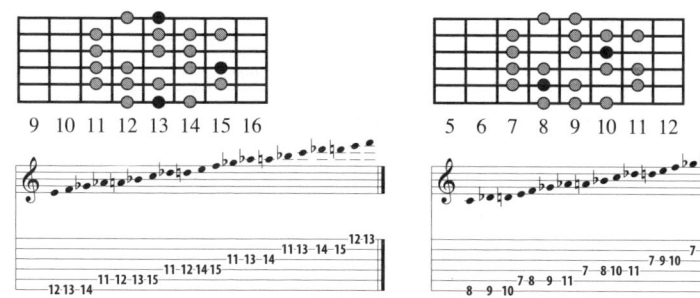

## Augmented 9 (1 2 ♭3 3 ♯4 5 ♭6 ♭7 7 8)

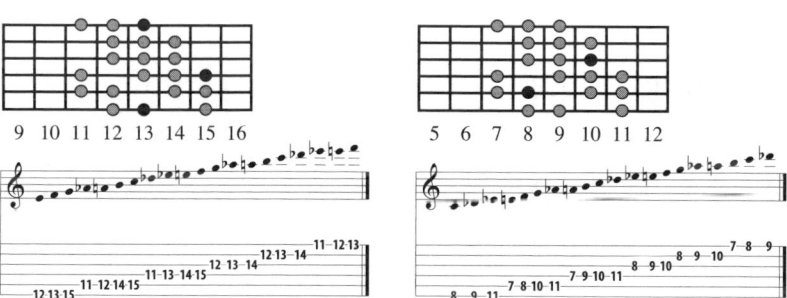

## Diminished Blues (1 ♭2 ♭3 3 ♯5 6 ♭7 8)

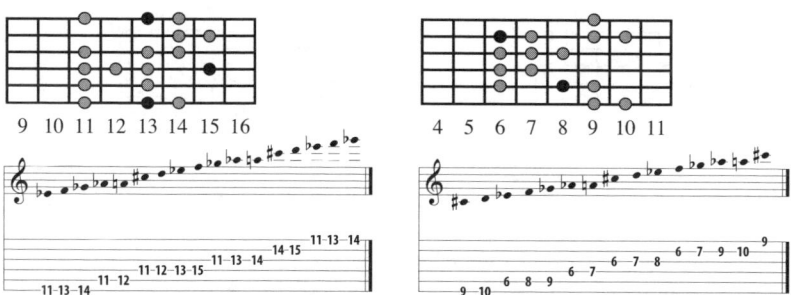

# Four Semitone Tritone (1 b2 2 b3 3 #4 5 b6 6 b7 8)

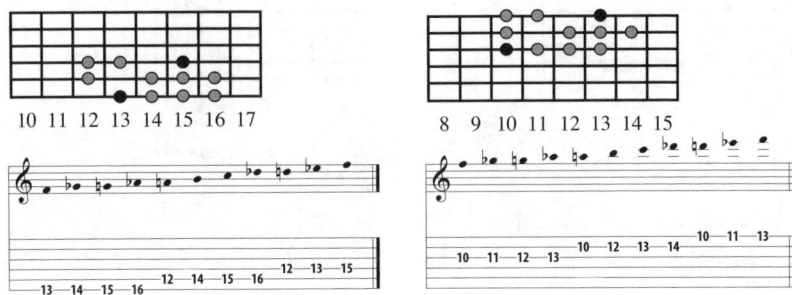

# Tetratonic (1 4 b5 7 8)

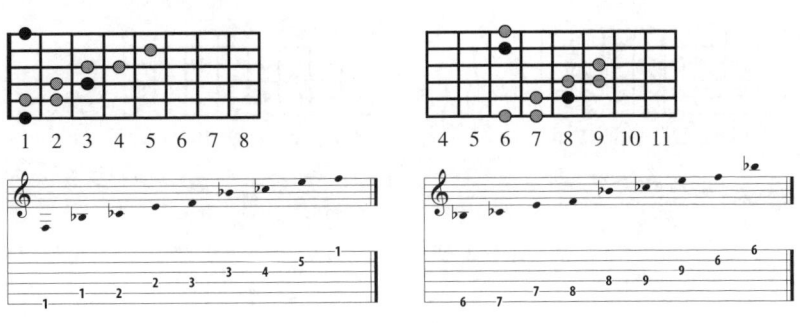

# Three Semitone Tritone (1 b2 2 b3 b5 5 b6 6 8)

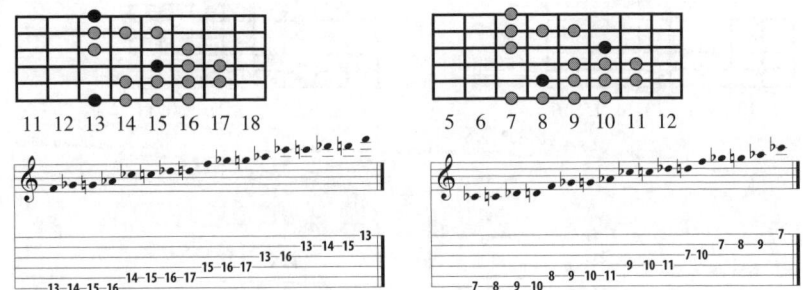

## Tritone (1 ♭2 3 ♯4 5 ♭7 8)

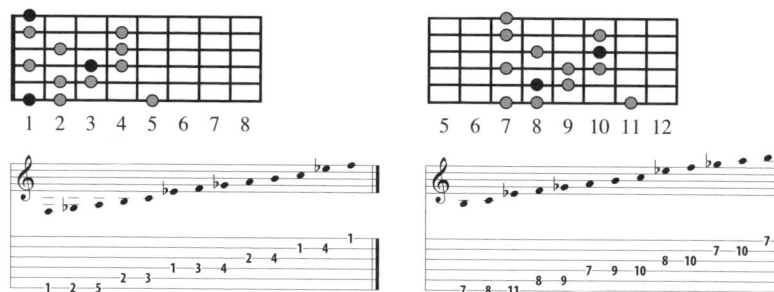

## Two-Semitone Tritone (1 ♭2 2 ♯4 5 ♭6 8)

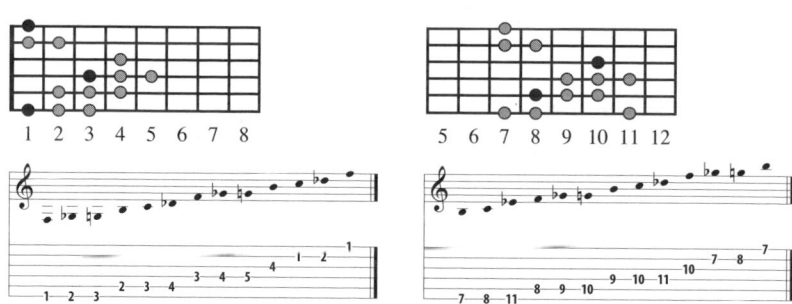

# Hybrid Scales

## Aeolian ♯11 (1 2 ♭3 ♯4 5 ♭6 ♭7 8)

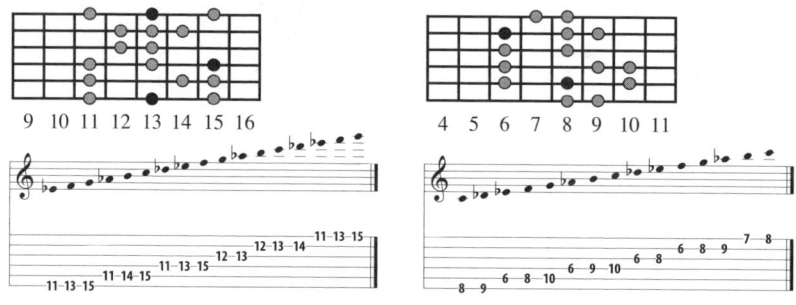

## Augmented Dominant (1 2 3 4 ♯5 6 ♭7 8)

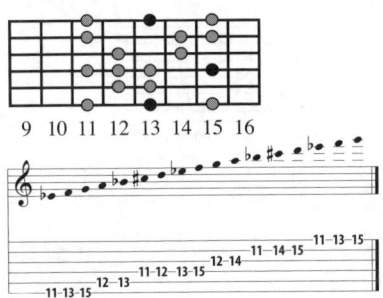
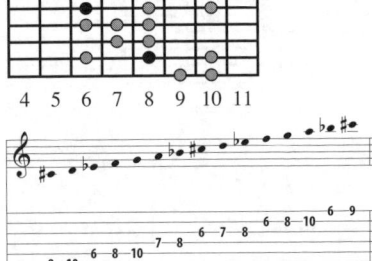

## Augmented Dominant ♭9 (1 ♭2 3 4 ♯5 6 ♭7 8)

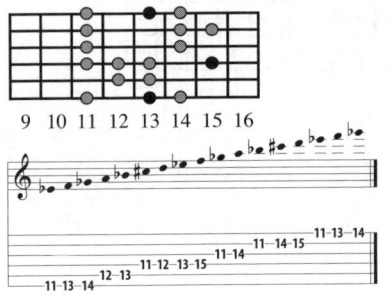
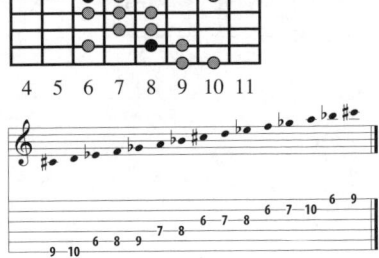

## Augmented Dominant ♯9 (1 ♯2 3 4 ♯5 6 ♭7 8)

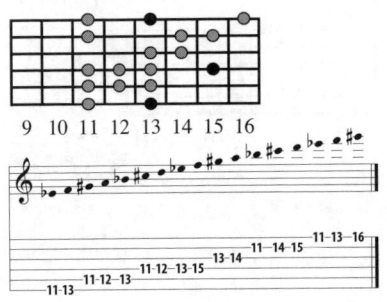

# Augmented ♯9 (1 ♯2 3 4 ♯5 6 7 8)

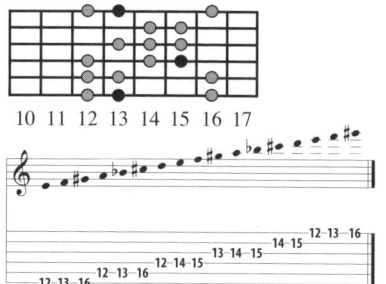
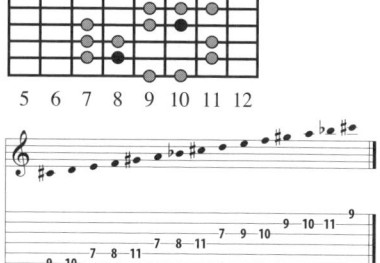

# Augmented Minor/Major 7 (1 2 ♭3 4 ♯5 6 7 8)

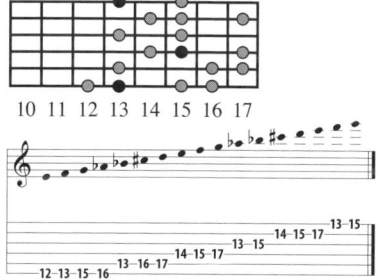
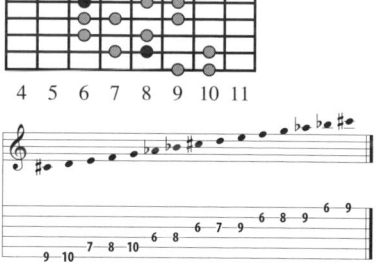

# Bebop Dominant (1 2 3 4 5 6 ♭7 7 8)

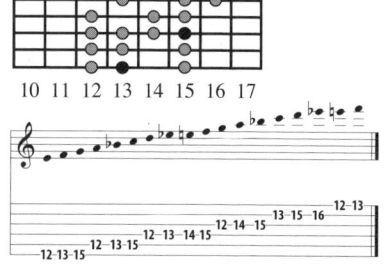
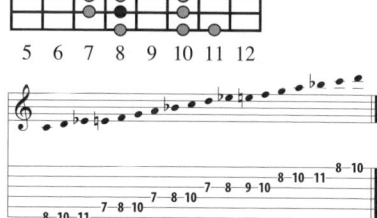

## Bebop Dorian (1 2 b3 3 4 5 6 b7 8)

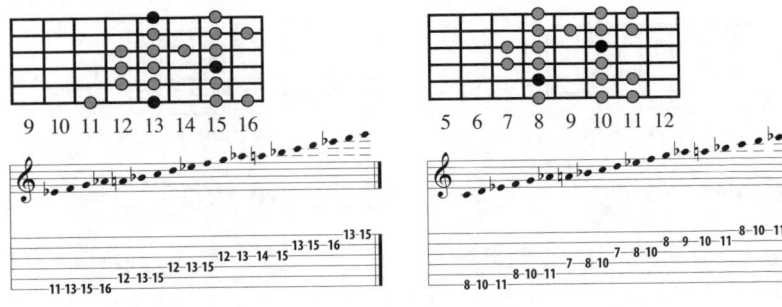

## Bebop Major* (1 2 3 4 #4 5 6 7 8)

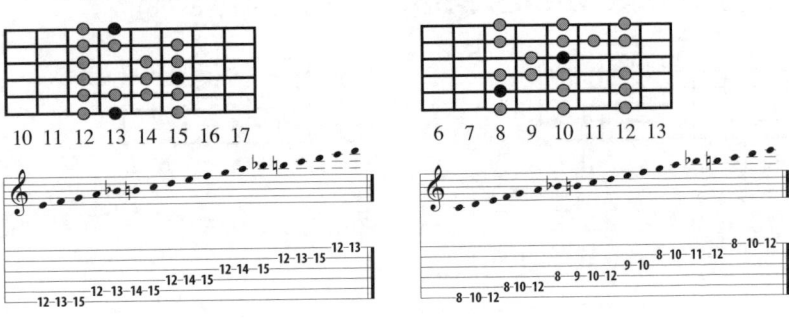

## Bebop Melodic Minor* (1 2 b3 4 #4 5 6 7 8)

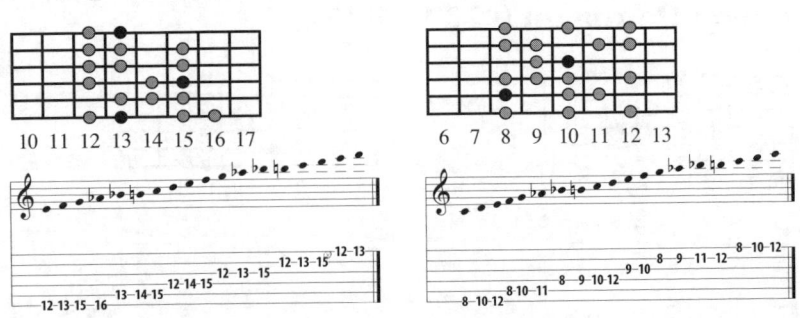

* Many musicians spell this scale with a #5 instead of a #4.

## Diminished Tritonic (1 ♭3 4 ♭5 8)

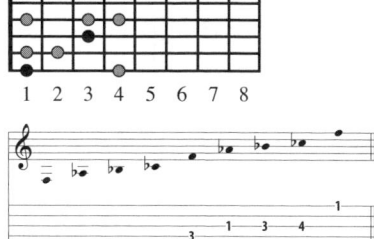
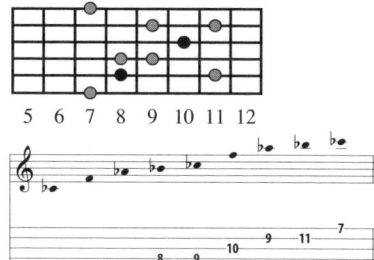

## Dominant ♭5 (1 2 3 4 ♭5 6 ♭7 8)

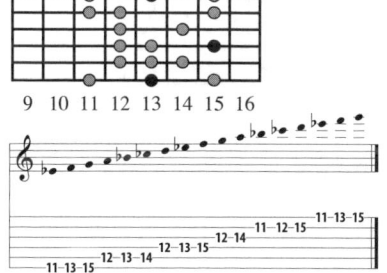
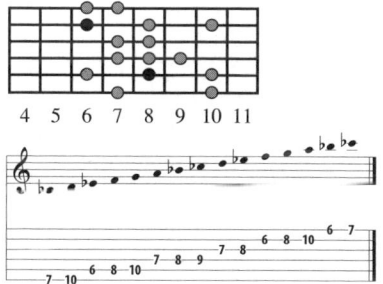

## Dominant ♭5 ♭9 ♯9 (1 ♭2 ♭3 ♭4 ♭5 6 ♭7 8)

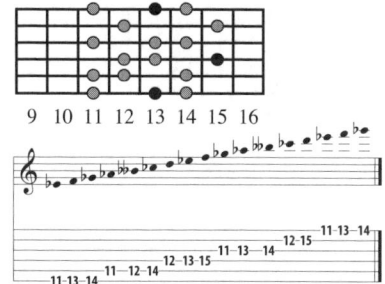
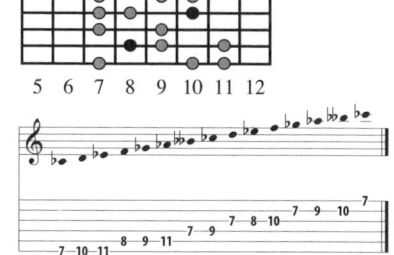

# Dominant ♭9 ♯9 (1 ♭2 ♭3 ♭4 5 6 ♭7 8)

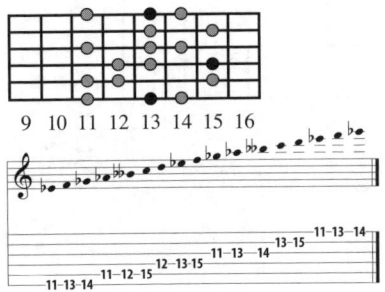
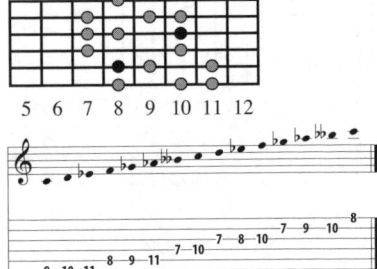

# Dominant ♭9 ♯9 ♭13 (1 ♭2 ♭3 ♭4 5 ♭6 ♭7 8)

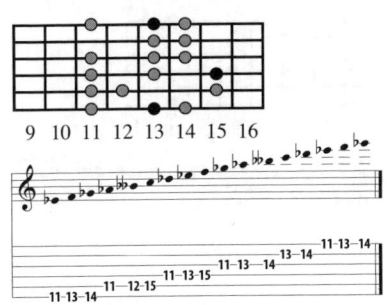
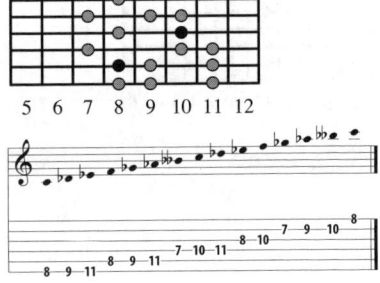

# Dominant ♯9 (1 ♯2 3 4 5 6 ♭7 8)

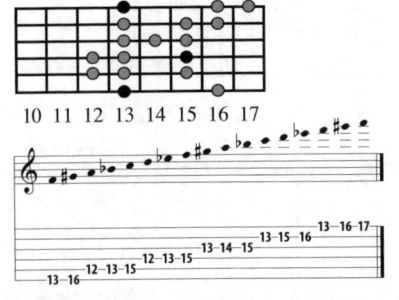
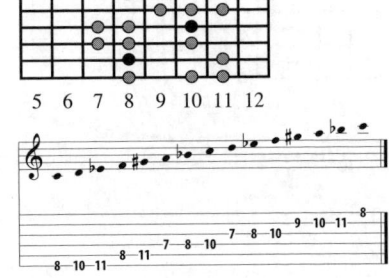

## Dominant ♭9 ♯11 (1 ♭2 3 ♯4 5 6 ♭7 8)

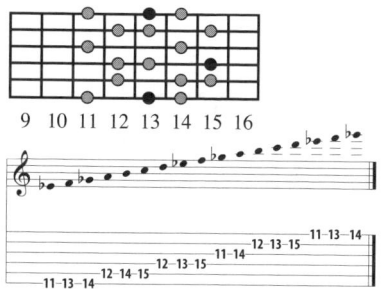
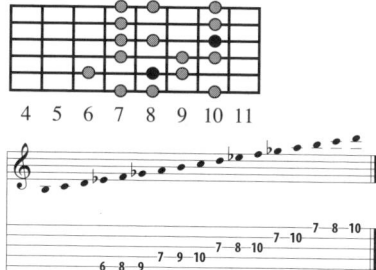

## Dominant ♭9 ♯11 ♭13 (1 ♭2 3 ♯4 5 ♭6 ♭7 8)

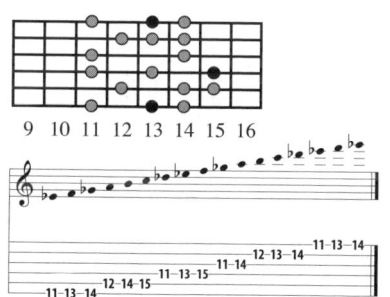
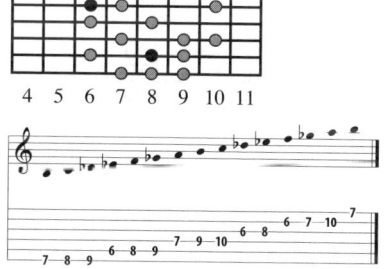

## Dominant 13 (1 2 3 5 6 ♭7 8)

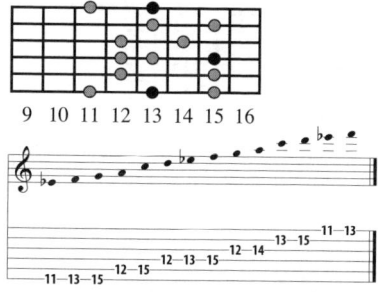
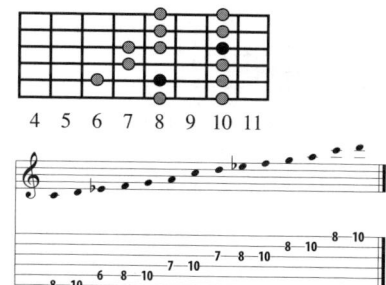

# Major and Dominant Scales

## Major/Ionian (1 2 3 4 5 6 7 8)

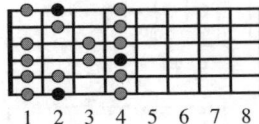
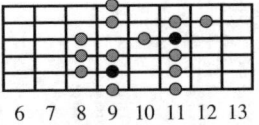
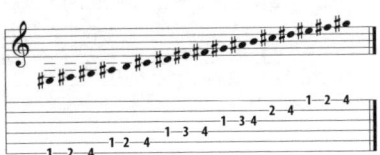
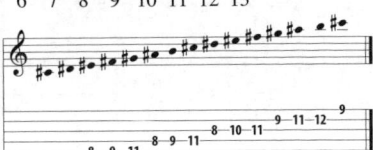

## Mixolydian (1 2 3 4 5 6 ♭7 8)
5th mode of the major scale

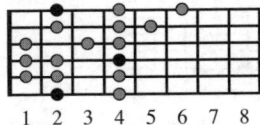
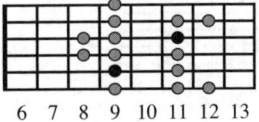

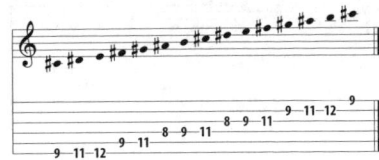

## Lydian (1 2 3 ♯4 5 6 7 8)
4th mode of the major scale

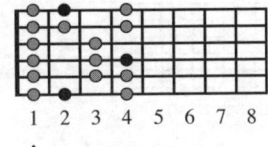
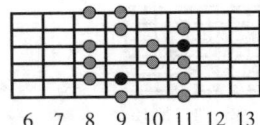

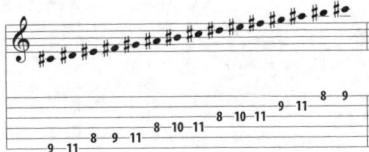

## Major Pentatonic (1 2 3 5 6 8)

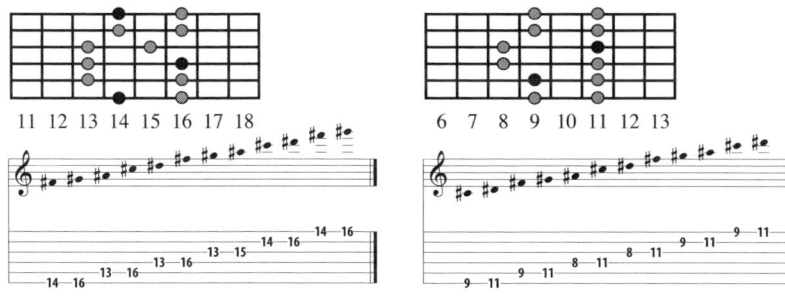

## Major 13 Pentatonic* (1 2 3 5 6 7 8)

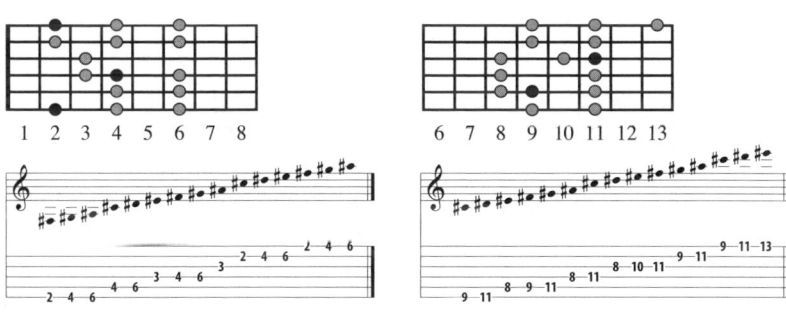

## Major Pentatonic Blues* (1 2 ♭3 3 5 6 8)

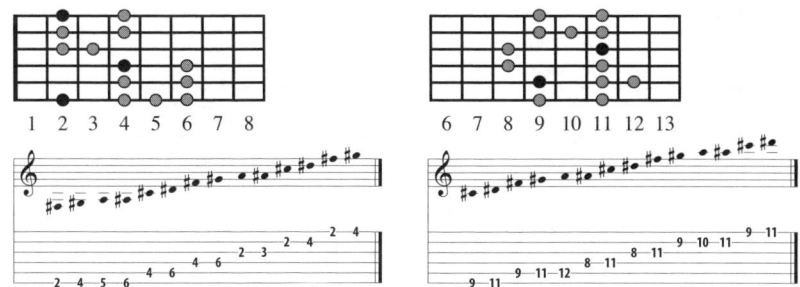

* While this scale has more than five notes, it is based on a five-note, pentatonic scale and it is best to think of it as a pentatonic scale.

## Lydian Pentatonic (1 3 #4 5 7 8)

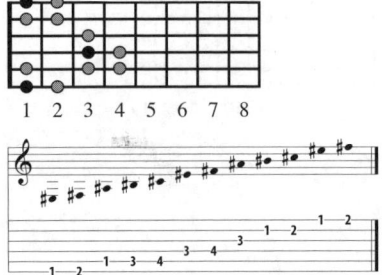
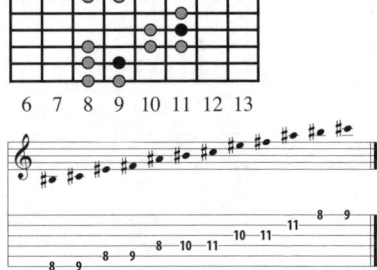

## Lydian ♭7 (1 2 3 #4 5 6 ♭7 8)
4th mode of the melodic minor scale

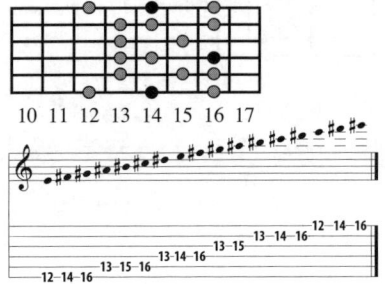
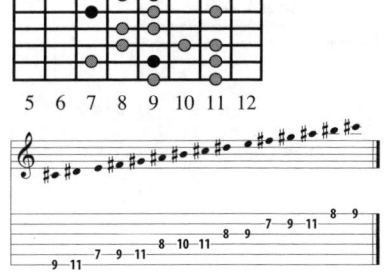

## Lydian #9 (1 #2 3 #4 5 6 7 8)
6th mode of the harmonic minor scale

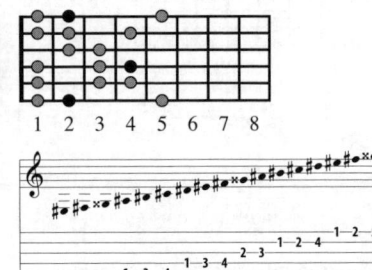
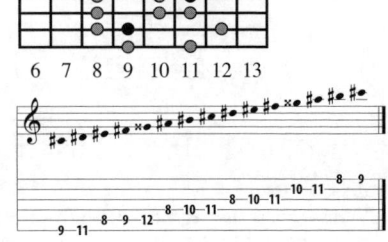

## Aeolian Major (1 2 3 4 5 ♭6 ♭7 8)
5th mode of the melodic minor scale

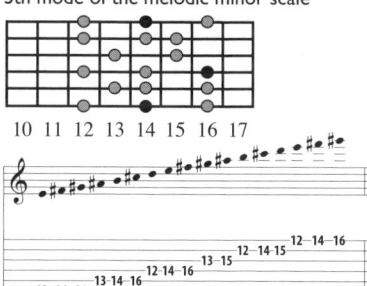
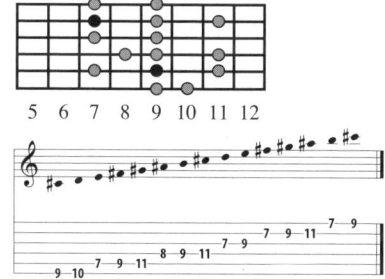

## Phrygian Major (1 ♭2 3 4 5 ♭6 ♭7 8)
5th mode of the harmonic minor scale

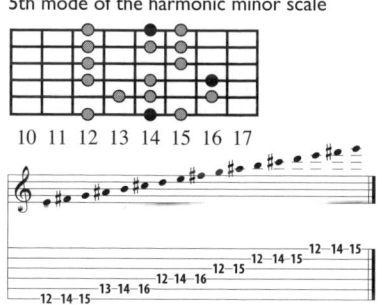
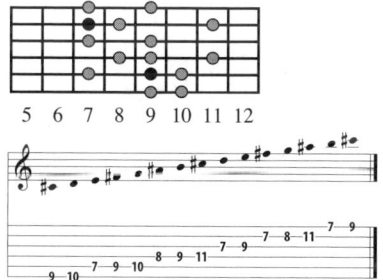

## Ionian Augmented (1 2 3 4 ♯5 6 7 8)
3rd mode of the harmonic minor scale

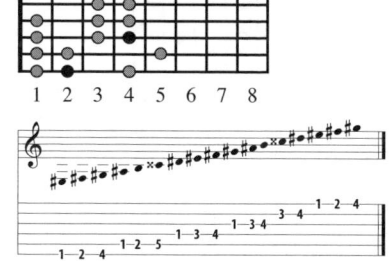
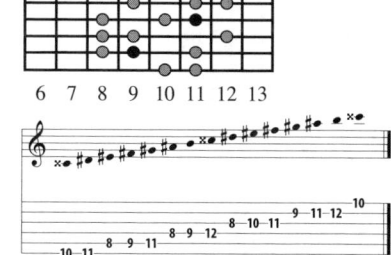

## Lydian Augmented (1 2 3 #4 #5 6 7 8)
3rd mode of the melodic minor scale

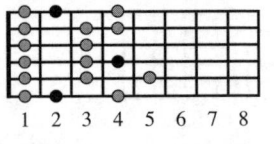
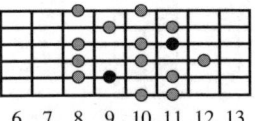
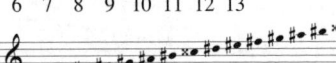
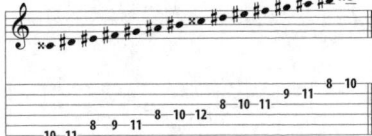

# Minor Scales

## Natural Minor/Aeolian (1 2 ♭3 4 5 ♭6 ♭7 8)
6th mode of the major scale

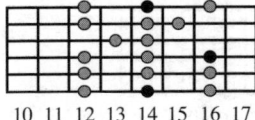
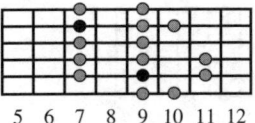
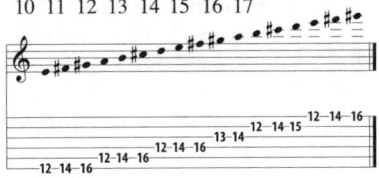

## Harmonic Minor (1 2 ♭3 4 5 ♭6 7 8)

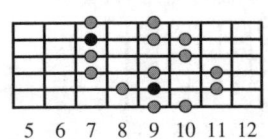
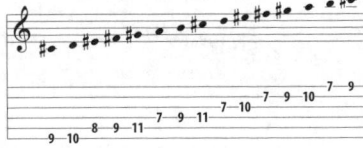

# Jazz Minor/Melodic Minor (1 2 ♭3 4 5 6 7 8)
Melodic Minor descends in Aeolian/Natural Minor

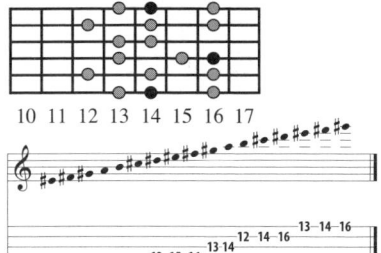
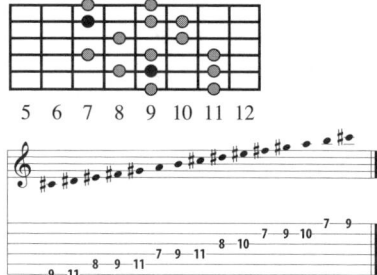

# Dorian (1 2 ♭3 4 5 6 ♭7 8)
2nd mode of the major scale

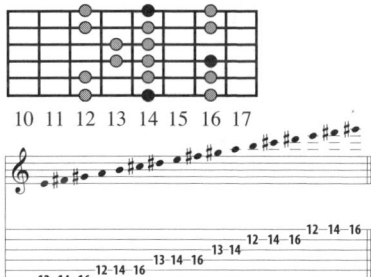
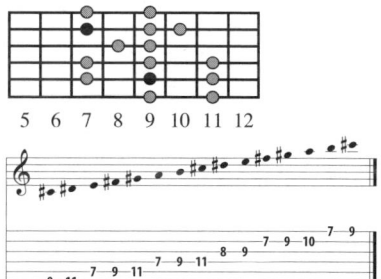

# Phrygian (1 ♭2 ♭3 4 5 ♭6 ♭7 8)
3rd mode of the major scale

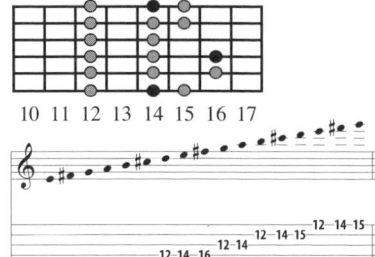
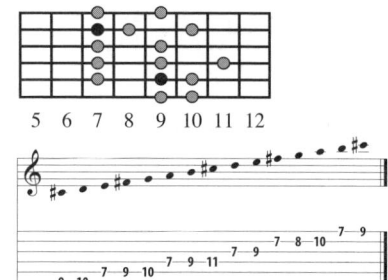

F#

## Locrian (1 ♭2 ♭3 4 ♭5 ♭6 ♭7 8)
7th mode of the major scale

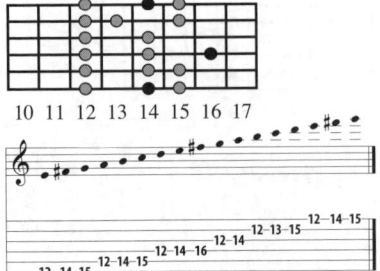
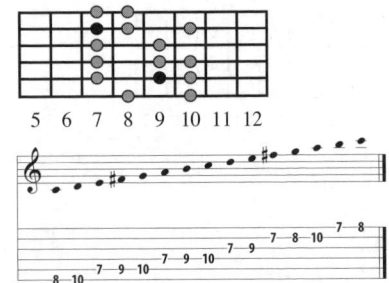

## Minor Pentatonic (1 ♭3 4 5 ♭7 8)

## Minor 13 Pentatonic* (1 ♭3 5 ♭6 ♭7 8)

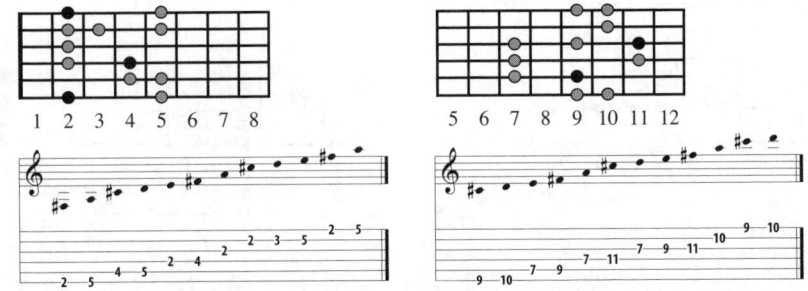

* While this scale has more than five notes, it is based on a five-note, pentatonic scale and it is best to think of it as a pentatonic scale.

## Minor Pentatonic Blues* (1 ♭3 4 ♭5 5 ♭7 8)

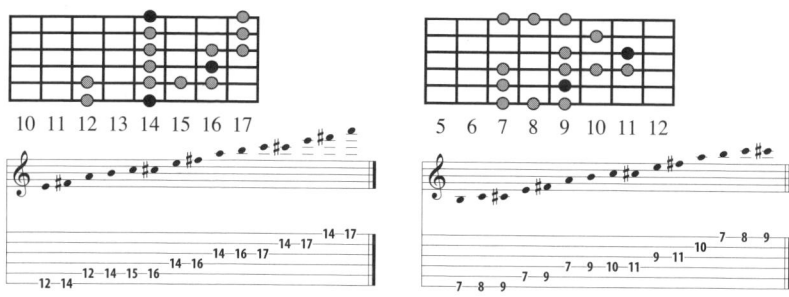

## Dorian Pentatonic (1 2 ♭3 5 ♭7 8)

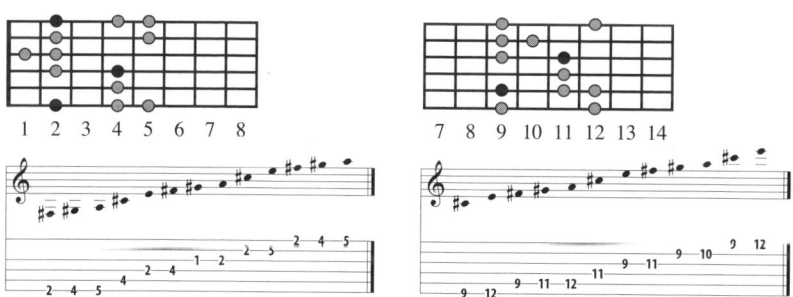

## Phrygian Pentatonic (1 ♭2 4 5 ♭7 8)

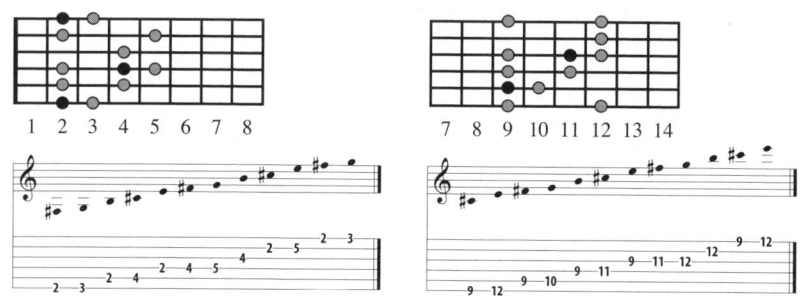

* While this scale has more than five notes, it is based on a five-note, pentatonic scale and it is best to think of it as a pentatonic scale.

# Phrygian ♮6 (1 ♭2 ♭3 4 5 6 ♭7 8)
2nd mode of the melodic minor scale

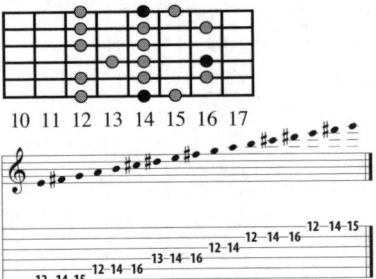
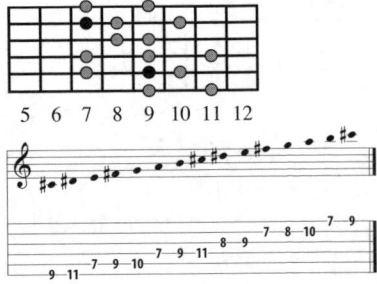

# Locrian ♮2 (1 2 ♭3 4 ♭5 ♭6 ♭7 8)
6th mode of the melodic minor scale

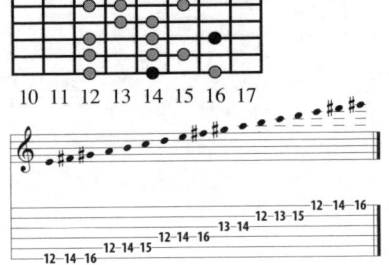
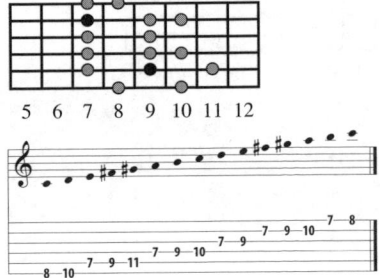

# Locrian ♮6 (1 ♭2 ♭3 4 ♭5 6 ♭7 8)
2nd mode of the harmonic minor scale

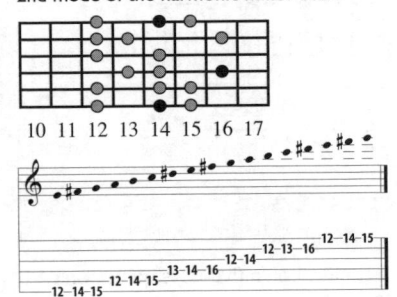

# Symmetrical Scales

## Chromatic (1 ♭2 2 ♭3 3 4 ♭5 5 ♭6 6 ♭7 7 8)

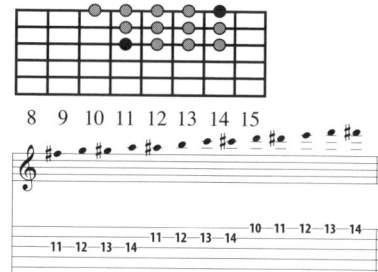

## Whole Tone (1 2 3 ♯4 ♯5 ♯6 8)

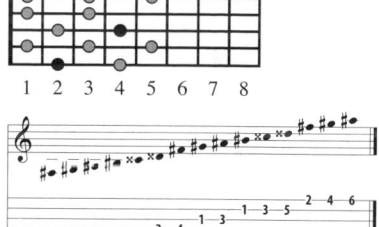
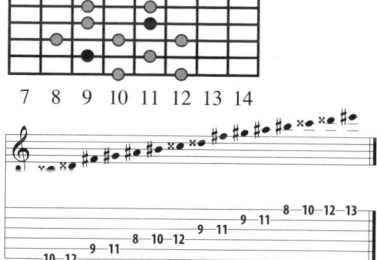

## Auxiliary, Whole/Half Diminished (1 2 ♭3 4 ♭5 ♭6 6 7 8)

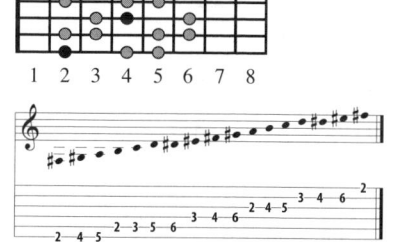
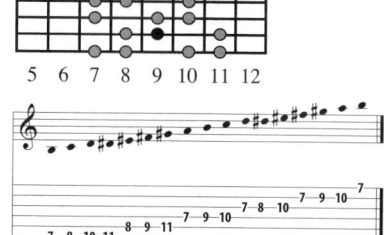

# Symmetrical, Half/Whole Diminished (1 b2 b3 b4 b5 5 6 b7 8)

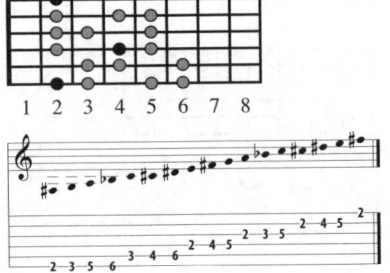
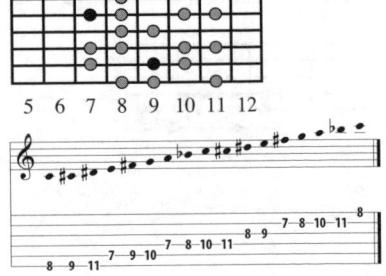

# Augmented (1 #2 3 5 #5 7 8)

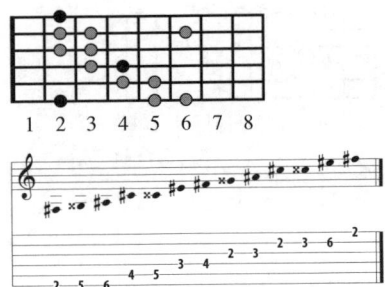
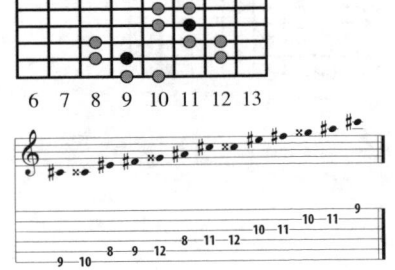

# Chromatic Augmented (1 b2 2 3 4 #4 #5 6 b7 8)

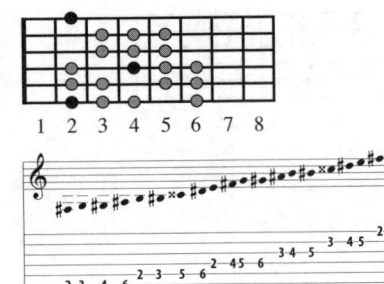
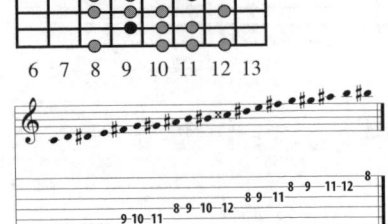

## Augmented ♭9 (1 ♭2 ♭3 3 4 5 ♭6 6 7 8)

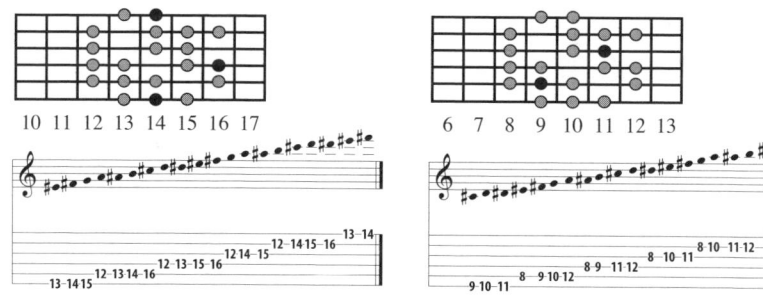

## Augmented 9 (1 2 ♭3 3 ♯4 5 ♭6 ♭7 7 8)

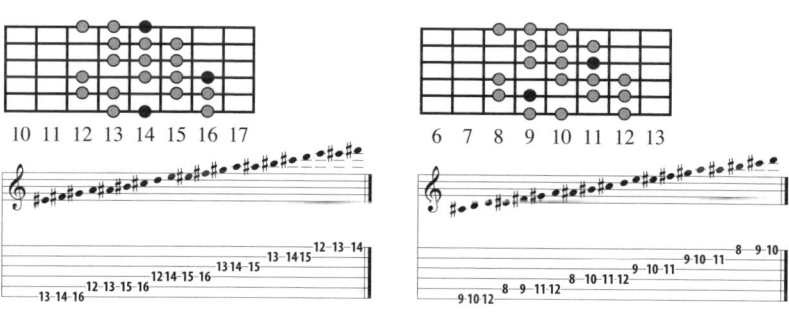

## Diminished Blues (1 ♭2 ♭3 3 ♯5 6 ♭7 8)

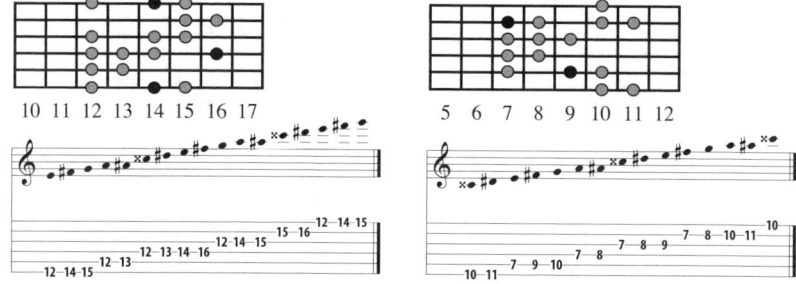

# Four Semitone Tritone (1 b2 2 b3 3 #4 5 b6 6 b7 8)

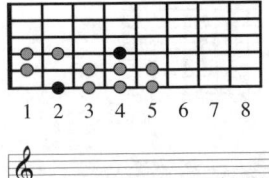
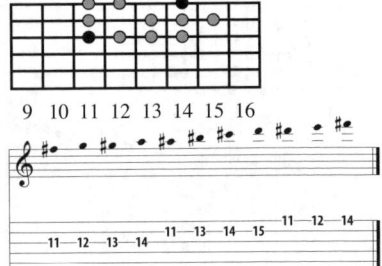

# Tetratonic (1 4 b5 7 8)

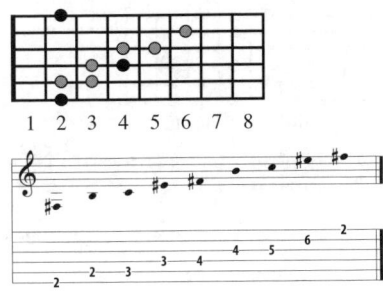

# Three Semitone Tritone (1 b2 2 b3 b5 5 b6 6 8)

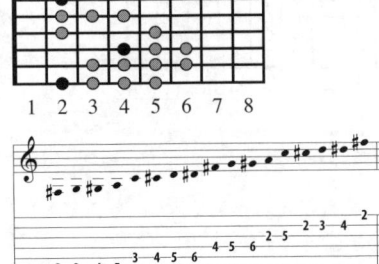
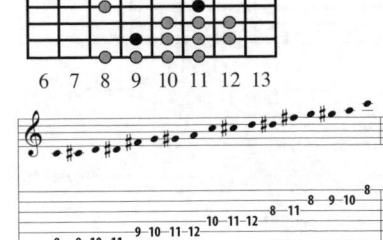

## Tritone (1 ♭2 3 ♯4 5 ♭7 8)

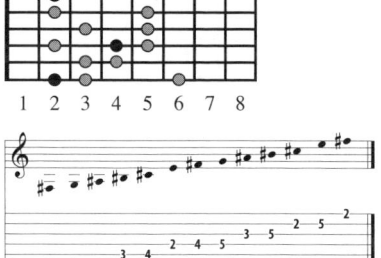
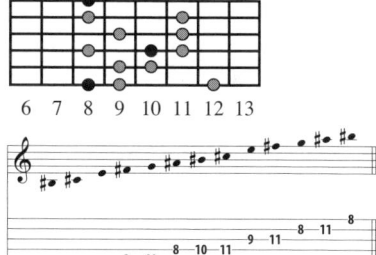

## Two-Semitone Tritone (1 ♭2 2 ♯4 5 ♭6 8)

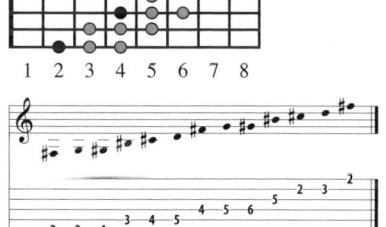
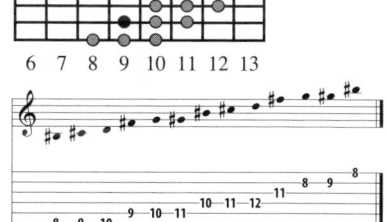

# Hybrid Scales
## Aeolian ♯11 (1 2 ♭3 ♯4 5 ♭6 ♭7 8)

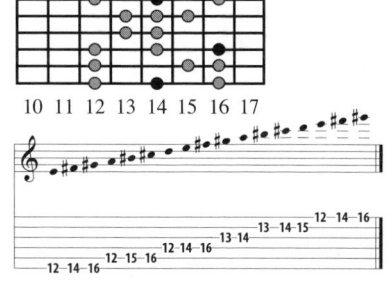

## Augmented Dominant (1 2 3 4 #5 6 b7 8)

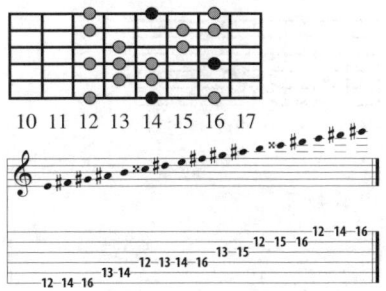
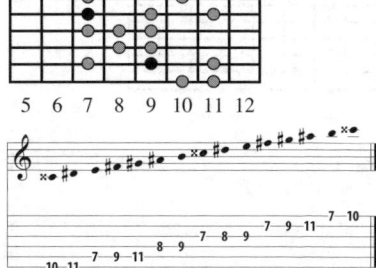

## Augmented Dominant b9 (1 b2 3 4 #5 6 b7 8)

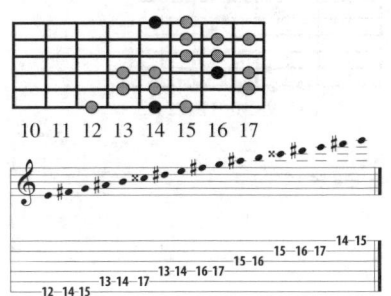
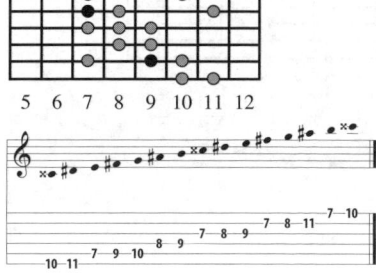

## Augmented Dominant #9 (1 #2 3 4 #5 6 b7 8)

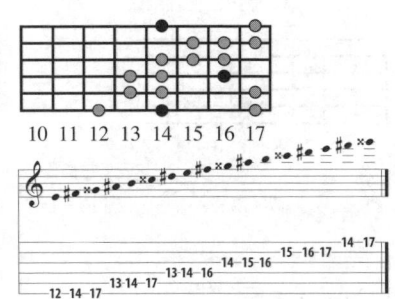
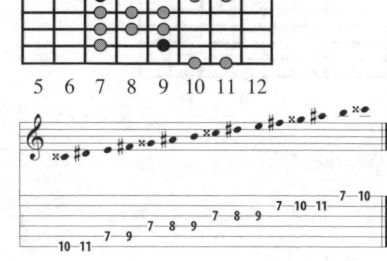

## Augmented ♯9 (1 ♯2 3 4 ♯5 6 7 8)

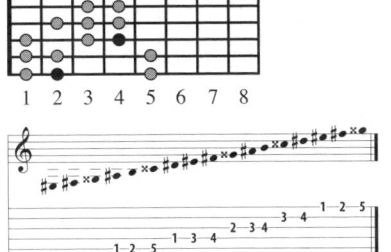
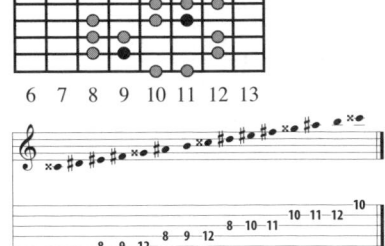

## Augmented Minor/Major 7 (1 2 ♭3 4 ♯5 6 7 8)

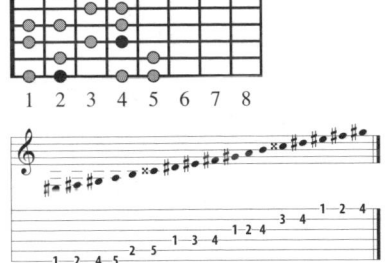
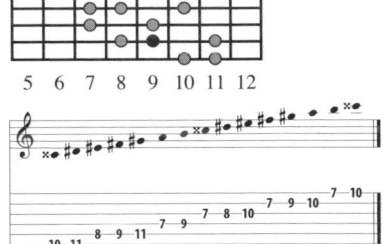

## Bebop Dominant (1 2 3 4 5 6 ♭7 7 8)

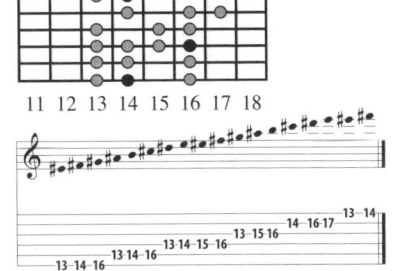
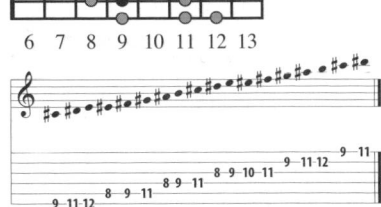

## Bebop Dorian (1 2 ♭3 3 4 5 6 ♭7 8)

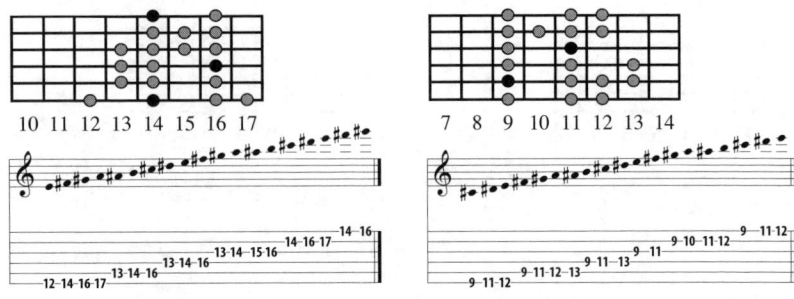

## Bebop Major* (1 2 3 4 ♯4 5 6 7 8)

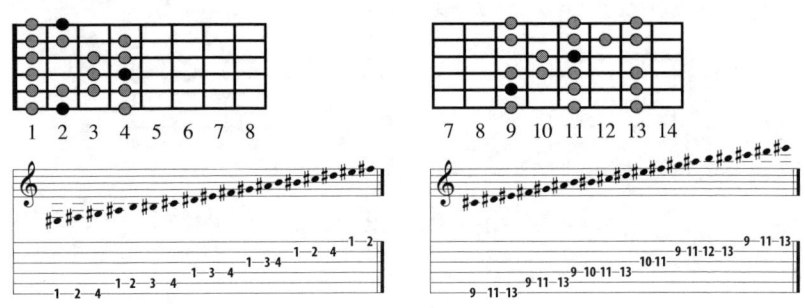

## Bebop Melodic Minor* (1 2 ♭3 4 ♯4 5 6 7 8)

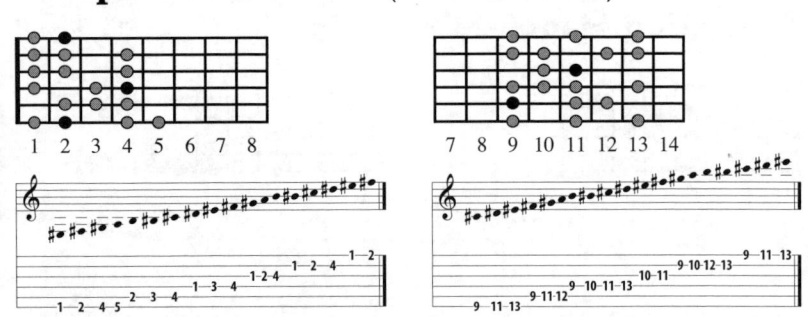

* Many musicians spell this scale with a ♯5 instead of a ♯4.

## Diminished Tritonic (1 ♭3 4 ♭5 8)

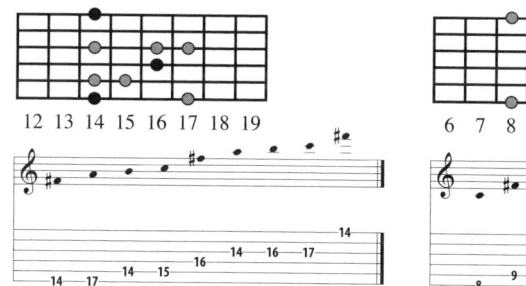
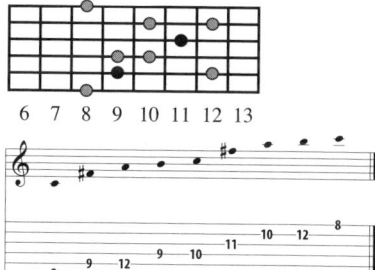

## Dominant ♭5 (1 2 3 4 ♭5 6 ♭7 8)

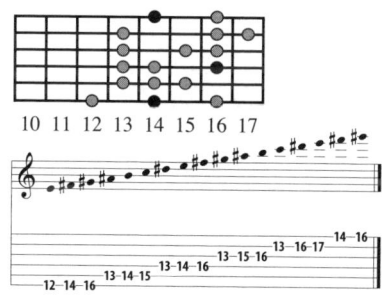
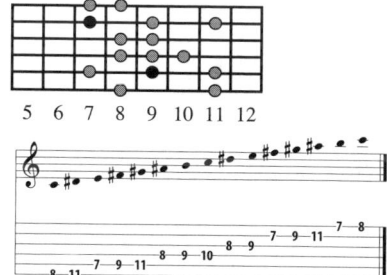

## Dominant ♭5 ♭9 ♯9 (1 ♭2 ♭3 ♭4 ♭5 6 ♭7 8)

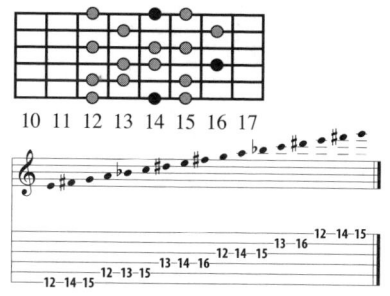
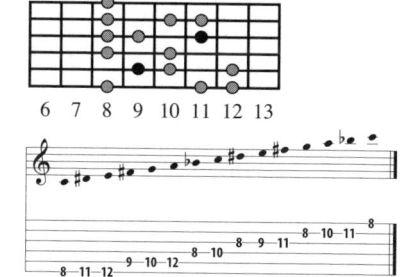

## Dominant ♭9 ♯9 (1 ♭2 ♭3 ♭4 5 6 ♭7 8)

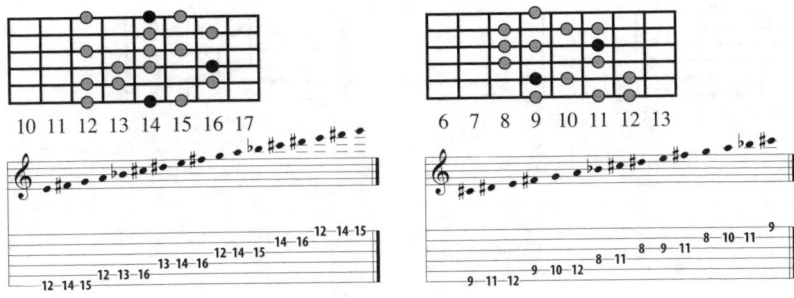

## Dominant ♭9 ♯9 ♭13 (1 ♭2 ♭3 ♭4 5 ♭6 ♭7 8)

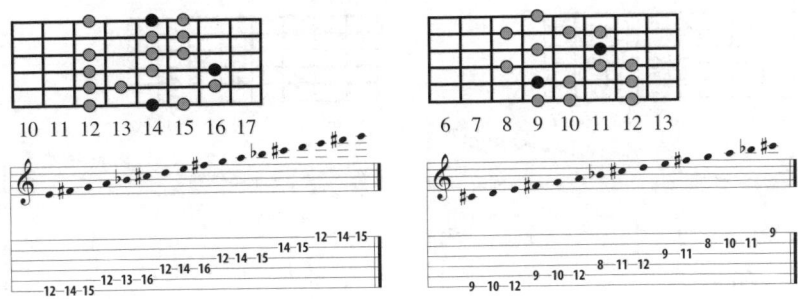

## Dominant ♯9 (1 ♯2 3 4 5 6 ♭7 8)

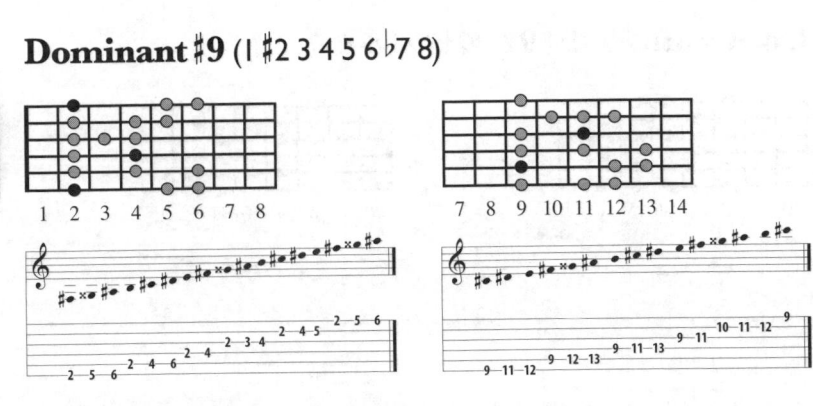

## Dominant ♭9 ♯11 (1 ♭2 3 ♯4 5 6 ♭7 8)

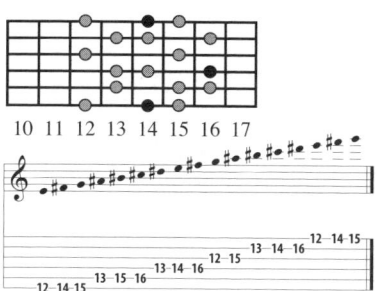
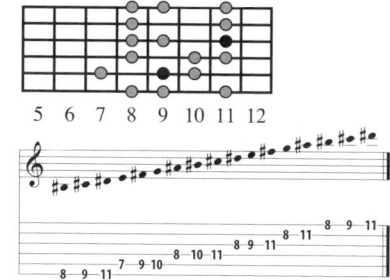

## Dominant ♭9 ♯11 ♭13 (1 ♭2 3 ♯4 5 ♭6 ♭7 8)

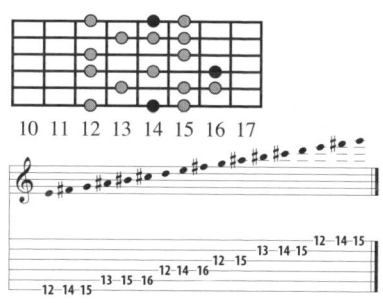
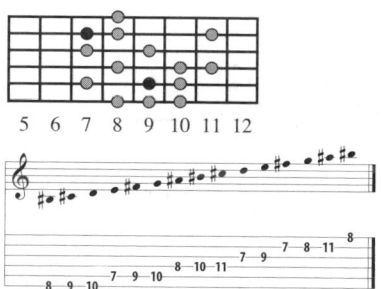

## Dominant 13 (1 2 3 5 6 ♭7 8)

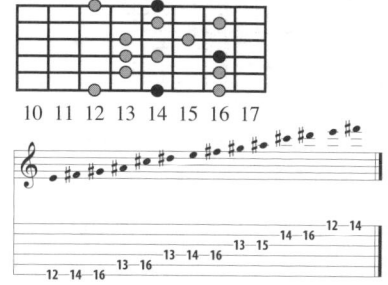
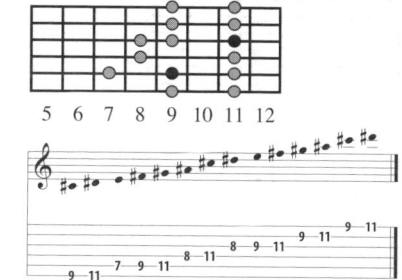

# Major and Dominant Scales

## Major/Ionian (1 2 3 4 5 6 7 8)

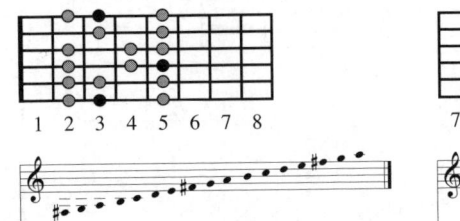
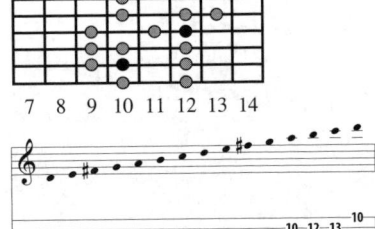

## Mixolydian (1 2 3 4 5 6 ♭7 8)
5th mode of the major scale

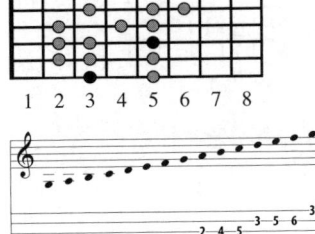
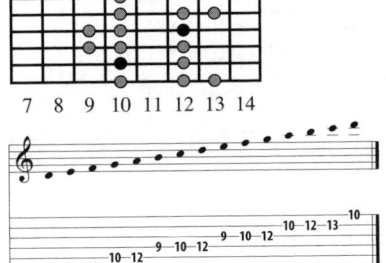

## Lydian (1 2 3 ♯4 5 6 7 8)
4th mode of the major scale

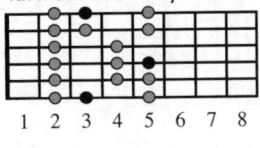

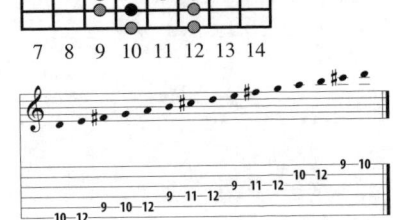

## Major Pentatonic (1 2 3 5 6 8)

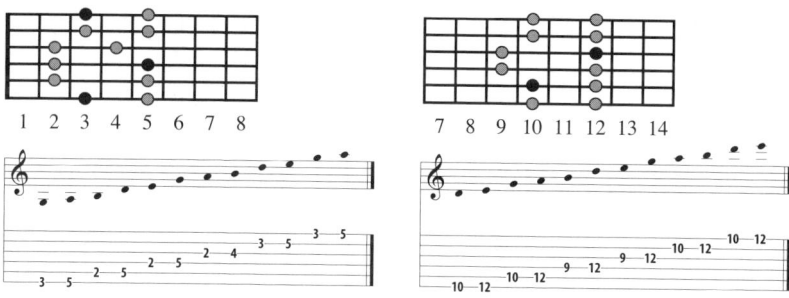

## Major 13 Pentatonic* (1 2 3 5 6 7 8)

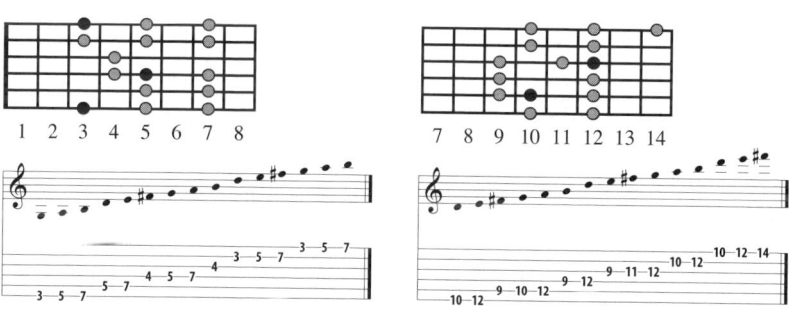

## Major Pentatonic Blues* (1 2 ♭3 3 5 6 8)

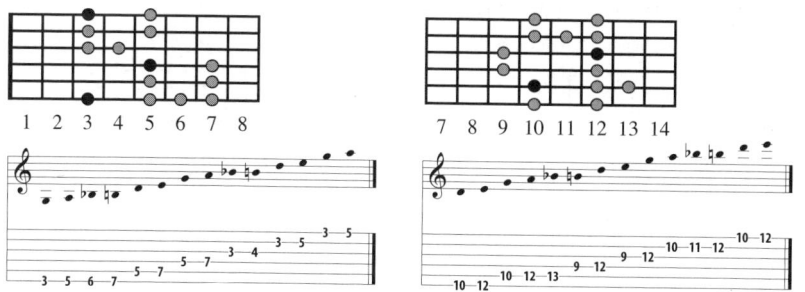

* While this scale has more than five notes, it is based on a five-note, pentatonic scale and it is best to think of it as a pentatonic scale.

## Lydian Pentatonic (1 3 #4 5 7 8)

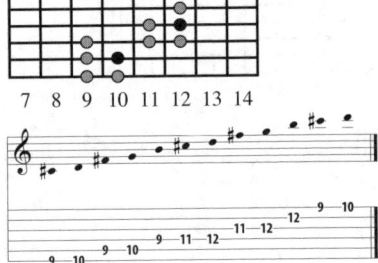

## Lydian ♭7 (1 2 3 #4 5 6 ♭7 8)
4th mode of the melodic minor scale

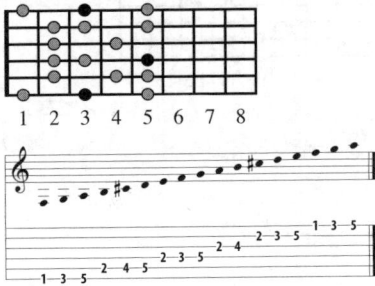
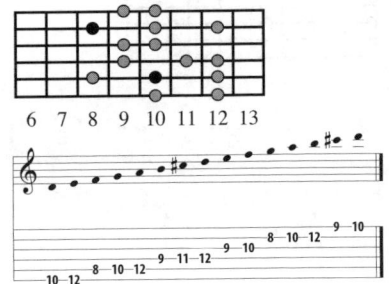

## Lydian #9 (1 #2 3 #4 5 6 7 8)
6th mode of the harmonic minor scale

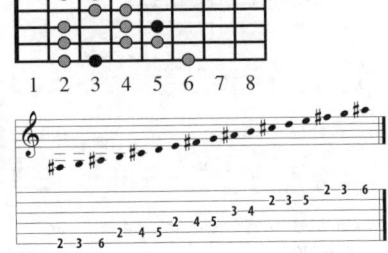
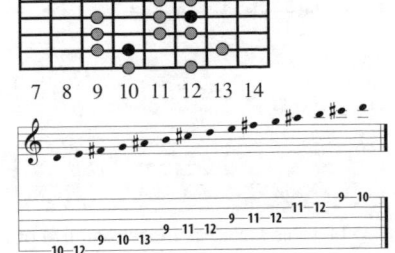

## Aeolian Major (1 2 3 4 5 ♭6 ♭7 8)
5th mode of the melodic minor scale

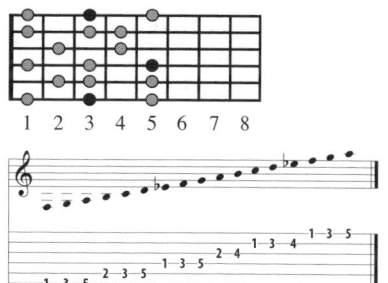
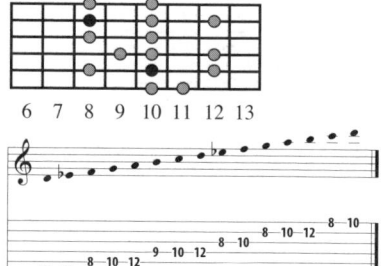

## Phrygian Major (1 ♭2 3 4 5 ♭6 ♭7 8)
5th mode of the harmonic minor scale

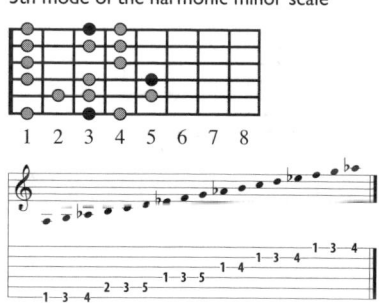
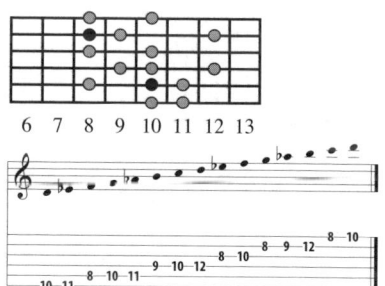

## Ionian Augmented (1 2 3 4 ♯5 6 7 8)
3rd mode of the harmonic minor scale

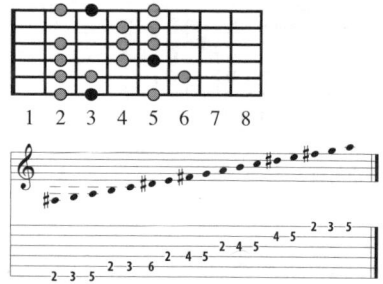
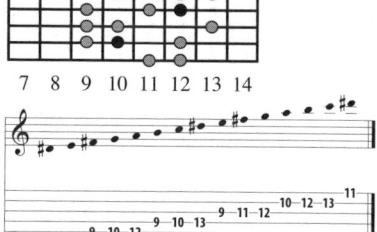

## Lydian Augmented (1 2 3 #4 #5 6 7 8)
3rd mode of the melodic minor scale

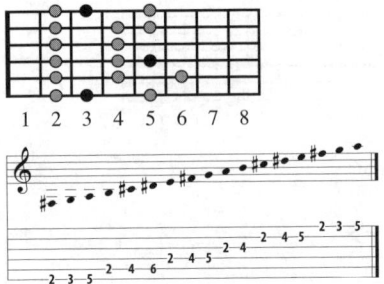
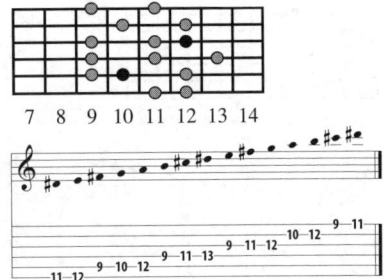

# Minor Scales

## Natural Minor/Aeolian (1 2 ♭3 4 5 ♭6 ♭7 8)
6th mode of the major scale

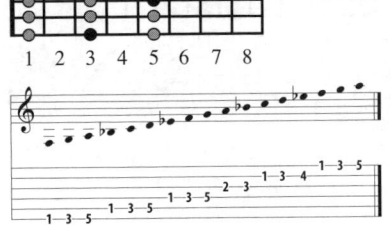
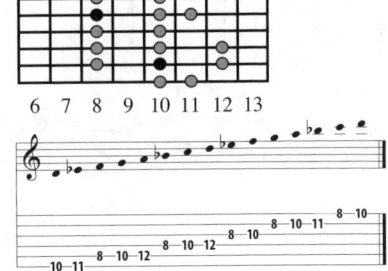

## Harmonic Minor (1 2 ♭3 4 5 ♭6 7 8)

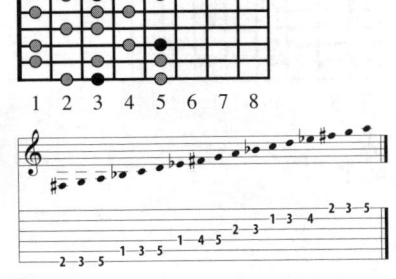
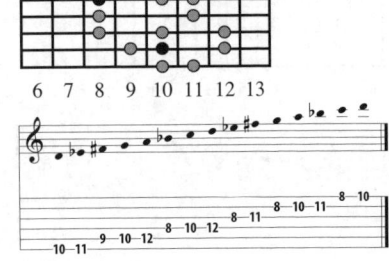

## Jazz Minor/Melodic Minor (1 2 ♭3 4 5 6 7 8)
Melodic Minor descends in Aeolian/Natural Minor

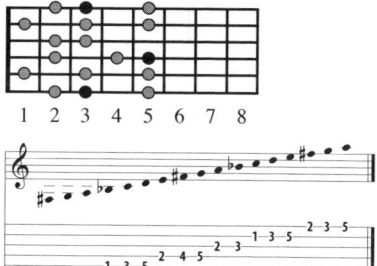
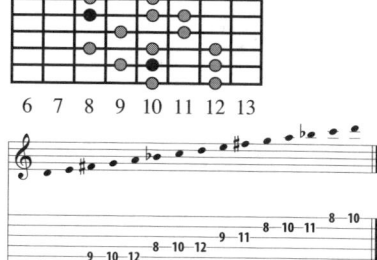

## Dorian (1 2 ♭3 4 5 6 ♭7 8)
2nd mode of the major scale

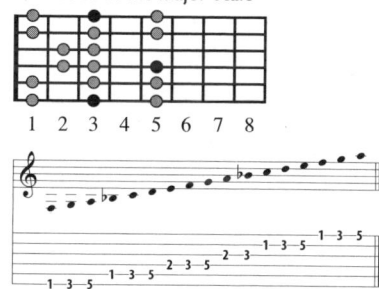
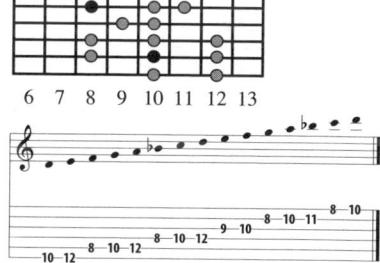

## Phrygian (1 ♭2 ♭3 4 5 ♭6 ♭7 8)
3rd mode of the major scale

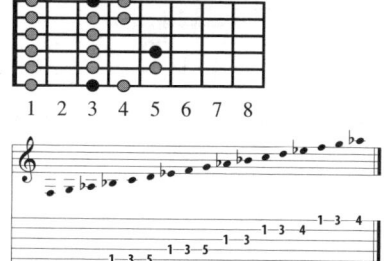
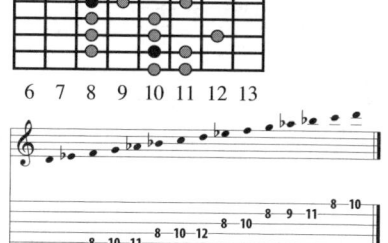

## Locrian (1 ♭2 ♭3 4 ♭5 ♭6 ♭7 8)
7th mode of the major scale

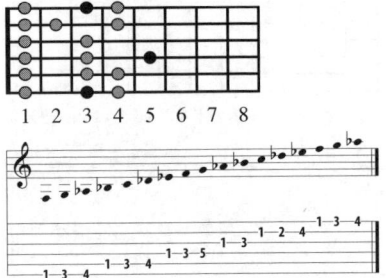
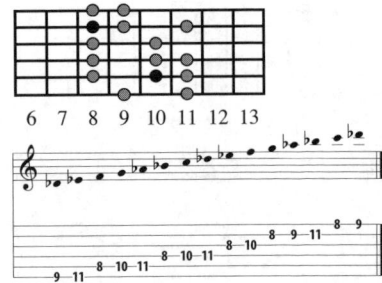

## Minor Pentatonic (1 ♭3 4 5 ♭7 8)

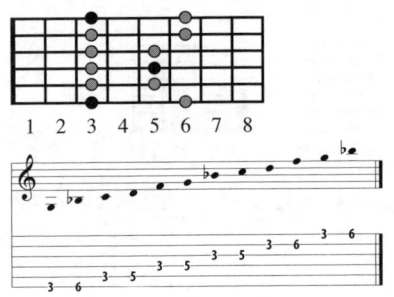
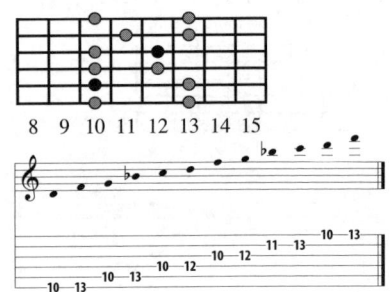

## Minor 13 Pentatonic* (1 ♭3 5 ♭6 ♭7 8)

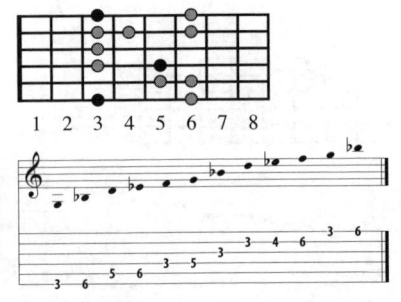
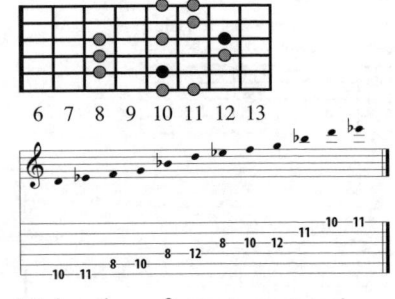

* While this scale has more than five notes, it is based on a five-note, pentatonic scale and it is best to think of it as a pentatonic scale.

## Minor Pentatonic Blues* (1 ♭3 4 ♭5 5 ♭7 8)

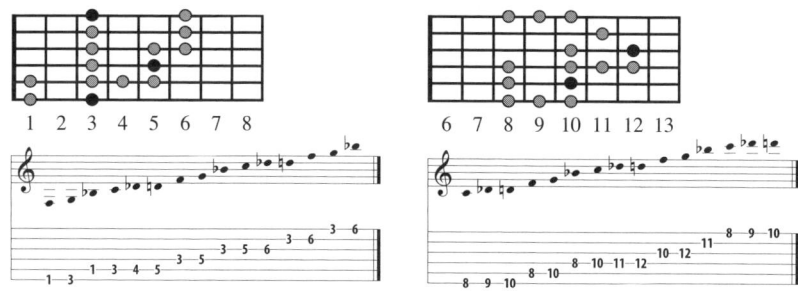

## Dorian Pentatonic (1 2 ♭3 5 ♭7 8)

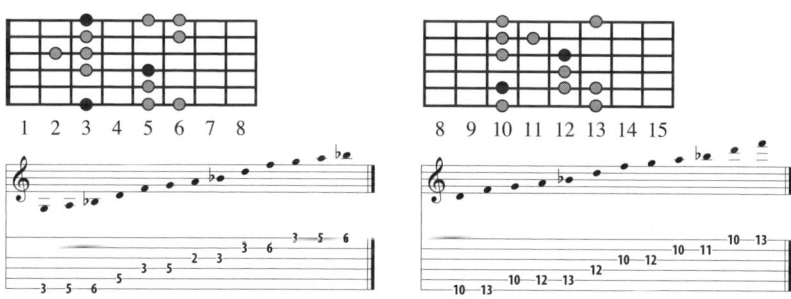

## Phrygian Pentatonic (1 ♭2 4 5 ♭7 8)

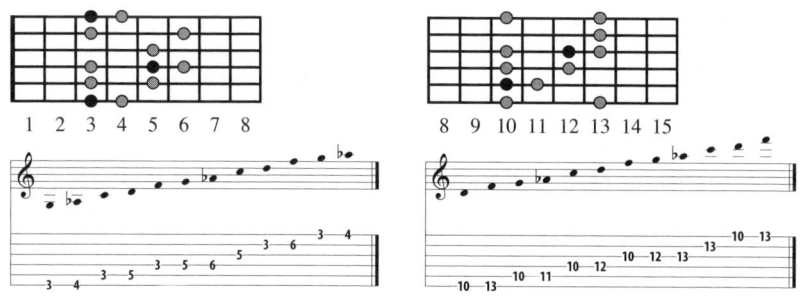

* While this scale has more than five notes, it is based on a five-note, pentatonic scale and it is best to think of it as a pentatonic scale.

# Phrygian ♮6 (1 ♭2 ♭3 4 5 6 ♭7 8)
2nd mode of the melodic minor scale

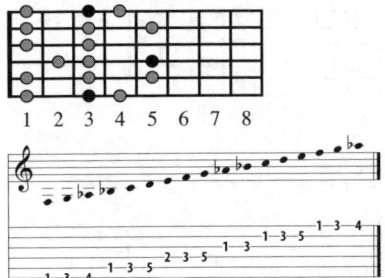
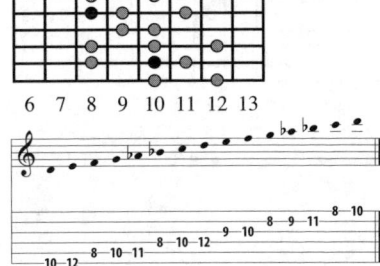

# Locrian ♮2 (1 2 ♭3 4 ♭5 ♭6 ♭7 8)
6th mode of the melodic minor scale

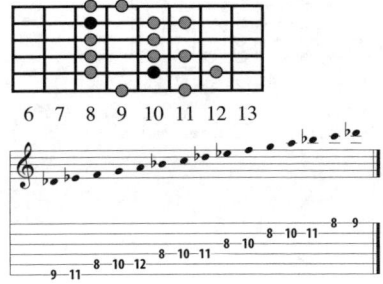

# Locrian ♮6 (1 ♭2 ♭3 4 ♭5 6 ♭7 8)
2nd mode of the harmonic minor scale

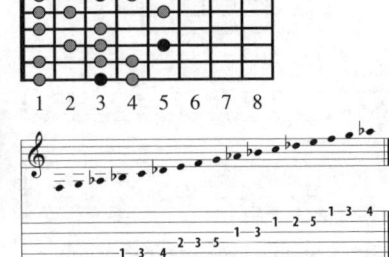
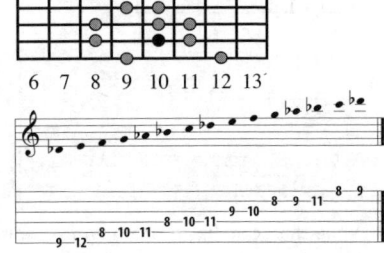

# Symmetrical Scales

## Chromatic (1 ♭2 2 ♭3 3 4 ♭5 5 ♭6 6 ♭7 7 8)

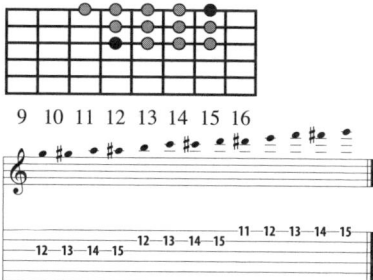

## Whole Tone (1 2 3 ♯4 ♯5 ♯6 8)

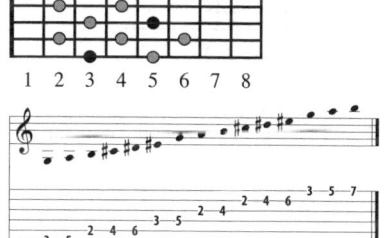
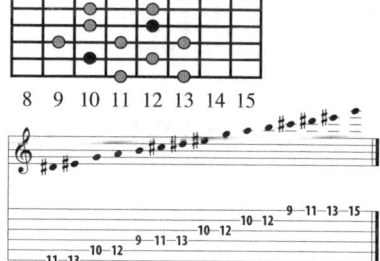

## Auxiliary, Whole/Half Diminished (1 2 ♭3 4 ♭5 ♭6 6 7 8)

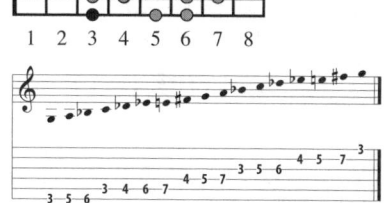

# Symmetrical, Half/Whole Diminished (1 ♭2 ♭3 ♭4 ♭5 5 6 ♭7 8)

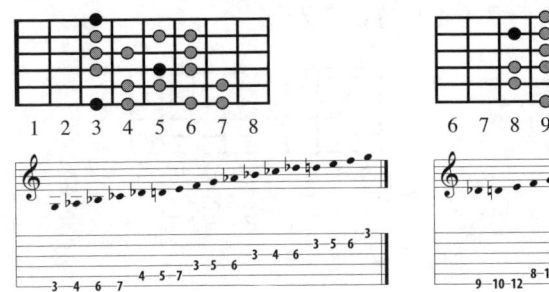
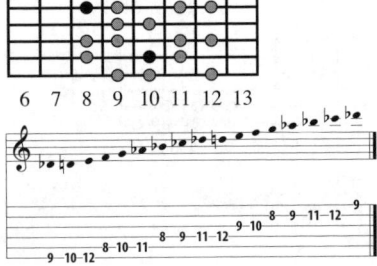

# Augmented (1 ♯2 3 5 ♯5 7 8)

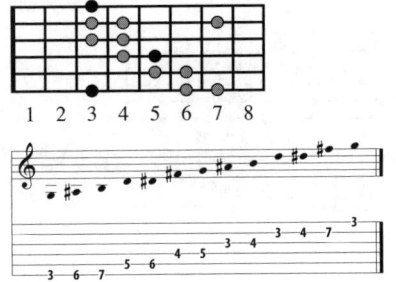
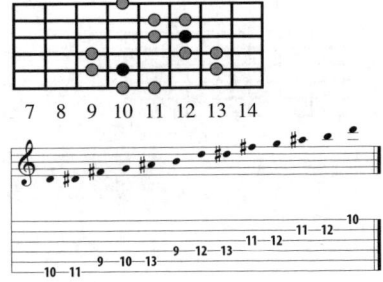

# Chromatic Augmented (1 ♭2 2 3 4 ♯4 ♯5 6 ♭7 8)

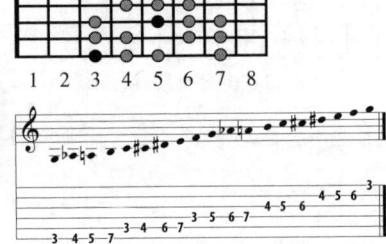
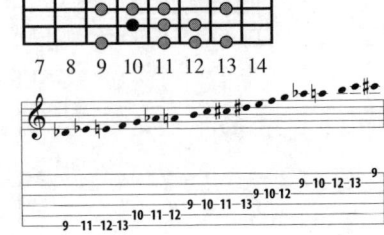

## Augmented ♭9 (1 ♭2 ♭3 3 4 5 ♭6 6 7 8)

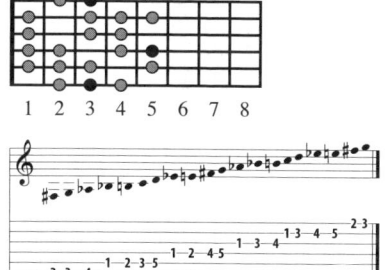
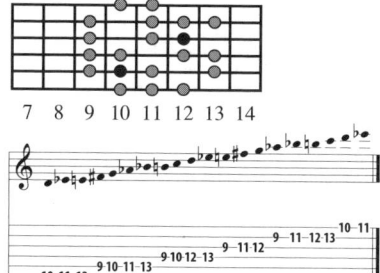

## Augmented 9 (1 2 ♭3 3 ♯4 5 ♭6 ♭7 7 8)

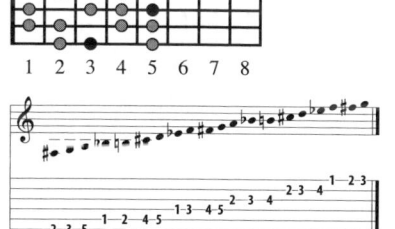
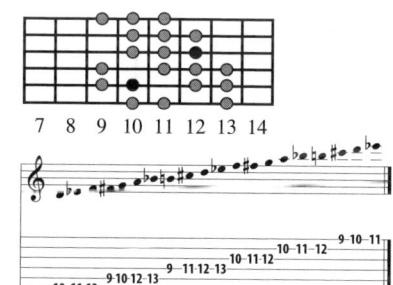

## Diminished Blues (1 ♭2 ♭3 3 ♯5 6 ♭7 8)

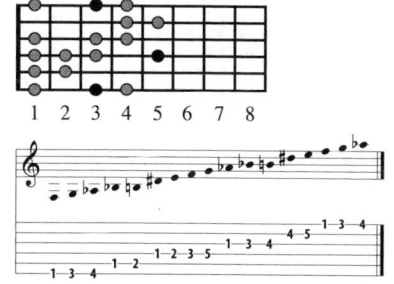
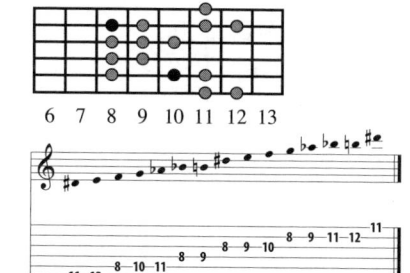

# Four Semitone Tritone (1 b2 2 b3 3 #4 5 b6 6 b7 8)

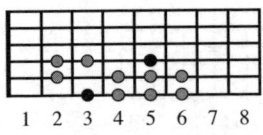
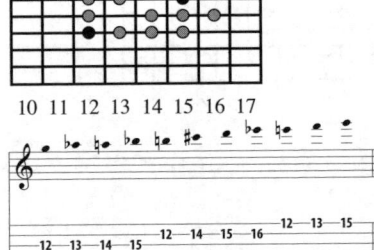

# Tetratonic (1 4 b5 7 8)

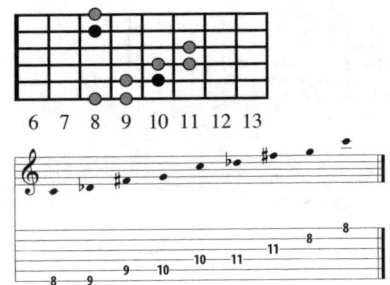

# Three Semitone Tritone (1 b2 2 b3 b5 5 b6 6 8)

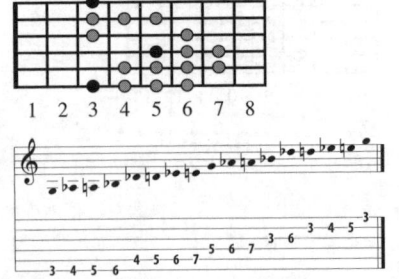

## Tritone (1 ♭2 3 ♯4 5 ♭7 8)

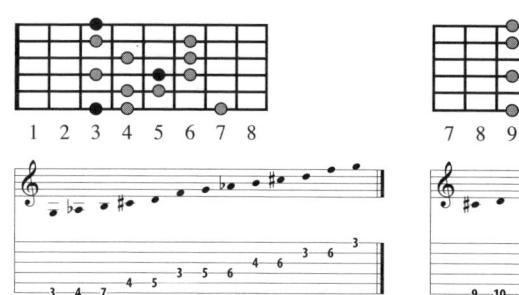
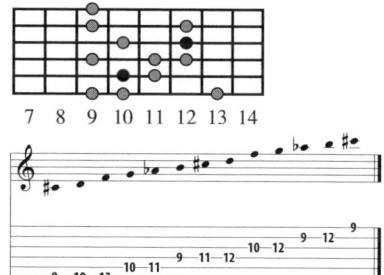

## Two-Semitone Tritone (1 ♭2 2 ♯4 5 ♭6 8)

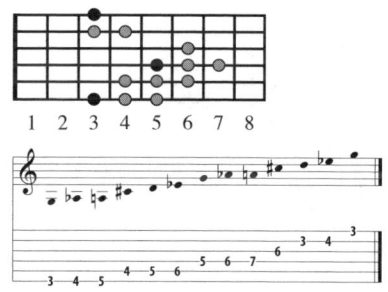
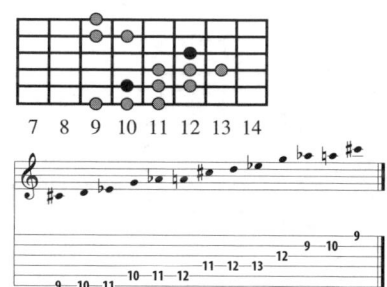

# Hybrid Scales

## Aeolian ♯11 (1 2 ♭3 ♯4 5 ♭6 ♭7 8)

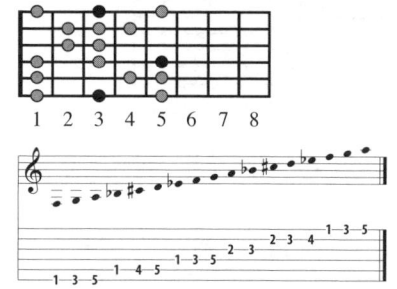
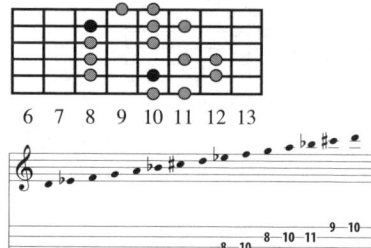

## Augmented Dominant (1 2 3 4 #5 6 b7 8)

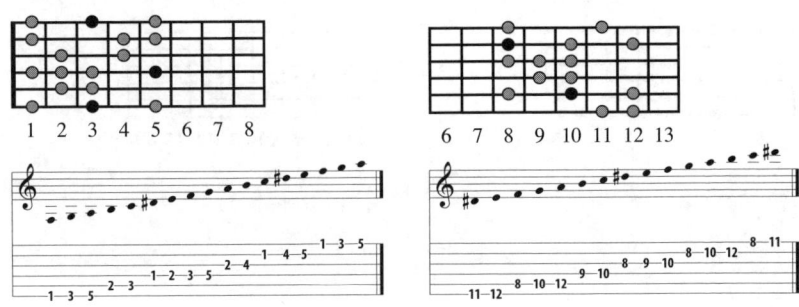

## Augmented Dominant b9 (1 b2 3 4 #5 6 b7 8)

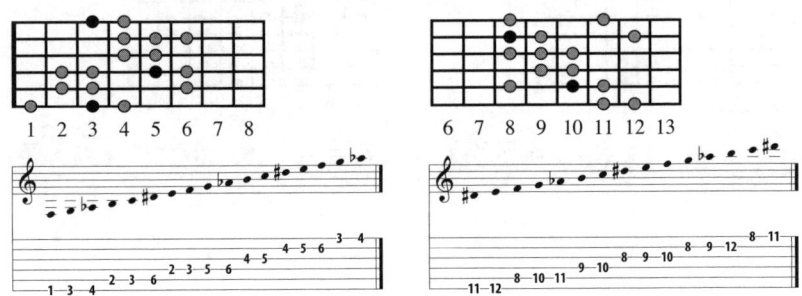

## Augmented Dominant #9 (1 #2 3 4 #5 6 b7 8)

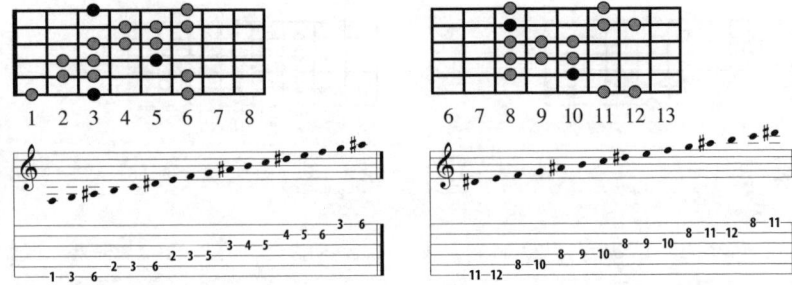

## Augmented ♯9 (1 ♯2 3 4 ♯5 6 7 8)

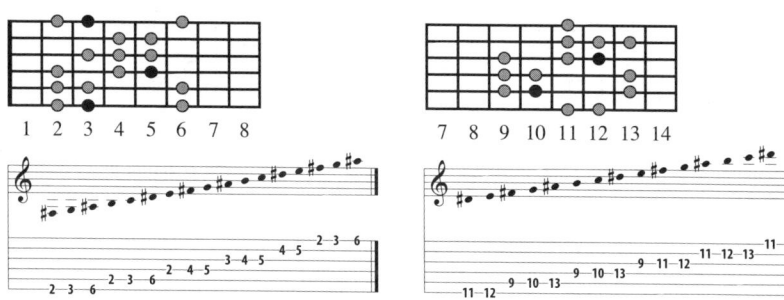

## Augmented Minor/Major 7 (1 2 ♭3 4 ♯5 6 7 8)

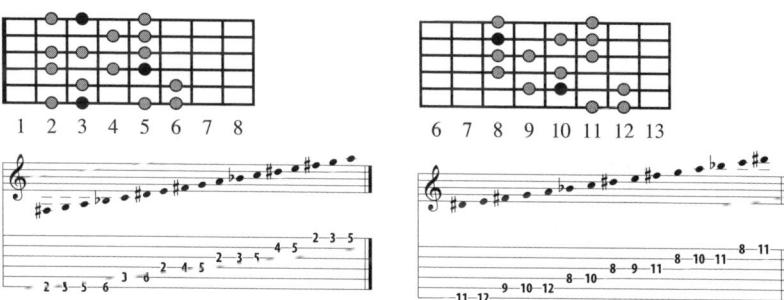

## Bebop Dominant (1 2 3 4 5 6 ♭7 7 8)

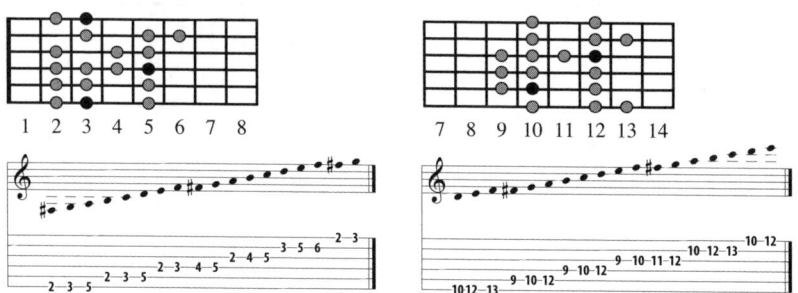

## Bebop Dorian (1 2 ♭3 3 4 5 6 ♭7 8)

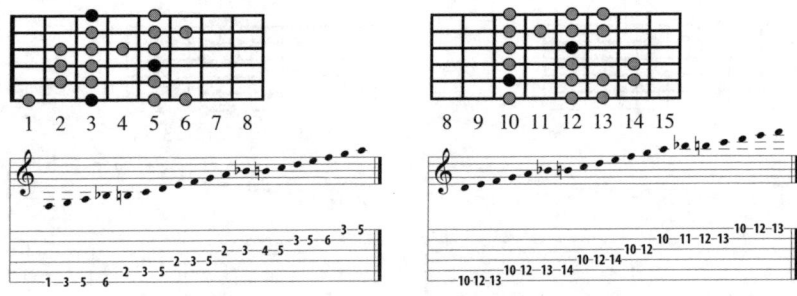

## Bebop Major* (1 2 3 4 ♯4 5 6 7 8)

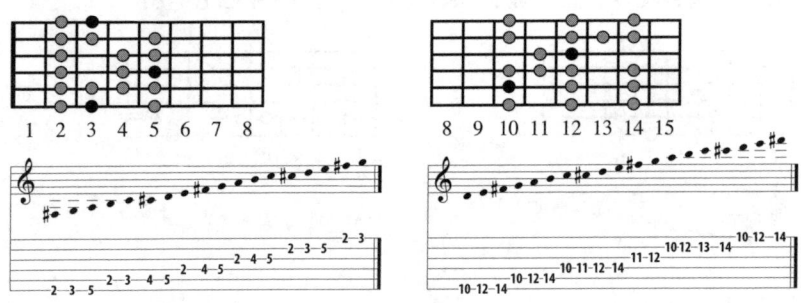

## Bebop Melodic Minor* (1 2 ♭3 4 ♯4 5 6 7 8)

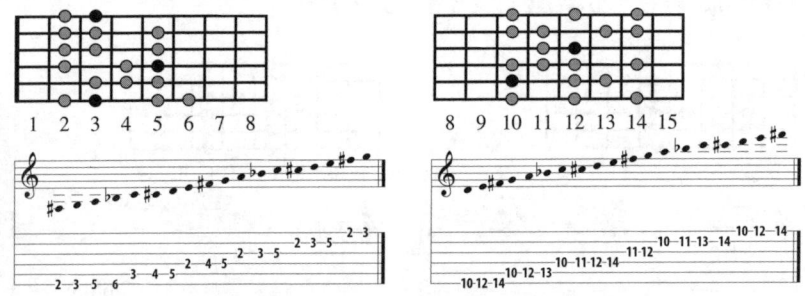

* Many musicians spell this scale with a ♯5 instead of a ♯4.

## Diminished Tritonic (1 ♭3 4 ♭5 8)

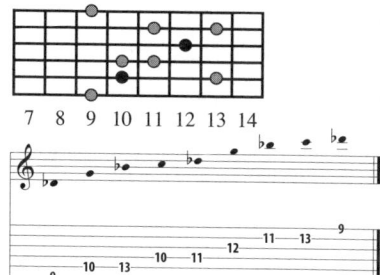

## Dominant ♭5 (1 2 3 4 ♭5 6 ♭7 8)

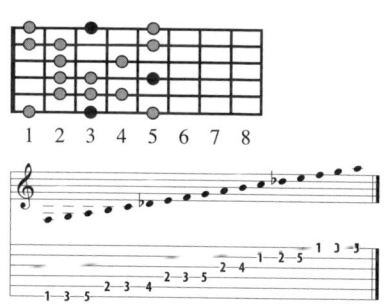
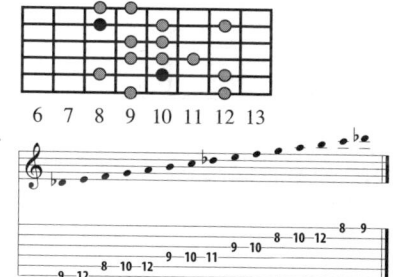

## Dominant ♭5 ♭9 ♯9 (1 ♭2 ♭3 ♭4 ♭5 6 ♭7 8)

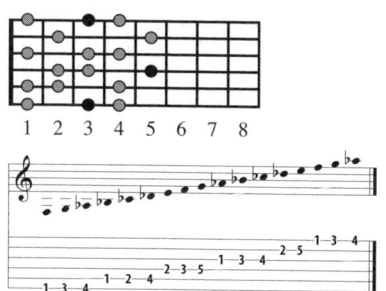
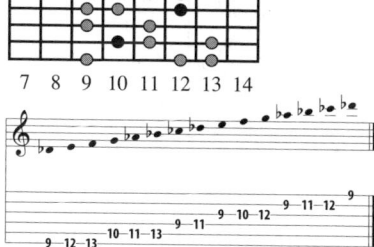

## Dominant ♭9 ♯9 (1 ♭2 ♭3 ♭4 5 6 ♭7 8)

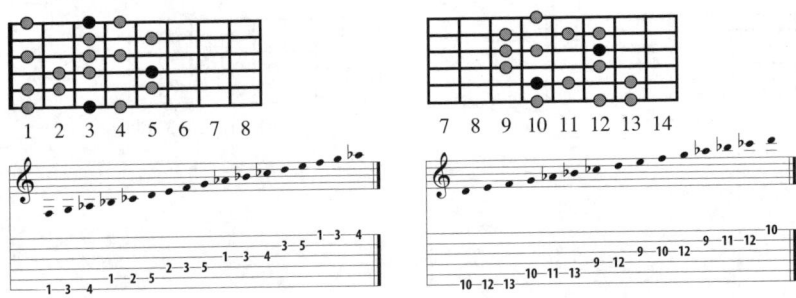

## Dominant ♭9 ♯9 ♭13 (1 ♭2 ♭3 ♭4 5 ♭6 ♭7 8)

## Dominant ♯9 (1 ♯2 3 4 5 6 ♭7 8)

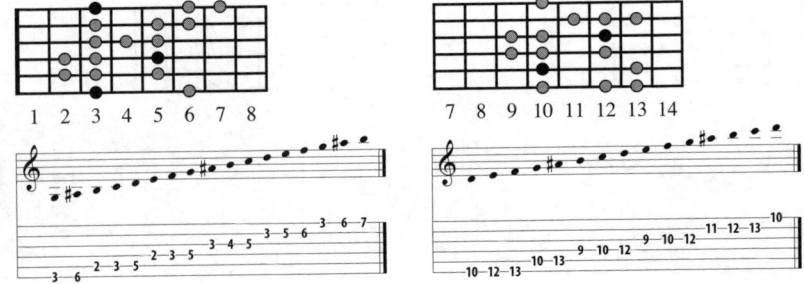

## Dominant ♭9 ♯11 (1 ♭2 3 ♯4 5 6 ♭7 8)

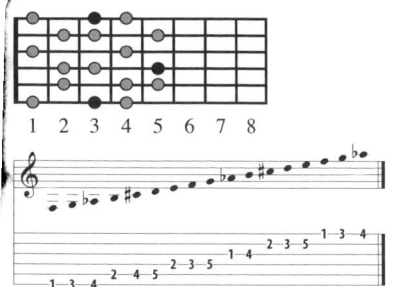
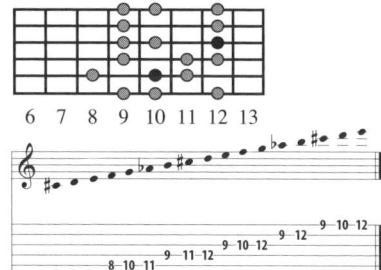

## Dominant ♭9 ♯11 ♭13 (1 ♭2 3 ♯4 5 ♭6 ♭7 8)

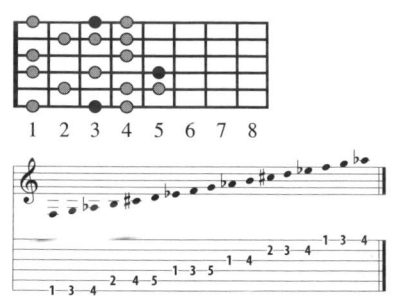
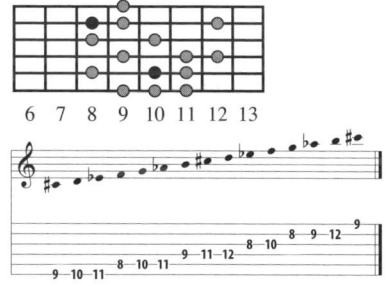

## Dominant 13 (1 2 3 5 6 ♭7 8)

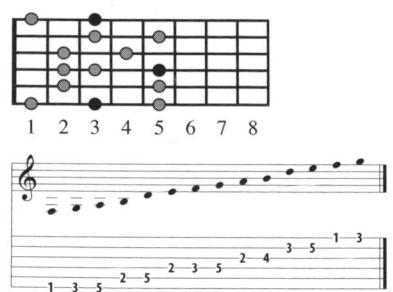
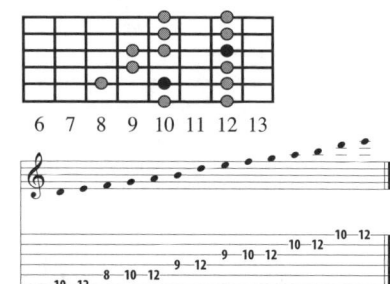